RESTLESS ECOLOGIES

Restless
Ecologies

CLIMATE CHANGE AND
SOCIOECOLOGICAL FUTURES
IN THE PERUVIAN HIGHLANDS

ALLISON CAINE

THE UNIVERSITY OF
ARIZONA PRESS
TUCSON

The University of Arizona Press
www.uapress.arizona.edu

We respectfully acknowledge the University of Arizona is on the land and territories of Indigenous peoples. Today, Arizona is home to twenty-two federally recognized tribes, with Tucson being home to the O'odham and the Yaqui. The university strives to build sustainable relationships with sovereign Native Nations and Indigenous communities through education offerings, partnerships, and community service.

ISBN-13: 978-0-8165-5417-1 (hardcover)
ISBN-13: 978-0-8165-5416-4 (paperback)
ISBN-13: 978-0-8165-5418-8 (ebook)

Cover design by Leigh McDonald
Cover photo by Allison Caine
Typeset by Sara Thaxton in 10.5/14 Warnock Pro with ITC Mendoza Roman Std
and Ainslie Sans

Short sections of the introduction, chapter 1, and the conclusion are derived in part from "Herding at the Edges: Climate Change and Animal Restlessness in the Peruvian Andes," published in *Ethnos*, November 6, 2022 (copyright Taylor & Francis), available online: https://www.tandfonline.com/doi/full/10.1080/00141844.2022.2142266#abstract. Short excerpts of chapter 3 appear in "'Who Would Watch the Animals?': Gendered Knowledge and Expert Performance among Andean Pastoralists," published in *Culture, Agriculture, Food, and Environment*, February 15, 2021, available online: https://doi.org/10.1111/cuag.12261.

Library of Congress Cataloging-in-Publication Data
Names: Caine, Allison, 1985– author.
Title: Restless ecologies : climate change and socioecological futures in the Peruvian highlands / Allison Caine.
Description: [Tucson] : The University of Arizona Press, 2025. | Includes bibliographical references and index.
Identifiers: LCCN 2025003817 (print) | LCCN 2025003818 (ebook) | ISBN 9780816554171 (hardcover) | ISBN 9780816554164 (paperback) | ISBN 9780816554188 (ebook)
Subjects: LCSH: Quechua Indians—Peru—Sierra. | Herders—Peru—Sierra. | Climate change adaptation—Peru—Sierra. | Social ecology—Peru—Sierra.
Classification: LCC F2230.2.K4 C35 2025 (print) | LCC F2230.2.K4 (ebook)
LC record available at https://lccn.loc.gov/2025003817
LC ebook record available at https://lccn.loc.gov/2025003818

Printed in the United States of America
♾ This paper meets the requirements of ANSI/NISO Z39.48-1992 (Permanence of Paper).

For Concepción Rojo Rojo
and in honor of all the beings nurtured
in her wisdom and care.

Contents

Illustrations

Acknowledgments

First and foremost, I owe my deepest and most heartfelt gratitude to the community of Chillca. I am especially indebted to the Rojo family, as well as the other families and individuals that opened their homes to me, introduced me to their herds, and helped me know and sense the landscape of Chillca. I am immeasurably grateful to Concepción Rojo Rojo for taking me in and raising me. I also thank Julio Huaman Mamani, Emilia Rojo Condori, Mario Huaman Rojo, Maritza Tunque Huaman, Vilma Huaman Rojo, Julio Callo Iberto, Jorge Huaman Rojo, Juanita Achusi Huaman, Basilia Rojo Rojo, Julian Huanca Choquechampi, Carmen Rojo Rojo, Julio Rojo Rojo, Josefa Huillca Mendoza, Aniseta Tunque Huaman, Hernan Mamani Rojo, and many others. Their wisdom, humor, and patience continue to shape me and my own practices of care. My appreciation likewise extends to the 2015–16 Chillca junta directiva and comité de alpacas for facilitating my time there and allowing me to take part in many community meetings, especially Ernesto Rojo, Justino Quispe Huaman, Eloy Condori Suyo, Juan Carlos Rojo, and Marcos Rojo Mamani. I am also grateful to the places of Chillca, for sustaining me, calling me sharply into the present, and providing endless wonder for the thinking, daydreaming, and scribbling that would eventually become these chapters.

The city of Cusco was a second home long before this research began. I return each time to the welcoming arms and generous plates of the Huaman Escalante family: Janet Escalante Barrios, Ernesto Huaman Zapata, Rosalía Daniela Mendoza Quispe, Leslie, Illapa, and Miski Wuaira Huaman Escalante, and Ernesto Guevara Huaman. I am especially grateful for Jean-Jacques Decoster and the staff at Centro Tinku, my first home in Cusco. The ideas, thoughts, and questions that animated this research were cultivated over many long walks, *cafecitos*, and conversations with dear friends and colleagues in Cusco. For that, I am deeply grateful to Génesis Abreu, Alex Chepstow-Lusty, Wendi Chiong, Alex Cusiyunca, Giovanni Estrada, Rich Everett, Jorge Flores Ochoa, Devin Grammon, Aaron Hyman, Steve Kosiba, Maidel Luevano, Yésica Pacheco, Kylie Quave, Sara Scherr, Iris Tinta Chunvislla, Gustavo Valdivia, Céline de Visser, Adam Walters, and Robin Weiss. I thank Julia McHugh for her wisdom, friendship, and wit. I am indebted to *Equipo Sapo* for introducing me to the people of Chillca and drawing my attention to the humble *telmatobius*, especially Kelsey Reider, as well as the Crispín family of Pukarumi, in particular Felipe, Juliana, Wilian, Verónica, and Miriam. My gratitude likewise extends to other members of the Sibinaqocha Watershed Initiative and the Cordillera Vilcanota Research and Conservation Initiative, including Jan Baiker, Katherine Doyle, Baker Perry, Julio Postigo, Charles Rodda, Anton Seimon, Tracie Seimon, Preston Sowell, Alfredo Tupayachi, and Karina Yager. I am especially grateful for Dina Farfán, and I remain in awe of her tireless dedication and continued work for the community of Chillca.

The groundwork for this book extends back to my years in the graduate program in anthropology at the University of Michigan. Bruce Mannheim has my utmost gratitude for being an endlessly encouraging and insightful mentor from the beginning into the present, and a bridge between the worlds of Peru and Michigan. I am thankful for my doctoral committee members: Stuart Kirsch, for bringing the larger threads of my research into sharper relief; Elizabeth F. S. Roberts for encouraging me to dive into the murky depths; Joyce Marcus for her generous and discerning eye; and Robin Queen, for not letting me short-shrift the sheep. Special thanks go to Benjamin Orlove for his continued enthusiasm, encouragement, and insight. This book bears the traces of conversations and classes with many other faculty members at the University of Michigan, and I'd like to thank Kelly Askew, Abby Bigham, Bilal Butt, Jason De León, Gillian Feeley-Harnik, Krisztina Fehervary, Kent Flannery, María

Elena García, Judith Irvine, Webb Keane, Maria Carmen Lemos, Laura MacLatchy, Barb Meek, John Mitani, and Erik Mueggler for the many vibrant hours spent in the halls and classrooms of West Hall and the Dana Building. My research has been sharpened by conversations over the years with Barry Lyons, Lisa Markowitz, Julio Postigo, Juan Rivera Andía, Linda Seligmann, and Enrique Mayer. I am immeasurably indebted to Regina Tupacyupanqui Arredondo and Adela Carlos Rios, who provided careful and detailed transcriptions of Quechua audio recordings, including Concepción's songs. Doris Loayza has likewise shaped both my understanding and translation of the Quechua language, and Alison Krögel and Bruce Mannheim assisted further in the translation of Concepción's song lyrics. Any errors in translation or interpretation, however, are entirely my own.

At Michigan, I was lucky to have landed in a supportive, tight-knit cohort of brilliant minds and quirky dispositions, and I am endlessly thankful for both. I especially thank many friends and colleagues: Anna Antoniou, Yeon-ju Bae, Amelia Burke, Anne Marie Creighton, Jordan Dalton, Adrian Deoanca, John Doering-White, Nicholas Q. Emlen, Georgia Ennis, Chelsea Fisher, Brady G'Sell, Drew Haxby, Onyx Henry, Benjamin Hollenbach, Adam Fulton Johnson, Hayeon Lee, Jessica Lowen, Maire Malone, Brenna Murphy, Prash Naidu, Sandhya Krittika Narayanan, Michael Prentice, Guillermo Salas, Kimberly Sanchez, Joshua Shapero, Jennifer Sierra, Alex Sklyar, Howard Tsai, Jennifer Tucker, Travis Williams, Cheryl Yin, and Magdalena Zegarra Chiappori. Many thanks to Christine Sargent, who has seen the various components of this book unfold over the course of more than a decade.

The research upon which this book is based was supported by the Wenner-Gren Foundation and the U.S. Department of Education Fulbright-Hays Program, as well as many institutions at the University of Michigan, including the Rackham Graduate School, the International Institute, the Center for Latin American and Caribbean Studies, the Institute for Research on Women and Gender, and the Center for the Education of Women. The Foreign Language and Area Studies Fellowship of the U.S. Department of Education funded my Quechua language training, and I particularly thank my Quechua instructors: Regina Tupacyupanqui Arredondo, Arturo Villavicienco, and Alicia Galdós at Centro Tinku, and Martin Castillo at the University of Michigan. I also thank the staff at Comisión Fulbright del Perú for their support in navigating grant requirements and visas in 2008 and again in 2015.

In truth, the very first sparks of this research were lit long before I even knew I would spend so much of my life in the Peruvian Andes. For that, I am indebted to my mentor at Bates College, Loring "Danny" Danforth, who first nurtured my interest in anthropology and who has provided invaluable encouragement throughout my career. To Keely Maxwell, my biggest thanks for introducing me to the vicuña, the animal that would start this whole journey, and for continuing to be an insightful colleague, mentor, and friend. At the University of Edinburgh, my interests in climate change and ethnography were further honed under the mentorship of Magnus Course. I made lifelong friends in Edinburgh who continue to be my closest confidants and sources of inspiration as well as levity. Special thanks to Sammie Francis-Taylor, Jeffrey Larson, Max Taylor, Ian Nichols, Koreen Reece, and Steffi Schien, as well as Andrea Torres Slimming, whom we miss deeply.

Many of the central arguments in this book were honed over the course of three years in Grinnell, Iowa, between 2019 and 2022. What was meant to be a short stay extended well into the pandemic, and during those years, I found writing companionship in the Flaming Quillz: Eiren Shea, Marion Tricoire, Amanda Lee, Elias Saba, and John Petrus. I am grateful to our friends and neighbors in Grinnell during the challenging COVID times, including the aforementioned Quillz, as well as Charlotte Bowcutt, Gwenola Caradec, Yoel Castillo, Jan and Dan Gross, Emily Guenther, Kathleen Hershberger, Jackie and Paul Hutchison, Julie Lascol, Josh Marshack, Taylor Price, Jordan Scheibel, and Sejal Sutaria. Although less writing was accomplished during that time than any of us had hoped, this book would not have been possible without those hours of company and contemplation in Saints Rest.

The University of Wyoming has provided a productive and sustaining academic home in which to finish this book. I thank my colleagues in the anthropology department, especially Bree Doering, Randy Haas, Lauren Hayes, Jim Johnson, Melissa Murphy, and Todd Surovell for supporting this project and its completion. My writing process was bolstered through conversations in the classrooms, labs, and hallways of the George C. Frison building, and inspired by the company of our wonderful students, including Casey Black, Dakota Buhmann, Kassandra Dutro,

Briana Houghton, Aubrey Edwards, Lexi Huiras, Brad Murdock, Fox Nelson, Eric Nigh, Haley Purifoy, Ann Stephens, and Josie Corbett Waters. The final stages of writing were supported by the Wenner-Gren Hunt Fellowship, as well as the Wyoming Institute for Humanities Research. I thank Scott Henkel and fellow members of the Humanities Research Group for their careful review of several chapters, as well as their writing companionship and wisdom: Dan Auerbach, Kent Drummond, Alyson Hagy, Trisha Martinez, Nikolas Sweet, and Katharine Teykl. I also thank Eric Sandeen for his generous support of the Sandeen Lectureship, which allowed me the opportunity to share this research with the University of Wyoming and Laramie community. I consider it one of the great strokes of luck in my life to have landed in Laramie, and I am grateful to all our Laramigos for their support, kindness, and humor. It truly takes a village.

I am indebted to Allyson Carter, Alana Enriquez, and Amanda Krause at the University of Arizona Press for shepherding this project through the various stages of publication, Amy Benson Brown for sharpening my focus at key moments during the writing process, and to several anonymous reviewers for their generous engagement with this text. Many thanks to Mia Loia for her beautiful illustrations, Irina du Quenoy for her careful copyediting, Amron Lehte for preparing the index, and Leigh McDonald for her dedicated work on the cover design.

Finally, I thank my family and dear friends. My parents, Pam and Brian, who always supported me in an unconventional and at times perplexing career choice, and who have read and listened to many parts of this book through various stages of percolation. My brother Liam, whom I admire immensely. Sarah Maharjan and the Lynes family, for providing steady ground throughout the decades; Kaitlyn Sawyer and the Cooper Sawyer family, for encouraging me to finish my "book reports"; and Katy Rodden Walker, for broadening my understanding of multispecies entanglement and futurity through her art. Many thanks to my in-laws, Monika, Philip, and Matthias Sweet, for their unwavering support and warm company over the years.

A very singular thank-you to Nik, my partner in all things and our family's true north. And finally, to Rowan and Sophie, who have simply expanded the bounds of the universe and taught me more than I imagined possible.

Note on Orthography and Translation

For Quechua words and phrases, I follow the standard conventions for Peruvian Quechua, relying on the three-vowel system of orthography: /a/, /i/, and /u/. Spanish loans embedded in Quechua speech are transcribed following Quechua orthography when appropriate: for example, when the speaker is a monolingual Quechua speaker (i.e., for words and phrases like *awir* [a ver], *piru* [pero], or *phinu* [fino]), or when the word has been conjugated in Quechua (e.g., *dalimushan*, from Spanish "dale" [colloq. go, give] to mean goes, does, or moves). I include the Spanish vowels /e/ and /o/ when pronounced. Exceptions to the three-vowel rule include place-names (e.g., Quesiunu) and surnames (e.g., Huillca), in which case I aim to be consistent with local orthographic conventions. Since the orthography of both place-names and surnames tends to vary even within a single community, I include the most widely used representation.

All Quechua and Spanish language translations in the text are free translations, presented without interlinear glosses of any kind. I chose this method of presentation to enhance the readability of the text for a primarily English-speaking audience. However, in doing so, I must acknowledge the limits of translation. I attend to incommensurabilities in the text when I feel they must be addressed, and I include the original Quechua when possible. I do not, however, include a glossary, given that the expansiveness of many Quechua concepts elude a singular English-language gloss. Spanish-language dictionary translations are likewise presented throughout, not as authoritative translations but to further highlight the challenges of translation in contemporary as well as historical contexts. All errors in translation or interpretation in the text itself, however, are my own.

RESTLESS ECOLOGIES

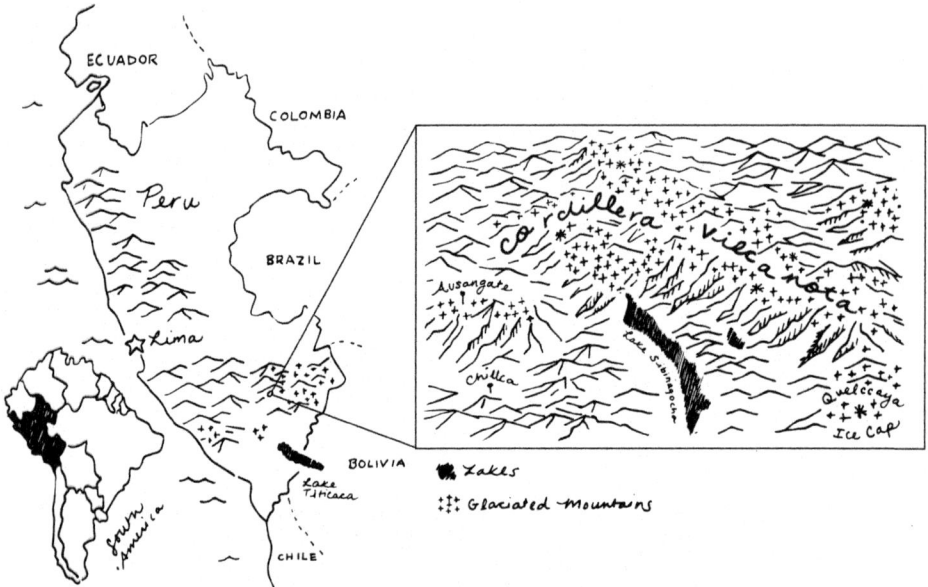

FIGURE 1 Map of Chillca and the Cordillera Vilcanota. Map design by Mia Loia.

Introduction

Restless Ecologies

> *The cosmos emerges, again and again, out of diverse ways of composing worlds, of crafting attachments and connections that link soil and earth, compost, humus, mud, grass, dogs, sheep, humans, and more. All of this is to say that there are some places on Earth where the cosmos passes through the mouths of sheep.*
> —VINCIANE DESPRET AND MICHEL MEURET (2016)

Illachiy was Concepción's favorite place to herd her animals. It was the smaller of the three glacial valleys behind her dry-season home in the community of Chillca, but it held within it a lush and expansive terrain. It was here, at forty-five hundred meters above sea level, that a bit of transformative magic happened beneath her feet. Usually, those feet were on the move, in pursuit of the alpacas, llamas, and sheep that grazed the valley floor or ran up and over the valley walls. But below the pasture is where everything came together, in the watery and peaty subterranean composite that was the *uqhu*, an alpine wetland. Also known as a *bofedal*, the *uqhu* is a teeming ecological community knit together by the consistent flow of water from nearby glacial peaks and seasonal rain clouds. The green and fleshy stems and leaves of its plants—mostly dense vascular and cushion plants, barely more than a few inches high—emerge out of the dark peat to transform water, sunlight, and soil into nutrients for the animals to consume. Alpacas are especially drawn to these plant communities, given their higher biomass and protein content (Castellaro et al. 2004). The animals then transform the waters and plants of the *uqhu* into their wool, flesh, and dung, which sustain the human communities living at the wetlands' edges.

For the people in Concepción's Quechua community in the Peruvian Andes, these *uqhu* are known to be integrated with the entirety of the world's water, flowing from the ocean up into the cosmos and back again in a vast "metabolic assemblage" of which humans are likewise a part (Paerregaard 2021; 2023). Far from a pristine, untouched landscape on which human and animal life unfolds, the wetlands are cultivated landscapes implicated in the broader relations of care, reciprocity, and predation that sustain the humans, animals, and landscapes of the Andean social world (White-Nockleby et al. 2021; Yager, Prieto, and Meneses 2021). *Uqhu* themselves are tended and cared for: through the irrigation canals that people often build to sustain the flow of water, and also indirectly through the practices of care between humans and animals (Vining 2016, 99; Squeo et al. 2006). While animals will always drift toward these nutrient-dense spaces, humans will urge them elsewhere when it is time for the wetlands to rest.

At its root(s), the *uqhu* is a relation, an assemblage, a network, a community. And, as such, it contains within it the risk of fragmentation. Indeed, the Andean wetlands are increasingly vulnerable to other

FIGURE 2 A young herder in an *uqhu* (alpine wetland). Photo by author.

processes at work: specifically, the transformations wrought by global climate change. The transformation of fossil fuels into greenhouse gases has altered temperatures and precipitation patterns around the world, including in the high Andes. Alpine wetlands are breaking apart, splintering into fragments with the continued disruption of water flow from melting glaciers. Climate scientists have referred to these fragments as "ecosystem sentinels for climate change" (Dangles et al. 2017), visible signals for otherwise stealthier shifts. For alpaca herders like Concepción, these wetlands are also spaces of inquiry, although the signals of change are myriad, diverse, and embedded within practices of sensing and caring for one another in this landscape. Concepción has always known a place like Illachiy to be revelatory: its very name, *Illachiy*, comes from the Quechua word "to illuminate."[1] It contained within it both the evidence and impacts of a fragmentation that extended more widely throughout the community of Chillca. But it also contained within its depths enduring streams of continuity and connection.

This is a book about the beginnings of fragmentation, specifically the first notes of agitation—of *restlessness*—as relations between people, animals, and landscapes began to strain and shift. When I arrived in the herding community of Chillca in southeastern Peru in 2015, the rumblings of a larger process of fragmentation were beginning to accelerate. Indeed, in the years after I left, the community would vote to divide their communal pasturelands in the face of increasing conflict over diminishing grasslands and restless animals. This book is, in many ways, the prelude to the breakdown of the commons. But more than that, it is an ethnographic exploration of the attentive forms of attunement, care, and communication through which people both sustain the multispecies assemblages within which they live and notice the first hints of estrangement and detachment in those relationships.

In more concrete terms, this book asks how herders in the community of Chillca *sensed* and *made sense* of changing socioecological conditions in the shifting qualities of their interactions with the humans, animals, and landscapes of the Cordillera Vilcanota mountain range of southeastern Peru. Much of this work was undertaken by the women of Chillca, who are the primary pastoralists in the Cordillera Vilcanota and continue to be "stewards of the rangelands" throughout the Andes mountains (Valdivia, Gilles, and Turin 2013). The central theoretical thread of this narrative draws on their utterances and provocations, specifically those shouted at wandering animals: *k'ita uywa*! Restless animals. In this book, I draw upon the Quechua concept of restlessness (*k'ita*) to articulate the breakdown of sociality between human and nonhuman social beings, as capricious mountains, distracted alpacas, wayward children, and aging bodies deviated from their expected spatial and temporal trajectories. When practices of sociality began to fall apart in Chillca—when animals no longer listened to the herder's whistles, humans no longer communicated with mountains, and both bodies and landscapes began to dry out— these failures signaled a broader ecological instability, one that threatened the viability of the herder's world and their own survival. And the Quechua analytic of restlessness that herders used to describe these changes both aligned with and challenged prevailing theoretical understandings of what it means to be vulnerable in a time of planetary crisis.

To explore the relationships that hold humans, animals, and landscapes together in the high Andes, I conducted two years of ethnographic and mixed-methods fieldwork (2014–16) in the Cordillera Vilcanota. Between June 2015 and July 2016, I lived in the community of Chillca, a small pastoralist community where people herded their animals in an approximately sixteen-hectare glacial valley system on the southern slopes of the mountain of Ausangate. For one of those years, I herded alongside the women of Chillca, following in their footsteps, observing their interactions with their animals, landscapes, and each other, until eventually I was deemed competent enough to tend a few animals myself. My methods entailed the careful analyses of the "ecology of obligation" of pastoralism (Despret and Meuret 2016, 27)—the multispecies relations of attention, care, affect, and predation—that coalesced in human and animal bodily orientation, communication, recognition, and shared labor in the pasture. While studying the daily practices through which herders and their animals coproduced their lived world, I became especially intrigued by the moments when the work of herding fell apart, and how these moments of frustration and antagonism were interpreted by herders as signals of broader socioecological trouble.

By analyzing climate change from the ground up, this book asks what herders in the high Andes can tell us about climate change in their communities. In the coming chapters, I will suggest that the Quechua concept of *k'ita* provides a compelling articulation of the social and ecological unpredictability that defines the world under a changing climate. Quechua analytics of restlessness both merge with and diverge from recent interpretations of unruly, wild, or feral ecologies. On the one hand, *k'ita* neatly articulates the confluence of temporal, spatial, and relational qualities that define precarity in a time of climate change. Traces of restlessness are palpable around the globe, as phenomena come untethered from their expected and anticipated positions in time and space, and predictable forms of relationality between beings and entities become increasingly elusive. And yet *k'ita* also pulls us back from the apocalyptic leanings of wildness, ferality, and unruliness to emphasize the continued practices of relation that endure through disruption.

The central narrative in this book pivots around the life history and experiences of Concepción Rojo Rojo, an alpaca herder and folk singer whose stories and songs provide a touchpoint for the broader discussions around change and continuity, endurance and precarity, and aspirations of improvement that rippled throughout the broader community. This isn't to suggest that this is her story alone: Concepción would not claim to speak for all herders in Chillca, and indeed there are many voices running throughout this text. Her experience stands not as the definitive story of this time and place but as a guiding line through what is a much larger and more complex story, the details of which will unfold throughout the ensuing chapters.

The chapters that follow root these stories in the daily life of the high Andean pasture, to explore how the breakdown of communication between humans and animals signals ecological trouble (chapter 1) and how relationships between humans, animals, and landscapes have shifted over time (chapters 2 and 3), rendering the work of sensing the world and cultivating relationships crucially different and generative of new potential futures (chapter 4). I explore the potentialities of this future and how this bears upon the sensory experience of living, and aging, in a rapidly changing place (chapter 5). All these stories unfold across the landscape of the Andes Mountains, a place that has drawn the attention of researchers because of its larger significance for understanding the intricacies of ecological connection and the rupturing possibilities of global climate change.

Tracing Climate Change in the Andes

This book is situated in one of the "climate laboratories" of the world. The Cordillera Vilcanota is a glaciated mountain range in southeastern Peru that extends roughly eighty kilometers east to west, with its highest peak, Ausangate, visible from the nearby city of Cusco. The Cordillera Vilcanota also houses the largest ice cap in the tropics, the Quelccaya, the site of an extensive climate science program that generates cryospheric and atmospheric data for the long-term assessment of global climatic changes (Thompson et al. 2011; 2013; 2017; 2021). Before the first climate stations were carved into Quelccaya's icy terminus, however, the Andes mountain range had long been a site of knowledge production concerning the Earth's climate and the interrelation of atmospheric, terrestrial, and aquatic life. Extending nearly seven thousand kilometers along the western edge of South America, the spine of the Andes emerges from the northern coastal shrublands of Venezuela before traversing Colombia, Ecuador, Peru, Bolivia, Chile, and Argentina, finally submerging at the continent's southern tip. At the turn of the nineteenth century, German geographer and philosopher Alexander von Humboldt's expeditions in the Andes laid the groundwork for the ecological sciences by positing a holistic understanding of the earth's processes: an interrelatedness of biotic communities and earth, atmospheric, and oceanic systems in a total "unity of nature." On the flanks of Chimborazo Mountain, von Humboldt mapped lines of relation between phenomena—altitude, temperature, atmospheric pressure, humidity, and the corresponding plants and animals—and, in doing so, ordered the world in such a way that continues to inform our understandings of the paired trajectories of climatic zones and the species housed within.

In recent decades, international climate researchers have continued to use Andean proxies to map the progressive and accelerating warming of the earth's climate. Changes in the Andean mountain ecosystem have revealed, unequivocally, that the past fifty years of climatic warming have been well outside the range of climate variability for the last several millennia (Thompson et al. 2013). Atmospheric warming in the Andes has been especially rapid compared to the rest of the planet: average surface air temperatures in the tropical Andes increased at a rate of 0.1 degree Celsius per decade in the late twentieth century (Vuille et al. 2003; 2008).

This warming trend has been predicted to continue and likely accelerate in the future, with projections indicating that temperatures in the high tropical Andes could increase by 3 to 6 degrees Celsius by the end of the twenty-first century, compared to late twentieth-century averages (1961–90), leading to more major El Niño events, more frequent heat waves, and fewer frost events (Bradley et al. 2009; Urrutia and Vuille 2009).

A devastating result of this temperature increase has been the loss of glacial ice cover throughout the Andes. Tropical Andean glaciers have been retreating progressively for an extended period of time, with periodic moments of stabilization and mass gain during the Little Ice Age between seventeenth and eighteenth centuries, and other intermittent periods of stabilization (Jomelli et al. 2009; Mark et al. 2002; Vuille et al. 2018). However, glacier retreat has accelerated in the tropical Andes since the 1970s, with most glacier cover decreasing significantly in volume and surface area due to the persistent ice loss associated with the rise in freezing-level height (Rabatel et al. 2013; Schauwecker et al. 2017). Increasingly strong El Niño events, characterized by augmented air temperatures and associated decreases in snow accumulation, have contributed to lowered albedo, higher radiation absorption, and further glacial mass loss (Vuille et al. 2018). The El Niño event during 2015–16, for example, produced greater ice wastage along the margin of the Quelccaya Ice Cap than in the previous fifteen years, and future El Niño events are predicted to be even stronger (Thompson et al. 2017). In the lead-up to the United Nations Climate Change Conference (COP 20), held in Lima in December 2014, the Peruvian government updated its national glacier inventory to reflect a 40 percent reduction in the country's glacial cover since the 1970s (UNFCCC 2014). This rapid deglaciation is clearly visible in satellite imagery from the Cordillera Vilcanota (Hanshaw and Bookhagen 2013; Kamp et al. 2021, Salzmann et al. 2013; Veettil and de Souza 2017).

Glacial retreat is projected to continue in the future regardless of various emission scenarios, and many of the smaller Andean glaciers—particularly those under one square kilometer, which constitute about half of the total glacierized surface area—are predicted to disappear in the coming decades (Rabatel et al. 2013; Drenkhan, Huggel, and Frey 2018). Many small, low-elevation glaciers in the tropical Andes are projected to disappear within a few decades, and 90 percent of all remaining permanent ice cover could be lost by 2090, part of a global trend of glacier loss (Huss et al. 2017). Indications suggest that the Quelccaya Ice Cap could disappear entirely within the next century (Yarleque et al. 2018). Currently, glacier retreat has led to a temporary increase in stream output, river flow, and a surplus of water availability in the dry season (La Frenierre and Mark 2014). However, glacial meltwater contribution to glacier-fed streams will eventually peak and then taper off as the ice disappears and glacier-fed water catchments shrink. Future water scarcity is all but inevitable throughout the Andes, and in the coastal regions and cities that depend on glacier water, particularly given the increasing demand of urban population growth and expansion of water-intensive industries like agriculture, mining, and hydropower.[2]

The scientific community has widely suggested that alpine wetlands, like Concepción's beloved *uqhu* in Illachiy, will be the ecosystems most heavily impacted by changes in meltwater discharge (Dangles et al. 2017; Loza Herrera, Meneses, and Anthelme 2015). Future decreases in hydrological output from glaciers and glacial catchments will likely lead to wetland shrinkage and fragmentation, creating patches that can no longer sustain the multitude of species that rely on them for both habitat and sustenance (Polk et al. 2017). Many high Andean wetlands have already lost aquatic connectivity to glacial meltwater, and have undergone plant community changes indicating severe reductions in the dry-season water table (Cooper et al. 2019). Further compounding this loss of glacial water, precipitation in the central Andes is projected to decrease significantly by the end of the century, leading to the further fragmentation of the *uqhu* ecological community (Kronenberg et al. 2016; Neukom et al. 2015).

※

By the time I arrived in 2015, Chillca's grasslands had already hosted many teams of climate scientists, each in search of the traces of global environmental processes in the ice, soils, plants, and animals of the Cordillera Vilcanota. Indeed, my first introduction to the community was facilitated by a team of frog biologists who were tracking the upward migration of the *Telmatobius marmoratus*, a spotted semiaquatic frog that inhabits the rivers, lakes, and montane wetlands of the Andean highlands. As melting glaciers create new pools and streams for them to explore, the frogs have started appearing higher and higher in the watery corridors of the glacier's wake (Reider 2018; Seimon et al. 2017). Following closely behind was *Batrachochytrium dendrobatidis*, a deadly chytrid fungus that appeared to be thriving under conditions of climate change in the lowlands and highlands of Peru, threatening to wipe out the frog population. The biologists had set several frog traps in Chillca's wetlands and found that people there were genuinely interested in their research and eager to talk about the changes that they, too, were noticing.

In 2015 climate scientists and Quechua alpaca herders were both deeply involved in the process of *tracing* climate change: producing knowledge about the world and theorizing about its roots and its consequences. People living in Chillca were encountering and interpreting a range of phenomena through the daily practice of caring for animals, and like the scientists on nearby Quelcayya, they were "learning to see climate change" (Irvine et al. 2019) in collaboration with the intuitive others with whom they shared their landscapes. As they traversed the landscape with their herds of alpaca, llamas, and sheep, they developed a cultivated attunement: a way of seeing, understanding, and analyzing their surroundings. As I mentioned in the beginning of this introduction, the word *illachiy* means "to illuminate," and it warrants some explanation of how the process of illumination works in Quechua. Much like its translation in English, the concept of *illachiy* holds a same duality of meaning, referring both to the act of "shining a light" upon something and the process of clarifying or making sense of it. The actual work of illumination is done through a practice that I call *tracing*. As I will elaborate in a later chapter, I draw this concept from the Quechua word *sut'i*, which describes a legible marker that indexes a previous event or action, tells of an underlying condition, or hints at an event or action to come. While no perfect translation exists, herders expressed the Spanish-language equivalent of *sut'i* as *al aire* (literally "in the air"; in plain sight, revealed, exposed, laid bare).[3]

Tracing, in this interpretation, is like any scientific methodology in that it is a process that involves the "selection and reassemblage of ideas and practices, of their creative elaboration and modification, undertaken by specific groups of people in specific institutional, political, and cultural locations" (Stepan 1991, 7). Tracing is dynamic, hybrid, flexible, and deeply immersed in a broader social and material context (Ingold 2011). People in Chillca knew, for example, to read the traces of two species of small birds (*waychu pichinchu* and *chusllunku*), who would announce the impending arrival of rain with a particular call ("kak'ay kak'ay kak'ay" for *waychu pichinchu* and "shhhchuchuchuchu" for *chusllunku*). Certain cloud patterns, particularly those that formed small spheres (*k'umpachakuy*), could announce the arrival of drought. In the wide field of literature on climate change, there is often a marked distinction made between "climate science" and "local" or "Indigenous" knowledges, without the clear acknowledgment that all knowledges are produced through culturally situated practices (Schnegg, O'Brian, and Sievert 2021; P. Harvey and Knox 2015; Gupta 1998). The data collected by climate scientists on Quelcayya glacier may align more closely to the generic "academic prototype" (Barth 2002, 2) of objective, ahistorical, and "pure" knowledge (Latour 1993), but it is no less situated within the broader social and material relations that give it its shape (Haraway 1988; Quijano 1999). Furthermore, these different practices of knowledge often arrive at the same conclusion (Orlove, Chiang, and Cane 2002).

Herders in Chillca traced changes in their world through observation as well as through various forms of communicative practice, and they made sense of those changes within Andean ontologies of place, person, and animal. As Catherine Allen has written, "To participate in a *pacha*, a world-moment, is to share in its *sut'i*, its clarity" (1998, 22). My goal was to share in the processes of tracing, of *sut'i*, through which herders rendered their world legible, bringing to light the transformative changes that constituted that particular moment in the high Andes. In Chillca, the emergence of ecological disruption often manifested in the shifting social relations between humans, animals, and landscapes, such that a capricious mountain or an inattentive sheep became critical interlocutors in articulating socioecological precarity. As both a methodological and ethical stance, I took *seriously* ontological premises of socioecological relatedness in Chillca (Viveiros de Castro 2011; de la Cadena 2010, 361). To that end, this book is grounded in the modes of identification and methods of analysis of the herders themselves, using that framework as the starting point from which to interrogate the emergence of incongruity, tension, and danger in a shifting world.

Within this frame, what could be identified as the traces of climate change are not so easily separated from the intricacies of everyday life in highland Peru. In addition to finding cause for concern in droughts and delayed migration schedules, herders also detected subtle changes in the emotional states of their animals and the rhythm of their daily herding tasks; shifting soundscapes of running water and cracking glacial ice; the disparate presences of plastics and smoke; and in the shifting tenor of their interactions with others, both human and nonhuman. These subtle shifts indexed broader transformations in the social relations between herders and their neighbors and animals; neighboring communities, city-dwellers, development agencies, and the state; and the sentient beings that inhabit their landscapes (mountains, glaciers, rock outcrops, and other socially agentive places). Rather than appearing as singularly linked phenomena, climatic changes emerged inextricably within a constellation of socioenvironmental concerns. Methodologically, this complexity was reflected in the ways that conversations and practices unfolded in the pasture, moving through a multiplicity at once, and leaving me—in the early days of fieldwork—stumbling and searching for the legible threads of continuity that aligned with how I strung phenomena together in chains of causality. It required a shift on my part to share in the herder's *sut'i*.

As will become apparent in the following chapters, the Quechua language was central to this work. Although I studied Quechua intensively for three years before beginning my fieldwork, the bulk of my language learning would happen during my time in Chillca, and it was the foundation of my ethnographic practice. I chose to foreground Quechua language and logics in my analysis and in this text for many reasons. First, thinking with and through Quechua herding analytics during my fieldwork allowed me to engage more deeply with the situated modes of practice and reflection through which ecological change emerged. This commitment also had ethical grounds: as Marilyn Strathern notes, "It matters what ideas we use to think other ideas (with)"—or, as Donna Haraway adds, "It matters what stories we tell to tell other stories with; it matters what knots knot knots, what thoughts think thoughts, what descriptions describe descriptions" (Strathern 1992, 10; Haraway 2016, 12). Practices of tracing are also practices in theory-making, and Quechua women are theorists in their own right. My ethnographic commitment was rooted in this premise, articulated by anthropologist Marieke Winchell, that "interlocutors' practices and activities carry their own conceptual stakes—they are doing theory" (2022b, 14). I aspired for my research to resemble, in part, the type of "recurrent threading" or collaborative "knotting" that scholars like Winchell urge us as anthropologists to undertake (Winchell 2022b, 14; 2022a, 4). While I tug specifically on the concept of *k'ita* as a provocative analytic for considering global climatic changes more broadly, inhabiting Quechua ideas "to think other ideas" allows for endlessly generative possibilities.

That being said, I have also kept my own presence and voice central in this book. This is a deliberate choice, informed by feminist critiques of disembodied methodological distance as the unfortunate archetype of empirical research (Haraway 1988). I am very present in these chapters, not to demonstrate my proximity or authority over this material, but rather to situate myself in relation to it. My positionality as a white American woman shaped the spaces I was allowed into, the conversations I could have, and the stories that people trusted me with. Furthermore, as a researcher from the Global North, I was acutely aware of how I was (and continue to be) implicated in the histories of extraction, globalization, and neocolonialism that have altered the trajectory of Chillca, as well as my own homelands. As I tell this story—a story that I have been entrusted to tell—I make that positionality present as an inextricable component of the narrative.

Restlessness in the Multispecies Collective

In the high Andes, humans and animals have long been partners in world-making and world-sensing. Alpacas and llamas share a lengthy history of co-domestication with humans, likely emerging multiple times in various locales throughout the Andes between 7000 and 5000 years BP (Mengoni Goñalons and Yacobaccio 2006; Mengoni Goñalons 2008; Wheeler 2012). "Domestication" is a fraught term, one that continues to hold connotations of human mastery despite ample evidence throughout the world that human-animal relationships vary tremendously from, for example, the brutal domination of industrial farming in the United States (Blanchette 2020) to the "intermittent coexistence" of nomadic herding in North Asia (Stépanoff et al. 2017). In the context of Andean pastoralism, camelid domestication is an ongoing process of attunement, cohabitation, and "mutual rearing" (Bugallo and Tomasi 2012). The 7000 and 5000 BP temporal marker refers to a significant period of species change, in which the wild camelids—"aggressive and territorial, well adapted for rapid flight in open terrain, and . . . difficult to habituate to human physical control"—became more akin to the llamas and alpacas we recognize today (Moore 2016, 18). The llama (*lama glama*) was bred from the wild guanaco in Peru, Chile, and Argentina as a pack animal and a source of meat and hides. The alpaca (*lama paco*) was bred from the wild vicuña in the central Peruvian Andes for its fine fiber. In both species, herders selectively bred camelids over generations that were gregarious, intuitive, and yielding to humans but also crucially self-directed.

The history of this human-animal relationship is both emplaced and place-making, and inextricable from the broader history of the Andean landscape (Nielsen 2016). Animals and humans together cultivated homes, pastures, pathways, and even empires: South American camelids contributed to the expansion and centralization of multiple large state societies such as the Chimu, Wari, Tiwanaku, and Inca through circulation of their fiber, meat, dung, transport labor, and ritual sacrifice (Browman 1989; deFrance 2016; Goepfert and Prieto 2016; Mengoni Goñalons 2008; Webster 1973; Vining 2016). The use of llama transport led to a vast integration of altitudinal production zones known as the "vertical archipelago" of the Andes, from the mountains to the altiplano, jungle, and along the coast (Gil Montero 2009; Murra 1972; Tripcevich 2016). Alpaca fiber and alpaca ritual sacrifice provided the material basis for social stratification and the consolidation of power in urban centers like Cusco (Brotherston 1989; Wheeler, Russel, and Redden 1995).

The camelid-centric infrastructure of the Andes was then co-opted by Spanish colonizers to fuel the extractive economy that would shape the region for the next five hundred years. When the Spanish arrived in what is now Peru in the 1530s, they quickly sutured an emerging system of colonial administration and labor extraction to the existing Indigenous infrastructure. Camelids played a central role in the supply of materials for mining and the provisioning of resources for the mining labor force. Even the animals' dung was co-opted in this vast extractive project: dried camelid droppings were collected in enormous quantities to provide fuel for smelting silver at the Potosí mines in Bolivia (Gade 2013, 225). In contrast to their immediate interest in the llama and its use as a pack animal, the Spanish were initially ambivalent regarding its smaller, softer cousin, the alpaca. It was not until much later, in the nineteenth century, that alpaca fiber became a commercialized export product (Gade 2013, 231; Orlove 1977a).

Camelids continue to be enmeshed in the inevitable reckoning of extractive resource economies throughout the globe. Since the industrial revolution, human activity has irreversibly altered atmospheric, oceanic, and terrestrial ecosystems. Arguably, these developments have rendered our interdependence with nonhuman others more readily palpable. Acknowledging that humans, animals, places, and their various "lifeways" are continuously entangled in processes of mutual becoming inevitably yields a discussion of our shared processes of mutual undoing (Tsing 2015). Or, perhaps, it offers us a moment to consider how we can continue to exist in "unexpected collaborations and combinations" with each other (Haraway 2016, 4). As this book will attest, the humans and animals of Chillca are indeed "staying with the trouble" (Haraway 2016) inextricably bound to one another through the most tumultuous of times.

Restless Ecologies joins in conversation a growing body of research dedicated to the dynamics of human and other-than-human relations in the anthropocene. Some of these works take an expansive view to interrogate the global entanglements of humans and other living beings, including animals, plants, fungi, and microbes, weaving together global narratives of meaning, exchange, and consumption to explore the possibilities of collaboration in an era of environmental crisis (Tsing 2012; Haraway 2016). Other works immerse these questions within particular localities (Stoetzer 2022; Chao 2022; Flachs 2019), locating central tensions in the situated material, sensory, and affective relationships between species (Parreñas 2018; Miller 2019). These texts emerge out of a longer interest in "contact zones" (Haraway 2008) and the permeability of previously held boundaries between human and other-than-human (Kirksey and Helmreich 2010). Indigenous and Native scholars have pushed back on the celebrated novelty of these approaches, however,

citing the centrality of other-than-human entanglement as an organizing principle in Indigenous and Native ontologies and epistemologies
(Tallbear 2011; Todd 2016; Whyte 2018). Indeed, anthropologists have
acknowledged the Indigenous antecedents of contemporary anthropological theoretical trends—for example, framing the core tenet of the
ontological turn as "taking seriously" (Viveiros de Castro 2011) or taking
"literally, rather than metaphorically" (de la Cadena 2010, 361) the practices and presuppositions of Indigenous peoples—although, notably, this
approach predates the ontological turn.[4]

Restless Ecologies likewise situates itself at the sensorial interstices of
a human-animal relationship in the anthropocene, yet it yields theoretical authority to the people at the center of the story and whose lives
and livelihoods are at stake. While herders in the Andes were tangling
with restless animals, variations on the concepts of *unruly, feral,* and
wild began to circulate in anthropological circles as tools with which
to think through the myriad impacts of a changing planet (Krishnan,
Pastore, and Temple 2015; Bubandt and Tsing 2018). In many ways, in
their frustrated shouts at their animals, Andean herders were articulating in powerful ways what these floating analytics of nondomestication
urged us to understand: our landscapes and livelihoods are, for better
and worse, shaped by an inherent wildness outside of human control.
The pasture has been forged over generations of human and animal wanderings, often with the animals leading the way. As I explore throughout
this book, domestication—of animals and of landscapes—is always only
partial (Pazzarelli 2020; Arnold 2022).

My translation of *k'ita* as restlessness—and not wild or feral—also has
political stakes. Daniel Heath Justice, an Indigenous literature scholar
and a Colorado-born member of the Cherokee nation, reminds us that
"when it comes to stories about Indigenous peoples, words—especially
those in non-Indigenous languages—bear a particularly burdensome
representation weight, usefully encrusted with hard, jagged layers of co-
lonialist misunderstanding" (2018, 6). Potawatomi environmental philosopher Kyle Powys Whyte likewise emphasizes how the words *wild,*
wildness, and *wilderness* "signal a culturally specific set of assumptions
about how humans relate to land, plants, and animals" that are based on
narrow interpretations of their potential interconnection (2024, 72). This
translation relies on ontological assumptions about what kinds of entities

compose the world, and what kinds of relationships and practices humans can and *should* have within ecosystems. As Whyte remarks, many Indigenous peoples of the Americas have "never really used anything like wild concepts to describe their relationships with land, water, plants, animals, and ecosystems," nor have they consented to those concepts being applied to them (2024, 72). In the Americas, demarcations of wildness are deeply rooted in settler colonial logics of function, utility, and productivity and are often used to define (and forcefully usurp) "useless" lands (Cronon 1996; Fisher 2023). The history of the term "wild" is not only rooted in misunderstandings of Indigenous peoples' relationships to land in the Americas and related practices of cultivation and stewardship but also inextricable from the histories of land dispossession, language loss, and forced assimilation that have accompanied settler colonialism.

It is important to note, however, that there is indeed something novel at work in Chillca, something akin to what Anna Tsing has called the "new wild" of the anthropocene (2018). Industrial and colonial histories have not only unleashed unwieldy entities and forces that upend livable ecologies and relations, but they have also altered the "companionable habits" of native species. A previously agreeable species—in Tsing's essay, a woody vine that lived in unremarkable cohabitation with Indonesian landscapes—feverishly accelerates in altered surroundings, defying human boundaries of space and time and frustrating human collaborative expectations. For Andean herders and their restless animals, this wildness is not a question of *kind* so much as *scale*: it is not a new wildness, but an unexpected *excess* of wildness that is causing trouble (Pazzarelli 2020). Animal restlessness is, after all, a necessary part of the human-animal encounter: ideally, the animals will roam peacefully of their own accord, sensing and finding their way to the most nutritious pastures and leaving the herder to rest on hillsides and catch up on their weaving. It is the excess of wandering that is now troubling the human sense of time and place, through the transgression of human spatial and temporal boundaries (Govindrajan 2015b). This other-than-human refusal of the human's best-laid plans might mean a day of headaches and exhaustion for the herder—or it could mean a lot worse. Restlessness, *k'ita*, acknowledges this other-than-human refusal, and the broader implications of ruptured relations that it signifies for the Quechua women at the heart of this ethnography: the *michiqkuna*, herders of the Andes.

Pastoralism as Women's Work

This book highlights women's knowledge and skill as pastoralists. Women in the Cordillera Vilcanota have been heralded for their spinning and weaving (Callañaupa Alvarez, Franquemont, and Coca 2013; Heckman 2003; Silverman 2008), but there has been less attention to the work that they are doing simultaneously. While weaving on backstrap looms staked into the hillside, the women's eyes often drift upward, their attention always on their animals. Women in Chillca took the animals out every morning, they watched them throughout the day, and they brought them in at night. They were constantly co-present with their animals: scanning the herd for any signs of distress, diagnosing and treating illnesses, monitoring their reproduction, and designating animals for slaughter, sale, and exchange. They were also continuously monitoring the grasslands through an attention to both the physical and emotional cues their animals gave them, and to the relative distribution of grass types and the availability of water. And they did this work in the company of other women. The conversations that took place between women herders—when they encountered each other in the pasture and shared food and observations of their animals—were fundamental to the ability of herders to live in this challenging alpine glacial landscape. It was during these moments in the pasture that women identified stressors affecting the health of the grasslands and the animals, and calculated potential strategies and solutions. Adaptive strategies such as modifying the herding calendar, or placing animals in reserve enclosures, found their roots in the daily, lived experiences of women.

Women's herding knowledge has often been overlooked by researchers as well as the many development projects related to animal husbandry and grassland management in Andean pastoralist communities (Caine 2021). This follows a broader historical trend in pastoralist studies and global development programs, which until recently have largely neglected to recognize women's labor (Hodgson 2001). Early ethnographies of Andean pastoralism—which emerged out of south-central Peru in the late 1960s and early 1970s, relatively late in comparison to the broader canon of pastoralist literature—provided invaluable complexity and nuance to combat the persistent stereotype of the "noble herdsman" (Dyson-Hudson and Dyson-Hudson 1980, 15) and also

FIGURE 3 A Quechua woman and her alpacas in the Cordillera Vilcanota. Photo by author.

widely acknowledged the role of women in the animals' care.[5] However, representations of women's involvement varied: from the assumption that women's labor was merely the rote completion of tasks assigned to them by a male head-of-household to the acknowledgment of herding as "women's work."[6]

I became interested in women's herding labor when I first read Catherine Allen's classic Andean ethnography, *The Hold Life Has* (1988). In it, she reflected on her own omission of women's pastoralist knowledge when she lamented the passing of her friend Rufina. Recalling how her own interests "did not strike a responsive chord" in Rufina, she acknowledged how "[Rufina's] interests and abilities were in animal husbandry" (1988, 72). As Allen recalls, "Too late I realized that on this subject she became open and expansive, and I could have learned much from her" (1988, 72). After Rufina's death, the centrality of women's knowledge and labor in sustaining the herd became apparent in the ways that Rufina was mourned:

At night Luis [Rufina's widowed husband] would sit with Rufina's sister . . . talking brokenly about his herds. If he and the children tried to care for the animals they'd kill them all, he insisted. Already a couple of lambs had died. Now, a woman knows how to keep track of animals. She can doctor their illnesses. She knows which have conceived and how many months along they are. She knows the approximate hour to expect births and how to attend female animals in labor, for a woman understands pregnancy and birth. How can a man know about these things? (Allen 1988, 73)

In the decades following Allen's work, there have been a number of important contributions to Andean pastoralist studies that foreground the specialized knowledge and skill of women in their work with animals (Arnold and Yapita 2001; Dransart 2003; Göbel 2002; Valdivia, Gilles, and Turin 2013). This scholarship dovetails with a broader acknowledgment of Andean women's labor, skill, and knowledge across multiple realms of practice, from kinship (Van Vleet 2008b), foodways and carework (Harris 2000; Weismantel 1988), commerce and development (Babb 2018; Cookson 2018; Seligmann 2000), and politics (Picq 2018). This book adds to this rich canon by situating women's labor, knowledge, and skill in the pasture, as well as within the broader context of shifting land tenure practices and global climatic changes.

The *Comunidad* and Commons of Chillca, Peru

According to a census conducted by the health post in coordination with community officials, there were ninety-eight families (*familias*) living in the various sectors of the community of Chillca in 2015, corresponding to roughly 385 individuals.[7] The unit of the *familia* was recorded for community business, school attendance, and health initiatives, and was intended to correspond to a nuclear family, a physical household, and a singular herd of animals. However, kinship and residence dynamics in Chillca were predictably more complicated. I used the term "herd-household" throughout my research to represent a more animal-centric unit that began with the herd (a unified group of alpacas, sheep, llamas) and extended to the humans who oriented themselves around that herd. This wasn't an arbitrary choice: in their day-to-day life, people in

Chillca talked about people and their herds as a contiguous unit. Furthermore, the people who shared a herd weren't always members of a nuclear family unit but could be, for example: two adults, their children, and a widowed grandmother; a single widow; a widower, his children, and their maternal grandmother; a pair of siblings, their spouses, and their children. Furthermore, a single herd-household was not consistently bound to a particular residence or pasture but occupied different residences or enclosures throughout the year. The animals within a herd-household did not all belong to the same person or family: most belonged to the adult members of the herd-household, but as children grew up, they were also given herd animals, such that one herd might belong to as many as eight to ten people. What held the herd-household together was a shared commitment to the labor of herding and caring for the same animals.

In 2015 a typical herd-household in Chillca encompassed roughly one hundred alpaca, thirty llamas, and forty sheep.[8] Alpaca were kept for their wool, which was shorn once a year in the month of November. They also provided sustenance: young, castrated alpacas were often sold for their meat; while older, nonreproductive animals were consumed by the family. A typical herd of alpacas had one stud male (*qhayñachu* or *padrillu*) for every twenty to forty reproductive females. Llamas were kept largely as transport animals, bringing dung from the pastures to the potato farms for fertilizing (August, September, and October), and potatoes from the farms to the storehouses (May, June, July). They were also contracted by the local tourism operator to transport luggage on the Ausangate trek. Female llamas were herded with the alpacas, while male llamas were left to roam the hilltops with periodic supervision. Finally, sheep were also kept for their wool, which could be sold as a source of supplemental income along with their meat.

Like many pastoralist communities in the Peruvian Andes, Chillca was a place in transition when I arrived in 2015. What initially drew me to Chillca was the community-wide rotation of pastures, an increasingly rare pastoralist commons in a patchwork of enclosure. Chillca had a much longer and complicated history of sociopolitical organization. Prior to the Peruvian agrarian reform of 1969, much of its territory was occupied by three large haciendas and a smaller private landholding (*previo*). After the agrarian reform, the Peruvian state held title to those lands, while the rest of the area was incorporated into the neighboring *comunidad campesina* (peasant community) of Pampachiri. In 1985, Chillca separated from Pampachiri and became its own *comunidad campesina*, initiating a lengthy process of land retitling in which historical land claims were formalized into a sectoral system. In 2015 the community contained nine sectors and one annex, the most populated of which was a sector also named Chillca, followed in relative population by the sectors of Chimpa Chillca, Phinaya, Killeta, Antaparara, Quesiunu, Uyuni, Alkatarwi, and Qampa.[9]

In 2015 the land tenure system in Chillca followed a relatively widespread system of mixed property rights in the Andes, wherein individuals managed their herd and residential property, families mediated access to pasture, and the community administration managed the community herds and shared resources. Each sector of the community contained designated wet-season and dry-season pastures within its boundaries, and each herd-household had multiple residences located in residential clusters (*astanas*, from the Spanish *estancias*, or "hamlets") alongside seasonal pastures. Pastures were shared as common property among the herd-households of each sector, and their use was negotiated on a daily and seasonal basis.[10] Seasonal migrations between designated wet-season and dry-season pastures were formalized. They required a verbal agreement (*acuerdo*) between herd-households in a sector and were subject to the oversight of the central governing body (*junta directiva*, as well as the alpaca committee, *comité de alpacas*) since the migrations also concerned the seasonal location of the community's alpaca herd, the *majada*. In 2015 Chillca maintained a *majada* of around twenty-five hundred animals (approx. twenty-three hundred alpacas and two hundred sheep) divided into seven smaller herds by sex, age, and coat color. Each year in November and May, the herding responsibilities of the *majada* were rotated between the families in each sector, and all families were responsible for contributing to the herd's care through communal medicating events (*hampiy faina*).

The primary driver of seasonal migration in Chillca was the fluctuating availability in biomass, particularly within the wetland and grassland plant communities. Chillca is situated at 4,400 meters (roughly 14,500 feet) above sea level in an ecozone characterized by semiarid conditions, limited oxygen, sparse vegetation, high solar radiation, and diurnal temperature fluctuations that produce deep nightly frosts almost year-round. The soils are predominantly acidic and low in phosphorous and nitrogen due to cold temperatures that inhibit decomposition of organic matter, making the soil hostile for most plant communities except for open grasslands (*pajonales*); alpine wetlands (*bofedales*; *uqhu*); and limited areas of shrub-cover (*tolares*).

In the wet season (*puquy timpu*; *tiempo de lluvias*), roughly between November and April, conditions are slightly warmer with significantly higher average rates of daily precipitation. Typically, the rains arrive intermittently in September and October, strengthening into afternoon rainstorms by November. In the wettest months, thunderous hailstorms whipped across the landscape with a startling ferocity, first appearing as ominous, opaque curtains that descended into the valley and shrouded the hillsides in white. The months of February and March had notoriously high levels of daily precipitation, earning them the names *febrero loco* and *marzo borracho* (crazy February and drunken March). During this time, the seasonal grasses of the *pajonales* would regenerate: dense bunch grasses, predominantly of the genera *Festuca sp.*, *Stipa sp.*, and *Calamogrostis sp.*, interspersed with stunted vascular plants, such as *brachypodium* and *valeriana* (Flores Martínez 2005). These plant communities have a high root-to-shoot ratio, with well-developed and extensive root systems that allow them to survive the prolonged dry season. However, these grasses also have less nutritional value than the wetland varieties and are less favorable pasture for llamas and alpacas (Bryant and Farfan 1984).

The dry season (Quechua: *chirawa*, Spanish: *tiempo de sequía*), between approximately May and October, is slightly colder with deep nightly frosts. In this season, precipitation is scant to nonexistent in the driest months, and herders keep their animals close to the glacier-fed wetlands. The *uqhu* have year-round soil humidity and cushion vegetation (especially *Distichia muscoides* and *Distichia acicularis*) with thick cuticle layers that absorb and hold water (Rado Janzic 2011). These nourishing plant communities have higher biomass and protein content than similar non-wetland species (San Martin and Bryant 1989; Maldonado Fonkén 2014).[11] In each sector where a wetland was present, the herd-households would occupy wetland-adjacent residences during the driest months of the year but would move as soon as the rains returned to avoid damaging these delicate ecosystems. *Uqhu* were largely off-limits or reserved (*reservado*) in the wet season.[12]

However, in contrast to the neat spreadsheets of herding patterns I diligently mapped my first months in Chillca, what unfolded over the course of a year was quite different: in the dizzying hum of daily life, contingencies ranging from twisted ankles to school and church obligations, house construction projects, *hampiy fainas*, shearing events, and the yearly roundup (*chaku*) of the community's wild vicuña population waylaid herders' plans. While delayed rains, drought conditions, and restless animals prompted the initial sector-wide agreements to rotate pastures, what followed on the ground reflected the embeddedness of these migrations within a broader socioecological landscape. Caring for herd animals was inextricably linked with the practices through which people sustained relationships with their kin and neighbors through labor exchange (house-raising, farming, and herding) as well as larger institutional structures like the community, the church, school, NGOs, and the state.[13] To actually track the yearly migrations of Chillca's herders, it was necessary to watch them unfold over the course of the year.

As I alluded to in the beginning of the introduction, the community of Chillca has changed substantially since I lived there. For this reason, the descriptions of Chillca and my fieldwork there are written largely in past tense. This reflects not only how much has changed since I left in 2016 but also how quickly things shifted even while I was there. It is impossible to describe Chillca as if it were a stable entity at any point in time. Rather, this book constitutes a snapshot, a moment, in the years before the community of Chillca dissolved their communal land into privately owned parcels. I will address the process of parcelization briefly at the end of the book, but, ultimately, the detailed story of those discussions is not mine to tell. Rather, I "dwell in the dissolve" (Alaimo 2016, 4) here—not as a form of "salvage ethnography," an effort to capture a lost world—but rather to engage with particular moment of unraveling in a restless world that we all inhabit, and in whose restlessness we are all implicated.

Fieldwork

I arrived in June 2015 to an empty town center. I climbed the wooden ladder to the storage space the community had allotted me, wrenched open the small door to a bare room, and unpacked my sleeping bag and a small cookstove. I'd sleep three cold nights there, before Concepción's son Mario fetched me to meet his mother up in the hamlet of Antapata. The previous month, she had watched me present myself and my research at the community assembly. Standing on the stage before the community, I introduced myself in Quechua, glancing at the notes I had jotted down on the wrinkled piece of paper—I was an anthropologist from the United States, I had been learning Quechua at the University of Michigan, and now I wanted to learn about pastoralism in their community, with their permission. The community put it to a vote, handed me a key to the storage room, and told me to come back the following month.

And so it was, when I arrived in June, that Mario sought me out and told me that his mother was worried about me sleeping alone. Concepción herself hated to sleep alone in the high valley of Antapata when her husband, Julio, was away working as a porter on the tourist treks around Ausangate. Concepción was known in the community for taking in strays: a few years before I arrived, she had welcomed a Japanese anthropologist into her home. He had been studying diet and nutrition, among other things, so she enthusiastically asked me if I'd like to weigh her meals every day. I politely declined, explaining I was not doing that type of study, which she gingerly accepted. She appreciated my company, and we quickly fell into a familiar pattern of cohabitation. During the day, we would take her animals out to pasture, and she would provide a running commentary of her own and her neighbor's activities, concerned as she was with my education into the goings-on of Chillca. Petite and wiry, Concepción was a strong and energetic herder. She enjoyed that I could keep up with her and was quick to share a bit of gossip with a rueful laugh when we took our breaks together.

In the evenings, Concepción and I would lean in close, and she'd assume the role of a researcher: commenting on my hair, hands, feet, contact lenses, and clothing and asking questions about me, my family, and my home. She'd rummage through the bags that were stashed throughout the hut, finding little treasures to show me. A rock shaped like an ear of corn, a vicuña's foot, bits and pieces of sewing projects, old bottles of medicine or alcohol that she'd sniff and pat onto our foreheads to ward off the malevolent winds that keened through the thatched roof. And then she would talk out loud as we fell asleep, shuffling blankets and skins around us to make our beds, making sure I wasn't touching the cold stone wall, while she huddled by the fire. She'd often wake up in the night to sew, weave, or cook, and I'd feel the soft glow of her lantern hit my face as she checked in on me.

Concepción was a celebrated singer of *waynu*—known as the blues of the Andes, for its mournful themes cloaked in upbeat rhythms—and always kept a radio on her to listen to the latest regional music. When she was younger, she performed with her family band, Conjunto Huaman Ticlla de Ausangate. In each of the chapters that follow, I foreground her songs, even if she herself fades into the background of the story. Singing these songs wasn't just something that Concepción enjoyed; it was her way of making sense of the world around her and narrating her lived experience. Many of her songs begin in the landscape, before submerging into her emotional world—*My dear pampas of* Chillca, *my dear Q'inqu river, where do you take my young beloved? Where, wandering, will I find my beloved?* Concepción was not prone to lengthy monologues, preferring to talk about her lived history in short bursts while she taught me about the animals, lands, and waters of Chillca. I enjoyed Conce's quiet and contemplative presence during our days in the pasture, and I held

FIGURE 4 Concepción Rojo Rojo. Photo by Pamela Michie Caine.

onto her talkative moments like warm stones, turning them over and over in the days that followed. It was through her songs that I'd hear more of the resonances of her emotional landscape, the joys and sorrows of her years past. Some of the songs that animate these chapters are drawn from the recorded discography of Conjunto Huaman Ticlla de Ausangate, and some from the evenings she and Julio would sing and play the bandurria in the dark warmth of their home.

During the year I lived with her, Concepción cared for around one hundred alpacas, thirty llamas, sixty sheep, three dogs, and a cat. As with any herd-household, those numbers fluctuated as she bought, traded, sold, and butchered animals. Among the smaller animals—the dogs Chinchirkumacha, Sultira, Chulu Banditu, and an unnamed and despised cat—Sultira had six puppies, of which none survived; Chulu Banditu met a tragic and mysterious end; and Concepción may or may not have deliberately poisoned the family cat. For the remainder of the dry season, I lived with Concepción and her animals in the hamlet of Antapata, which was tucked alongside her corrals into a hillside crosscut with the worn herding paths leading into the valley of Illachiy. Periodically I would spend nights up in the dry-season hamlet of Uqi Kancha with Concepción's mother, Emilia, and with Concepción's son and daughter-in-law, Mario and Maritza, with whom I became especially close. When they returned to their wet-season pastures in the central valley later in the year, I ventured further afield to visit people throughout the community, with a bit more herding ability under my belt and my Quechua a little less halting.

The key insights of this book emerged from participating in the minutiae of daily practice and observing the attentive engagement of Chillca's herders. In addition to participant observation and the corresponding field notes, I also created maps of herding routes with the use of a GPS unit and collected audio recordings and detailed notation of herding practices, conversations, ritual activities, and community meetings. This mixed-methods approach allowed me to capture the holistic, sociospatial practices of herding animals in a rapidly transforming glacial valley ecosystem. By grounding my research in practices of daily life in the Andes, I sought to engage with the situated epistemological and ontological premises through which environmental changes came to be recognized and coded as risks or opportunities, and the material, social, and ritual practices through which herders defined the qualities of vulnerability and forged adaptive possibilities. As Morgan Scoville-Simonds has argued, while there is a large body of research on "perceptions" of climate change in the Andes and elsewhere, there is comparatively less engagement with the epistemological practices through which climate change phenomena are made legible (2018). This is especially true of the routine, mundane practices of everyday life through which people produce knowledge about changes occurring in the world. For this reason, I maintain an analytical focus on these everyday encounters, choosing to undertake an "ethnography of small spaces" (Canessa 2012): analyzing spontaneous intimate encounters rather than more formalized ritual events, recognizing that it is "in the banal and humble intimacies of everyday" that multispecies relationships of power and history are collaboratively (re) produced and challenged (Canessa 2012, 25).

The anthropology of climate change is a crowded field, and this book joins—and hopefully, extends—a wide body of literature on climate change and Indigenous communities. Anthropological attention to climate change has yielded valuable insights into climate-based impacts in communities and institutions throughout the world (Barnes et al. 2013; Crate 2011; Crate and Nuttall 2009; Fiske et al. 2014; Whitington 2016). This work has led to a critical reevaluation of theories of adaptation, with an emphasis on the culturally contingent nature of vulnerability within situated ontologies (Adger 2006; Adger et al. 2013; Agrawal et al. 2012; Berkes and Jolly 2002; Leonard et al. 2013; Orlove 2005; 2009). While notions of adaptation, resilience, and vulnerability consistently appear in policy and development discourse and practice, it was only relatively recently that these theoretical concepts were translated from the ecological to the social sciences, and their application to social systems has been problematic (Adger 2000; Lemos et al. 2007; Gallopín 2006). Anthropological research has revealed the limitations of this terminology in representing the evaluations and practices of climate-affected communities themselves (Orlove 2009; Eakin and Luers 2006). In particular, anthropologists have shown how environmental hazards are deeply contextualized within specific ontologies of human-environmental relatedness that belie rigid dichotomies of nature/culture, history/event, and normal/abnormal (Cruikshank 2005; Kirsch 2004).

In essence, I have adopted what can be called "bottom-up approach" to climate change in Andean ecosystems, or what Peruvian anthropologist

Juan Rivera Andía defines as "a symmetric openness" (Rivera Andía 2018, 1). It is an iterative approach that blends my own interpretations with those of my friends, herding partners, and interlocutors in Chillca. This methodology stands in dedicated opposition to the top-down, "experience-distant" (Geertz 1983) structure of generic climate vulnerability assessments, in which evaluations of local impacts are based on standard models of human systems and short-term survey methodologies. These evaluative structures reproduce dominant Western perspectives while glossing over the primary concerns and ontological premises of the affected communities themselves. Mobilized within policy discourse, notions of vulnerability and adaptation can become unmoored and abstracted from human experience, obscuring how climate-affected communities evaluate and address transformative changes in their daily lives. Throughout this book, I emphasize the importance of ethnographically grounded approaches to climate change adaptation that privilege the analyses of Quechua peoples sensing a changing world.

Structure of the Book

In the following chapter, we'll begin in the pasture. The narrative arc of chapter 1 is structured around a single day in the life of a herder, following Concepción as she pastures her animals in the glacial wetlands above Chillca. By focusing on the details of the everyday, this chapter attends to the quotidian practices of communication and cooperative labor through which herders and their animals coproduce their lived world. It lays the foundation for understanding how herders detect ecological disruption in the world around them and how, ideally, humans and animals co-produce the strategies that allow them to respond to shifting conditions. It focuses specifically on communication practices, and how the breakdown of communication between humans and animals signals ecological trouble.

Understanding restlessness requires understanding how relationships between human and animal lives are intertwined in the first place. In chapter 2, I explore the labor of caring for animals as a constitutive part of women's identity in Chillca. I detail the practices of raising animals, and the systems of animal and labor exchange through which women in

Chillca establish themselves as competent herders. I examine how these regimes of value and practice are changing as new opportunities are afforded to people in Chillca.

In chapter 3, I examine how relationships between humans, animals, and landscapes have shifted over time, and orient us within Concepción's lived history. Historically, practices of commensality between humans and the land have been considered essential to the continued viability of Chillca as a community. However, in recent decades, these relationships have fallen out of practice, due in large part to widespread evangelization efforts in the Cordillera Vilcanota by the Maranata church. As a consequence, humans no longer *sense* phenomena in the same ways, and the world itself has become less *sensible*: unpredictable, unstable, more intense, and less legible.

Chapter 4 examines how people in Chillca imagined and cultivated "better" futures for themselves through their conversations around land tenure change. These improved futures emerged in coordination with broader regimes of power, including the Peruvian state, international wool markets, and development initiatives aimed at the rural poor. They centered around human, animal, and landscape possibilities, and articulated novel forms of relationality and responsibility between social beings. And they often left out members of the older generations, like Concepción, for whom a life of herding is "all we've known."

In the final chapter, I discuss the felt experiences of health, aging, and ecological change in the lives of Chillca herders. The narrative thread returns to Concepción, as she contemplates her ill-health and the future of her community. The outmigration of many of Chillca's younger generation has left behind an aging population that root an increase in health issues in the breakdown of familial and territorial networks. This final chapter explores how aging women in Chillca felt their bodies and lived experience as bundles of relation that were unraveling in the face of persistent drought, glacier retreat, and an aspirational future from which they were excluded.

CHAPTER ONE

Restless Animals

AGUSTU WAYRAHINA (LIKE AUGUST WIND)

Yachayurankitaq, sabiyurankitaq	You must have known, you may have known
Yachayurankitaq, sabiyurankitaq	You must have known, you may have known
Agustu wayrachahina luku kasqaytaqa	That I was crazy like the August winds
Fibriru killachahina waqʼa kasqaytaqa	That I was mad like the month of February
Taytayman mamayman willayapuwanki	You'd tell on me to my father and mother
Mamayman taytayman willayapuwanki	You'd tell on me to my mother and father
Warmi wawaykiqa ripushanmi, nispa	Saying, "Your daughter is leaving."
Warmi wawaykiqa pasashanmi, nispa	Saying, "Your daughter is going away."
Hinaya ripuchun, nispa niwaqtinqa	"Let her go," they'll say about me
Hinaya pasachun, nispa niwaqtinqa	"Let her go," they'll say about me
Wichaypas uraypas ripukapunaypaq	So that I'd go away, ascending and descending
Uraypas wichaypas pasakapunaypaq	So that I'd leave, descending and ascending

Daybreak

Concepción rose every morning instantly attentive to her animals. Often awakening from a dream in which she was watching the herd, she'd jolt into consciousness just as a herding command or whistle left her lips. In the small hut I shared with her, I became accustomed to these whispered remnants of dreamt chases. Even in her sleep, her mouth formed around the acoustic signals that she used throughout the day, her tongue poised at the back of her teeth in anticipation. Her body carried other traces of her day's labor, and she was often kept awake by the lingering imprints of her daily work: her feet and knees hurt constantly, her waist was sore from the weight of her skirts, and her head ached from the frustration of chasing wandering animals. When she couldn't sleep at all, I would catch her awake at three or four in the morning, weaving or mending her clothing by the orange light of a miner's headlamp, the radio playing softly in the background as she kept her eyes trained on the animal bodies taking shape outside in the emerging light.

On an early morning in September 2015, toward the end of the late dry season, the herd-households of Antapata began to stir. Nestled at the base of three long glacial valleys, Antapata was the dry-season hamlet (*astana*) for the families of the central Chillca sector, including Concepción. The first rays of light appeared just over the hilltops, illuminating the trails of smoke seeping out from thatched roofs. Rays of icy sunlight pierced the smoky interior of the hut as Concepción wrenched the rusted metal door open, stepped over the stone threshold into the frigid morning to shout, "Winus días, siñurita!" ("Good morning, *señorita!*") into the morning air. Ducking back into the hut, she tightened her shawl around her shoulders and cursed the bitter morning cold. She had coaxed the previous night's embers into a strong flame, an art that seemed nothing less than magic in those frigid pre-sunrise hours. Crouching low by the fire, she stirred two large simmering pots, dropping slices of potato, carrot, onion, and chunks of meat into one pot to make our soup for the day. In the other pot—older and tarnished black—she tossed the scraps, peels, bones, and gristle for the dogs, finished off with a final glug of alpaca blood from a plastic gasoline jug.

Every year between the months of March and May, as the rains dried up and the deep chill of the dry season began to settle in, herders in the central sector of Chillca moved their animals from the valley floor to the high, glacier-fed wetlands at the base of Ausangate Mountain. Six households migrated to the hamlet of Antapata, while two households migrated to the valley of Unu Palqa, and four households (including Concepción's mother, son, and daughter-in-law) walked twenty minutes further to the hamlet of Uqi Kancha, where the piercing white peak of Ausangate hung over a wide gully. They would remain there until the months of October through December, when the rains returned, and they'd make the migration in reverse, each household descending from the mountains down to the valley floor in order of seniority. Their homes in the high, dry-season hamlets didn't allow for many nonessentials. The stone-and-thatch homes were no more than two meters wide by four meters long, dominated by a central alpaca-dung hearth. In the deep cold of the dry season, the embers were always kept warm, rendering the floor next to the hearth as the most desirable sleeping spot. The inside of the home was blackened by smoke, and the underside of the roof dripped tendrils of soot-covered thatch. The stone walls provided convenient nooks to stash plastic bags and bottles filled with various essentials (alcohol, salt, herbs, spices, medicine, beads, yarn, batteries). Outside the home, small conical peat structures called *pirwas* held the alpaca dung (*ucha*) that the herders collected over the course of the dry season. When they were ready to return to the central valley, they would haul the *ucha* back to their homes on their llamas' backs, where the dung served as their fuel for the rest of the year.

As the pots softly simmered, Concepción kept a watchful eye on the animals outside, springing up from her crouched position and darting to the door to shout—*ukya, yaw!*—at the small herd of sheep growing restless in their pen. Her alpacas, near one hundred animals in total, stirred with soft keens and grunts on the matted circle of grass between the neighboring houses. She ladled two big bowls of soup for us, and poured the thick, gray-brown sludge of dog-soup into a pair of overturned miners' helmets tumbled on the front stoop for the dogs: the two large black herding dogs, Sultira and Chinchirkumacha; and the little sausage-dog, Banditu, whom Concepción's husband, Julio, often smuggled in his jacket to sleep in the warmth of the hut at night. We'd sit and eat by the door, a moment of calm in the morning's rush.

The calm never lasted for long. As the sunlight swept across the narrow valley, it melted the previous night's frost that had coated the grass and the backs of sleeping animals. The space between the neighboring herds slowly began to shrink as the animals gathered and shuffled in anticipation of the morning's journey to the wetlands above. Concepción darted repeatedly out the door to whistle and shout at them to stay put, cursing under her breath as her soup sloshed onto her skirts and the floor. Greeting her cousin and his wife in the home next door, she asked where they were taking their animals for the day. "Mayta rinkis?" "*Illachiyman*, to the valley of Illachiy," they yelled back. Every morning, herders coordinated the daily rotations of their herds between designated grazing locations. Concepción lived in closest proximity to her cousin Faustino and his wife Elizabeth, and across the small valley from another cousin, Vicente, and his wife Julia, as well as her neighbors Victor and Santusa, and a young couple Hernan and Aniseta, who was the sister of Concepción's daughter-in-law, Maritza. These were the households she most often coordinated herding labor with, usually through informal conversations shouted across a rising herd, or tacitly by observing where the neighboring herds were headed.

Tossing her carrying cloth (*q'ipina*) on her back and her radio over one shoulder, Concepción made a quick calculation, anticipating where the three families across the valley would bring their herds based on where they were the day before. I was only halfway into my boots, my felt hat perched haphazardly on my sleep-worn braids, as we ducked out the door and sealed it hastily with a pile of rocks. Walking briskly toward the moving herd with whip in hand, Concepción followed the animals down the valley toward Hatun Wayq'u valley. The day's herding had begun.

※

A herder's daily life in Chillca was organized—temporally, spatially, and socially—through a continuous attentive engagement with her animals. The herders of Chillca awoke with their animals in the morning, accompanied them into the pastures all day, and returned in the evenings together to sleep. In the Western imaginary of the pastoral, this daily work sounds peaceful and romantic, set to the sleepy soundtrack of windswept grasses and gurgling brooks. For the herder, it was decidedly less so. Especially in the dry season, when the rains were long gone and the wild winds of August had lifted away whatever strands of dry grass remained, the urgency of hunger gripped the herd and the herder alike, and the day's work accelerated, punctuated by the aberrant movement of increasingly restless animals.

In the minutiae of the everyday, herders and their animals co-produced their lived world through practices of recognition, communication, and cooperative labor. It was through these interactions that herders and their animals detected disruption in the world around them—particularly the impacts of seasonal fluctuations in water and pasture availability. Ideally, humans and animals also coproduced the mobile strategies that allowed them to respond to seasonal shifts by rotating pastures. Indeed, the work of herding (*michiy*) was premised upon a cooperative mode of engagement between humans and animals: humans did not continuously control or dominate their herd animals but often trusted in the intuitive knowledge and initiative of the animals themselves to accomplish the work of herding. In particular, herders relied upon animal knowledge of the grasslands to detect ecological shifts, and made inferences about pasture health by reading the cues their animals gave them, ranging from contented ear-twitches to agitated stomps. They also worked with animals to implement strategies in response to ecological change, recruiting and depending upon the initiative of lead alpacas, herding dogs, and the broader herd to accomplish the shared labor of moving to more promising pastures. The shared work of evaluating grasslands and strategizing in response was enabled through processes of mutual attunement between animals and humans, grounded in successful communicative exchanges between them.

In the months after I arrived in Chillca, my ears became trained to the patterns of acoustic signaling that permeated the pasture from sunrise to sunset. In the morning, the herders' whistles would blend with birdcalls emanating from the hillsides, gently urging the animals to their pastures. By midday the whistles and calls burst through the mountain air crisp and sharp, as if descending directly from the brightness of the afternoon sky above. In the evenings, they grew long and low, melting into the inkiness of the darkening twilight. They were the constant soundtrack of life in Chillca, and at the same time, its audible heartbeat. However, I was most intrigued by the moments when these communicative exchanges fell apart. Perhaps one animal would start to wander, and another would follow, and then another. Or the entire herd would lilt to one side of the valley, veering too close to a neighboring herd or the herding boundaries. The animals would become increasingly fickle and unresponsive, refusing to heed the herder's frustrated shouts and calls. The expectations of trust and intuition that underpinned human-animal sociality would break down into unpredictable states of madness and wandering. Herders and animals struggled to coordinate the controlled movement that secured their ability to survive in a challenging and, at times, capricious environment: the animals had become *k'ita*. In this chapter, I take us deeper into the practices and logics of herding in order to understand what *k'ita* is, what it means, and how it emerges through the daily work of herding animals in the high pastures of Chillca.

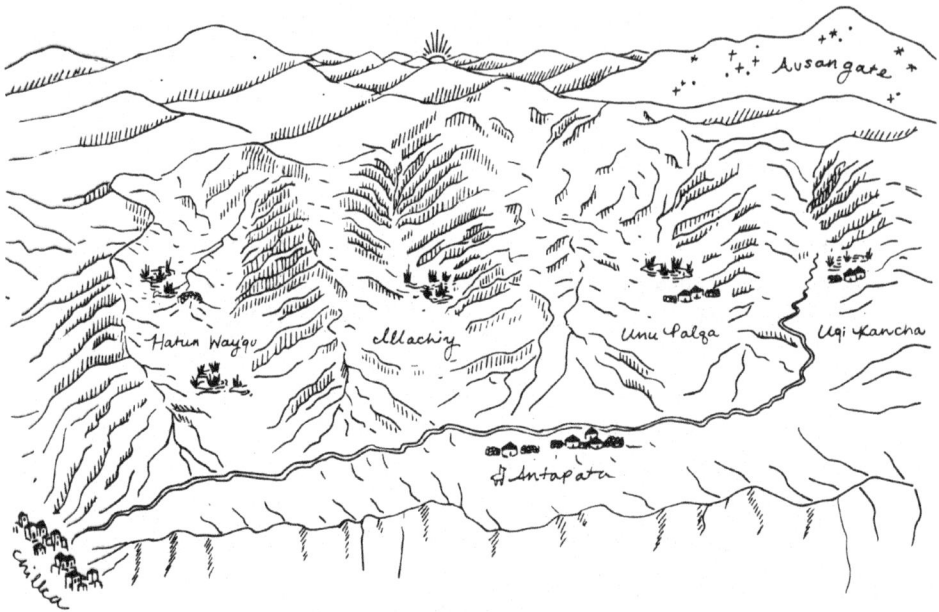

FIGURE 5 Map of the valleys of Antapata and Uqi Kancha. Map design by Mia Loia.

The Day Begins

Setting off from Antapata, the alpacas quickly took to the well-worn paths toward Illachiy, their preferred pasture. Concepción ran up the steep hillside and positioned herself above them, redirecting their movement down to the lower corridor of another valley, Hatun Wayq'u. She followed a few paces behind them until the animals' momentum was steady and directed, before turning back and racing down the hillside to the corrals. The sheep were agitated in their pen, crowding the gate as Concepción fetched the newest lamb, born the night before, to take it and its nursing mother to a reserved enclosure (*tullu kancha*, "skinny corral"), where a spindly sprinkler urged the last hints of green from the waning grasses. Too many lambs had already been lost that season. The body of another lamb lay just within the door of the hut, soon to be boiled for meat. The newest lamb was a delicate, tiny thing that Concepción had named *hukucha*, "little mouse." She plopped him gingerly in the enclosure and released the rest of the sheep in a tumble onto the hillside. The alpacas were already disappearing into the mouth of Hatun Wayq'u as we scrambled in pursuit.

Concepción bounded behind her animals with speed and agility, launching rocks with her whip (*wark'a*) at the hind feet of straggling animals with startling accuracy. Concepción's skills as a herder were especially apparent whenever we took the animals through the challenging corridor into Hatun Wayq'u valley. The widest of the three valleys in Antapata, Hatun Wayq'u (literally, "big valley") split into two slender ravines: the southern wing was longer and narrower, with a wetland (Llusquchu Q'uchu) at the center, while the northern wing was shorter and wider. At the base of the ridge that divides the two sides is the largest wetland (Uqhu Wayq'u). Both wetlands were reserved for the alpacas, which made entering Hatun Wayq'u with a mixed herd a challenge: ideally, one must deposit the alpacas near the wetlands before ushering their sheep toward the valley walls. On any given day, two herders would take their animals to Hatun Wayq'u, with one herder settling along the lower wetland and the other taking to the farthest wetland. Simultaneously redirecting both alpacas and sheep toward two different locales— all the while keeping them from mixing with the neighboring herds— was a challenging task, requiring incredible stamina to run up and down slippery valley walls to contain the animals along the valley floor. Her whip ready at her side, Concepción trained the alpaca herd on the wetland before concentrating her sheep into a tight group and directing their movement toward the southern wing of the valley.

An attention to the vocabulary of herding provides a window into the tacit assumptions of herding interactions. The word for "herding" (*michiy*) itself is perhaps best understood as an umbrella term for a variety of distinguishable tasks that contribute to the movement, protection, and care of the herd. However, this term wasn't used to describe the variety of tasks involved in that work. For example, if I asked a herder if she was herding (*michishankichu?*)—a common greeting when meeting someone in the pasture—the answer would be in the affirmative if the herder was, in general terms, out in the pasture with her animals. However, if I asked a herder in the middle of a specific task if they were *michiy*, the answer would be no, and the herder would respond with the more specific task they were accomplishing—"I'm turning (*kutichiy*) the alpacas around!" or "I'm launching (*chanqay*) the llamas over the hill!"[1]

In general, guiding animal movement—toward the preferred pastures and away from those of neighboring sectors—was the central task of *michiy*. Given my position as an apprentice to the work of herding, the unspoken tasks of managing animal movement were often verbalized to me by a more experienced herder, allowing me to hear the interactional dynamics as they were both anticipated and initiated. From her perch on the ridge, Concepción shouted directions down to me while pointing out areas of concern:

> We'll bring [*qhatisun*] them over here. They'll try to get into that enclosure over there, so we'll turn them back this way [*kutichimuychis*]. They'll try to go down to the sectoral boundary that way, so obstruct them there [*hark'amuy*], ya? Over that way they'll get mixed up with the neighbor's animals, they'll try escape up [to the hills], so obstruct them well [*allinta hark'akamuy*].

The verbs *qhatiy* and *hark'ay* are especially illustrative here, revealing the assumptions of agency, intention, and motivation that were distributed between the human and animal participants of a herding interaction. *Qhatiy*, for example, described the task of bringing animals to pasture, moving the animals from one place to the next by urging them on. While *qhatiy* is often translated as "urging," "hurrying," or "pursuing," in Quechua it carries a stronger connotation of accompanying or even trailing behind, rather than moving by force. The verb *qhatikuy*, for example, means "to follow," implying that the direction of the movement is determined by that which is being followed, not that which is following. The task of the herder was to guide the movement of the herd in the desired direction, while identifying and obstructing the places where they might spill over. The herder guided the animals in the same way that a canal guided water, and indeed, the verb *hark'ay* described both the action of obstructing animals and redirecting water in a canal.

Herders regularly encouraged and took advantage of the animal's environmental knowledge, skill, social organization, and gregarious disposition in producing results that were equally desirable for the herder as well as the animal. After all, both herders and their animals wanted to find the most nourishing grasses, and each knew the landscape well enough to find them. On an ideal herding day, the animals would calmly traverse the pastures of their own accord, walking calmly (*thak puriy*). The animals also knew when it was time to return home, and they would begin to amble back toward the *puñuna*, the open area between houses where the alpaca slept at night. Often, I was instructed not to *hark'ay* when the animals began to move home: looking up from her weaving, Concepción would tell me calmly, "They're going home on their own; let's not obstruct them (*mana hark'amusunchu*)."

However, it was crucial to anticipate moments where the intentions and motivations of the animals differed from the herders, and it would become necessary to either obstruct (*hark'ay*) their movement or re-direct it (*kutichimuy*, to make animals return toward the speaker), as Concepción suggested in her earlier directions. There were clear places where animals could not go. Potato farms, of course, were off-limits, but herders also needed to avoid areas that posed dangers to the animals or the herders (near deep water, or high exposed ridges during bad weather). Sheep weren't permitted to return to the *puñuna* alone, since their hooves might tear up the ground and disperse the alpaca dung the herders needed to collect for fuel. Most importantly, the animals had to be kept away from the pastures that belonged to other sectors of the community, or to the neighboring community of Pampa Chiri, to avoid conflict. The animals were not expected to know these rules; rather, they had to be taught. As one community elder articulated during a community meeting, the herders were responsible for teaching the animals the community boundaries:

> The animals become accustomed to [going to the other side], willing or not. We will teach them (*yachachikapusaqku*). We must teach them not to go over to that side . . . This is the right way, *compañeros* (*allinmi chayqa kanman, kunpanyirus*).

There were, therefore, critical moments when the herder needed to undertake more forceful and directed action: when turning a herd away from community boundaries, relocating them during seasonal changes, separating individual animals from the larger herd, or containing them in an enclosure for shearing, medicating, slaughter, or sale. In all these instances, a variety of visual and acoustic cues signaled to the animals that the character of the relationship had shifted. A running herder with her shuffling skirts marked the boundary of the herd's movement; the exaggerated up-and-down "shooing" movement of the herder's arms urged the herd the other direction; the wide arc of a whip hinted of a launched pebble.[2]

Acoustic signaling was the primary mode of communication through which both animals and humans marked interactional shifts from cooperative to human-dominated action. Herders utilized an extensive and rich lexicon of vocalizations—whistles, hisses, grunts, and commands—each of which corresponded to the specific species of animal to which it was directed, as well as the desired action. While acoustic signals varied between households, they were also partly conventionalized, with consistent correspondences between specific sounds and a common set of desired actions: move forward (away from herder), move along (with herder/herd), come back (toward herder), and stop. Short, quick whistles and vocalizations signaled an urgent action (such as removing animals from an enclosure). Longer, sustained whistles and shouts typically signaled the continuation of an ongoing action (to urge animals to continue walking, or to keep following the herd). A specific sound combination (a short, ascending whistle followed by harsh *kshhhk*) signaled to llamas that the herder wanted them to move forward, and a vocal command (*halay, halay!*) was used to urge both llamas and alpacas to stop.[3] An extensive repertoire of whistles—ascending, descending, short, long, punctuated, trailing, and so forth—might have sounded virtually indistinguishable to an untrained ear, but to the herder and the animal, they were immediately identifiable: a herder could easily distill one species of animal from a large mixed herd through whistles and commands alone.

Some of the vocalizations engaged or indexed other animals outside of the interaction, either through verbal recruitment or mimicry. One of the most common standard commands, for example, *wuqchiy*, was used to urge dogs to bark or chase, but it was also used in the absence of a dog to signal to the herd animals that a dog could be chasing them.[4] It was particularly effective in urging alpacas, llamas, and sheep forward, away from the speaker (and an imaginary dog). Herders also mimicked the bleat of a baby animal to prompt straying alpacas and llamas to return to the herd. The high-pitched whine (*eehn eehn*) mimicked the sound of a young alpaca (*uña* or *cría*) in need of its mother, thereby compelling an animal to return to the herd in search of her young. Herders also made a "baaa" sound to prompt a similar response from sheep.

Crucially, herders did not consider human-animal communicative exchanges to be trained stimulus-response sequences, in which the animal mindlessly responded to vocal cues. Rather, herding calls and whistles engaged the animals as sentient, social beings with a relative rank vis-à-vis the other participants in the interaction (Smith 2012). In the accomplishment of cooperative tasks, as well as in the frustration when that work fell apart, herders acknowledged their animals as social beings with intuition, motivation, emotion, and desire. They often represented the emotional states and needs of their animals, perhaps playfully venturing an underlying motive to the animal's behavior: "They don't want me to get any weaving done today"—or, more often, through direct quotation. Watching a herd of sheep eating peacefully, the herder might voice their contentment: "Why would I leave; I'll sleep here!" or voice the animals talking to one another: "Let's go this way" (*kayman risunchis, nispa*). These utterances presupposed the capacity for comprehension and intentionality, as well as the animal's desire to be playful or malicious.

Through acoustic signals, herders established a relative positionality between animals and humans, one that allowed for shifting levels of control, dominance, and subordination. While certain calls expressed the dominance of humans in an interaction, other calls were meant to engage the intuitive skills of lead animals, dogs, or the broader herd. The animals could (and often did) thwart the herder's plans, and they also took initiative by moving the herd to pasture, as is the case with lead alpacas (called *kapitán*, or herd captains). Herders also had expectations based on their shared history of interaction with their animals. They expected that when they used a particular whistle toward one animal, it would prompt the desired response: when they made a particular whistle to urge a lead alpaca forward, to compel a sheep to stop, or to keep the llamas in formation, there was always the expectation that those whistles would be heeded. Animals were regularly chastised for being disobedient (*mana kasukuqchu*, from the Spanish *hacer caso*)—a critique also frequently leveled at people who neglected their social obligations.

There were *also* expectations of failure, however, especially during shifts between seasons. As mentioned in the introduction, seasonal migrations between designated wet-season and dry-season pastures were formalized, requiring a verbal agreement (*acuerdo*) between households in a sector and the approval of both the community governing board (*junta directiva*) and the alpaca committee (*comité de alpacas*). Once all the households in a sector had decided on the date for their seasonal migration, everyone had to migrate within a time frame of a few days.

The community alpaca herd (*majada*) always went first, to take advantage of preferential pastures, and then the households followed in order of seniority. But first, the herders all had to agree upon the right time to migrate, and the first sign that they needed to rotate pastures often came from the animals themselves. As Concepción's son Mario explained it to me—tracing the arc of their seasonal migrations in the dirt at our feet—if the animals were calm, you stayed; if the animals were agitated and restless, refusing to have their movement obstructed (*hark'ay*), then you had to move.

It was the same in the daily system of pasture rotation between the small glacial valleys behind their homesteads. Mario explained how the animals wouldn't tolerate being taken to the same place every day:

> You must rotate. So, the first day you've got to go to Uqhu Wayq'u and the second day you absolutely have to go to Illachiy, and the other day you have to go to Lima Q'ucha. After, back again to Uqhu Wayq'u or Illachiy, but you can't go to the same place twice in the same day, no? The animals get tired, get bored, no? You can't go. [For example] our [animals] are only going to one place right now . . . they are already getting bored, they already want to go somewhere else.

Referencing the upcoming seasonal transitions from their high glacial wetlands to the valley floor, he explained that the decision to change pastures and move households ultimately came "from the animals." He clarified, "the animals were constantly going up [toward the glacial wetlands], they couldn't be held off (*atajar, hark'ay*) any longer, so we got together all of us and decided [to move]."

Sensing Disruption

The steep valley walls of the two wings of Hatun Wayq'u swept around the back of the valley, where they met and extended down in a wide and tabled ridge, Chawpi Sinqa ("Middle Nose"). Halfway up the ridge was a small stone windblock built by Concepción's grandfather, where we rested as the alpacas grazed in the wetland below and the sheep continued their ascent into the southern wing of Hatun Wayq'u. Here, Concepción set out the small battery-powered radio that was her constant companion and rolled out the weaving project she had been working on, a narrow scarf for a regional weaving competition. When the animals were calm, the day's work slipped into a quiet tedium: the radio played the daily news and *waynus*, announcing the time every half hour. When the radio batteries failed, the day could feel timeless, the hours stretching in the bright, stark silence of a dry ridge under a hot sun. The quiet tedium was punctuated by the steady syncopation of Concepción's alpaca-bone needle scraping the warp of her loom, the scratch of my pencil in a notebook, and the panting of our canine companions, Sultira and Chinchirkumacha, stretched out in the hot sand beside us.

On an ideal day, a herder would bring the animals to a spot where she could keep them concentrated and watch them from an elevated position. The high and narrow valleys of Antapata, like Hatun Wayq'u, were a favored herding spot for this reason: the steep valley walls provided natural boundaries for the herd as well as high perches for the herder from which she could mark the day's boundaries, creating a sort of map of the catchment area. Ridges, walls, fences, hillsides, farming areas, blindspots,

FIGURE 6 Concepción on the high ridge of Hatun Wayq'u. Photo by author.

and the outline of another herd were hard boundaries, and as soon as the herd animals began to meander toward those areas, they had to be called back. There were also soft boundaries, or buffer zones, that were acceptable for the animals but required more dedicated attention from the herder. When multiple herders were pasturing their animals in the same valley, they often coordinated their respective maps and herding efforts through elongated shouts from opposing ridges: "sayllamantalla qhatimunki, nuqalla kaymantaaauuu" ("just tend/obstruct/guide [the animals] from the rock cairn [toward me]; I'll [do the same] from heeere!").

If the herds were calm, women would often sit together, their conversations meandering from the patterns they were weaving, to where medicinal plants were growing and when to pick them, how the potato farms were faring, what their children were up to, and the latest news from town. Especially if a herder was coming from another sector to watch her relative's animals, the conversations could linger for hours, moving from one spot to the next as the clouds shifted. These conversations were always punctuated with speculation about what the animals were doing, especially if the animals started to wander out of sight or up toward the ridge that demarcated another sector or community. In one conversation earlier that season, Concepción's neighbor's mother was visiting from the neighboring sector of Alkatarwi, and she and Concepción discussed the stakes of their animals crossing community boundaries into the community of Pampa Chiri. As they watched Concepcion's sheep amble precariously closer to the ridge, the other woman, Rosa, became increasingly concerned:[5]

> ROSA: Look, that sheep is climbing up to the ridge—he'll turn around, right? Oh, and another is following . . .
> CONCEPCIÓN: I'll go up there and turn him around. Where is [the other herder]? Maybe she'll turn the animals around from up there.
> ROSA: Sheep are too much, *ukyan nishu*. They never let you get anything done.
> CONCEPCIÓN: Yesterday they tired us both out, me and the *siñurita* [Allison].
> ROSA: Look, that sheep is already heading over to the other side [of the ridge].

CONCEPCIÓN: If they didn't belong to my children, I'd get rid of the sheep.

ROSA: Ours too. There's too little pasture in Alkatarwi.

CONCEPCIÓN: It's too difficult, *imanasunmi*, what will we do . . .

ROSA: [The sheep] are already beating us (*atipakuspa*); they're passing over to Ausangate's side. [The people of Ausangate] are going to be summonsing us (*ñan waqyachakamushankuña*) . . .

Their conversation quickly turned from the difficulty of managing animals to the difficulty of managing people:

CONCEPCIÓN: They can be mean (*millay*) [over there], huh?

ROSA: Uh-huh, when our llamas wander over there, they detain them.

CONCEPCIÓN: They even take llamas from our side of the mountain!

ROSA: The male llamas, and hold them in their corrals.

CONCEPCIÓN: Ours too.

ROSA: Why, *yi*? I'd just turn the llamas around.

CONCEPCIÓN: They won't barter (*ingarayakamuy*) with us. They're happy like that.

ROSA: To get the money [from the fine].

CONCEPCIÓN: Uh-huh. I'd wonder how to get my llama back. It's hard to demand things (*mañakuy*) of people.

ROSA: Uh-huh, it *is* hard to demand things of people.

CONCEPCIÓN: People are difficult (*sasaya*).

ROSA: People are difficult, that's why I go about things carefully.

CONCEPCIÓN: *Imatan*, what to do . . .

These frustrations between people and animals, and disputes between people of neighboring pastures, only worsened as the dry season went on. During what was called *q'ara timpu* (the "bare time") at the very end of the dry season, the animals began to slip into chronic hunger. Even on that September morning in 2015—when we were still months from rotating to the wet-season pastures back in the central valley—the glacial valley walls were brittle and yellow, and people were beginning to worry about the wetlands. From our elevated perch that morning, Concepción and I could sense the nervous energy of the herd below. The animals ignored the high, persistent pleading of our calls: "*Yawww kuti kuti kuti*, come back!" In the distance, we could see another Antapata herder, Santusa, racing down the valley wall of Ch'uma Punta, struggling to contain her sheep.

Many herders, like Concepción and Rosa, placed sheep squarely at the root of the community's problems. Another herder explained to me that "sheep eat more; they're the ones that walk the longest distances, tearing up the pastures—not like the alpacas and the llamas. [Sheep] are the reason why we're always criticizing (*qhawanakuy*) each other." Sheep were widely maligned in Chillca for their erratic behavior and negative impact on the grasslands, as well as the problems they caused between people. Introduced to the Andes five hundred years ago by Spanish settlers, sheep are crucially different from alpacas and llamas: they have greater energetic needs than alpacas and llamas in relation to their metabolic weight, requiring a wider range of plant availability to meet their nutritional needs (San Martin and Bryant 1989; Tichit and Genin 1997, 177). The flocking tendencies of alpacas and llamas also vary significantly from sheep. Alpaca and llama herds have an internal dominance hierarchy through which a small number of adult males (the herd *kapitáns*) take the lead. Once those individuals are trained in one direction, the rest of the herd will follow in a largely coherent group. Sheep, however, are allelomimetic, prone to imitating the actions of random herd members (Orlove 1977a, 208). Any number of changes in the herd can produce a ripple effect through which the animals will start to shift direction, run, or scatter as if by random. Herders could leave their alpacas in a high valley on their own, and male llamas roamed the mountaintops with only minimal supervision. Sheep, however, required constant attention.

Only with their sheep did herders consistently describe the work of herding in terms of domination, or *winsiy* (from Spanish *vencer*: to overpower, dominate, conquer). One had to position themselves in front of the moving sheep and forcibly turn them back with aggressive, large movements, accompanied by a range of sheep-specific utterances. The word "sheep" (*ukya*) lent itself well to an urgent repetition *ukya-ukya-ukya* as well as a strained, frustrated call: *uuuuukyaw!* shouted periodically from a distance. When the sheep were being especially difficult, the usual commands devolved into a string of obscenities yelled in rapid order: *Hawalla saqra!* (Stop already, you devil!), *Mayta rinkis millaypuni!* (Where are you going, bad ones!) *kutiy karahu!* (Get back here, bastard!), *Kukuchi ukya!*

(Evil sheep!). Many women, like Rosa and Concepción, contemplated selling off the sheep entirely. But sheep were quick money—they reproduced twice as fast as alpacas or llamas, and the price of their wool and meat stayed relatively stable.

Watching Santusa's chase from across the valley, Concepción let out a deep sigh, loosened the backstrap from her loom, and packed her carrying cloth once again. We climbed Chawpi Sinqa to walk the sector boundary and find her herd of sheep. The wind whipped viciously at us as we struggled to reach the animals that had wandered close to the boundary of the ridge. Some sheep turned lazily toward us, while others ran off as we approached. Through the wind, I could hear Concepción's voice reaching a feverish pitch as she ran a wide arc around the animals to drive them back. Under the piercing sun, we were tired and thirsty, but we couldn't stop. Again and again, we scaled the sandy hillside to contain the herd's borders; yet every time we left an opening, the animals would escape to the ridge. I soon joined Concepción in shouting spiteful streams of obscenities, the two of us waving our arms, kicking at the dirt, and launching pebbles at the animals' hindquarters. The animals likewise bleated their frustration. It took more than two hours in this ambulatory standoff before the sheep settled on the valley walls and we could rest, exhausted and somewhat defeated, on the hillside below.

"Ukya ñakayta winsinchis," Concepción told me, breathless: the work of conquering sheep (*winsiy*) could indeed be accomplished, but only through suffering (*ñakay*). That afternoon, both of us came down with terrible headaches. While I attributed this to dehydration, Concepción informed me that it was always like this during this time of year. When the animals become *k'ita*, it could make you sick, and even drive you mad.

Unraveling Restlessness

In the later months of 2015, changes in seasonal weather patterns disrupted pastoralist migrations throughout the community of Chillca. "The seasons are going crazy" (*timpu muyupushantaq*), a herder named Margarita told me. Coming from the distant sector of Q'ampa, she greeted me on her way to the central valley with a lamb strapped to her back, hoping to sell it for a few *soles* to a passing meat truck. In the lingering dry season, her sheep weren't producing enough milk for their lambs, and she was determined to sell this one while it still had a little bit of fat on its body. Throughout Chillca, people worried about the lack of rain and remarked on the increasingly erratic weather patterns. The consensus was that weather patterns had become more intense and less predictable: one herder noted "little by little, every year it is changing . . . in the past, it wasn't like this. The rain is changing; it is becoming intense (*fwirti*) when it rains. Before [it rained] softly, slowly." This shift in intensity wasn't limited to precipitation. I heard multiple herders describe the wind as faster (*wayra wayran tantu*) and the sun as hotter (*inti intin tantu*) than it was before. As another herder summarized, "the heat, the sun, and the wind burn now."

Compared to previous years, the seasonal variations in precipitation had become difficult to predict, and the rains no longer came "in their time" (*timpullanpi*). By mid-November of 2015, the wet-season rains were weeks late, shifting agricultural schedules and seasonal herd migrations throughout Chillca. People recalled that the rains had also been slow to arrive in November and December of the previous year as well, and that several unexpected rainstorms in June had disrupted the yearly preparations they made during the dry season for the months ahead, especially the preparation of freeze-dried potatoes and the collection of dried alpaca dung. The appearance of weather phenomena outside of the expected time had also led to increased incidents of animal illness and distress. In particular, the late onset of rains meant that the animals were not recuperating from the typical period of hunger and weight loss wrought by the dry season. Herders had kept their animals within the dry-season wetlands for weeks longer than they had hoped, and there were few signs that the wet-season grasses were soon to return. As one herder reflected in September, "the animals are skinny now. But in the past this season wasn't like this; they were already recuperating. They should be recuperating already."

In severe drought conditions, sheep are the first to display the increasingly agitated mobile state of wandering referred to as *k'ita*. In time, the alpacas also begin to become *k'ita*, as these restless tendencies spread across the herd. I began to hear the word *k'ita*, shouted in frustration at the offending animals, in the later months of the dry season as the last dry patches of grasses turned a dusty brown. At first, *k'ita* struck me as a peculiar term, one that I couldn't get a firm grasp on and required multiple explanations and lingering conversations. At first, it seemed semantically identical to many of the other insults I heard yelled at straying sheep: *millay, saqra, kukuchi, karahu, mirda . . .* It could have been easily dismissed as just something that people yell at their animals when they were being "bad." But as I kept hearing it, I was intrigued: it was often used to describe animal behavior in a way that distinguished it not as the opposite of a moral state such as "good" or "virtuous," but as the opposite of the observable state of peaceful (*thak*, or *llaqhi*). Concepción would urge me to observe how her alpaca were walking or eating peacefully ("thak purishan, llaqhi mikushan paqucha, qhawariy"), in opposition to the sheep, who were always trying to escape to the hilltops to steal the llamas' grass ("bastu suwaq puntamanta rin, k'ita"). She was also the first to tell me that the animals started becoming *k'ita* during the dry season, when the pasture is low: "Watch, they are walking *k'ita*" (*qhawariy, k'ita purishanku*), she alerted me: "When there's no pasture, that's how they walk" (*mana bastu kaqtin aynallata purikun*).

When herders used the word *k'ita* with animals like sheep, alpaca, and llamas, they were describing animals that strayed or deviated from their expected trajectory, failing to respond to human vocal cues, flaunting their reciprocal obligations to humans, and, in some cases, even overpowering and dominating them. It could be used as an adverb to describe a temporary state—an animal could be "walking *k'ita*"—or it could be used in adjective form to describe a habitual state, when an animal had become *k'ita*. People could also walk *k'ita*, when seen to be staggering, swerve, or wander without direction. Only once did I hear it used as an adjective for people, in a case where someone was accused of habitually missing communal work events. Similar to its usage with animals, it suggested a deviation from social norms and a lack of attention to reciprocal relationships with other social beings.

The semantic breadth of *k'ita* became more evident when Concepción's daughter-in-law and my close friend, Maritza, dug a wild potato from a distant pasture as we were herding one morning: "Papaq k'itan," she announced, holding the tuber up for me to see, the potato's *k'ita*. It was inedible to humans, she explained, but animals can eat it, and it could be used as medicine. What else could be *k'ita*? I asked. The alpaca's *k'ita* was the vicuña (*paquchaq k'itan*), she explained. The domestic cat's was the puma (*michiq k'itan*), and humans even had our own: the monkey (*runaq k'itan*). "K'ita purishanku," she added; all these animals "walked *k'ita*," or, in other words, they *ran wild*: they were not habitually controlled or contained by human beings.

Turning to the documented literature on the word *k'ita* provided further intrigue. The term has been translated in several contemporary and earlier Quechua-Spanish dictionaries in adjective form as "feral" (*cimarron*), "wild" (*silvestre*), "elusive," and "unsociable" (*esquivo, arisco*); in noun form as "fugitive" or "runaway" (*fugitivo*); and in verb form as "evade," "run away," "escape," or "flee" (*evadirse, fugarse, escaparse, huir*).[6] *K'ita* also appeared in an early Aymara language dictionary with the Spanish translation "herd animal without owner" and *mostrenco*, a word that carries connotations of placelessness (Ludovico Bertonio 1612, 80, 221). This last translation—of an animal that, while still domesticated, does not have an owner or a home—seemed most similar to what I encountered in Chillca, and what other researchers had heard in nearby areas. In her fieldwork in Hanansaya Ccullana Ch'isikata (Cusco), for example, Eugenia Ch'aska Carlos Ríos described the usage of *k'ita* in reference to plants that "have potency in an [inedible] unsoftened [*no ablandado*] state," with the concept of soften (*ablandar*) drawn from the Quechua *llamphuy*, to make soft, tender, or tame (Carlos Ríos 2015, 237). She translated *k'ita* as untamed (*indomable*) and differentiated it from both *sallqa* (wild, *salvaje*), and *purun* (wilderness, *yermo*) (2015, 239). Beings who are *k'ita*, in her interpretation, resist the taming (or "softening") rituals and techniques of *llamphuy*, and are prone to fleeing and escaping into untamed places (2015, 242). It seemed to me that, just as *k'ita* plants were inedible, *k'ita* animals were indominable to humans. Neither had been *softened*.

Throughout its representation and translation in text, the state of *k'ita* was also clearly associated with movement, especially evasive movement like fleeing, escaping, or running away. After a while, I began translating *k'ita* in my fieldnotes as "restlessness" to capture this spatiotemporality: an agitated, accelerating wandering that frustrated and complicated social connections.[7] Wandering is considered suspicious, asocial behavior in many part of the high Andes: undirected, aimless movement indicates that a social being is operating outside of social conventions and is either emotionally unwell (angry, frustrated, or sad) or in an altered state brought on by intoxication, madness, or bewitchment. While I initially glossed *k'ita* as "wild," it does not necessarily map onto the connotations that accompany the English terms "wild" or "feral." Conceptualizations of domesticity and wildness operate differently in the Andes: a vicuña, for example, may not be a domesticated animal to humans, but it *is* a domesticated animal for the mountains, occupying a structurally similar position in parallel and partially overlapping realms of sociality. As Francisco Pazzarelli writes, "One could say . . . that domesticated animals have some shade of 'wild,' and wild animals are also 'raised' (*criado*)" (2020, 106).

K'ita behavior in herd animals manifested most evidently in the interactional context of the herding task *hark'ay*, when a herder attempted to obstruct or redirect undesired movement. As previously noted, this verb was used to describe both the obstruction of animal movement as well as the redirection of water in a canal, thereby presupposing the independent (and intentional) movement of herd animals, much like water.[8] When animals became restless, they were notoriously difficult to *hark'ay*. For herders, this was often the first sign that the animals were not getting the nutritional resources they needed from their current pastures and had to be moved to a new location. While herders utilized their own observations of grass abundance and rainfall patterns to adjust their migration schedules, the foremost indicator was the emotional state of the animals themselves.

When the animals' demands for new pastures couldn't be met—due to diminished grasses, drought, or other constraints on pasture availability—*k'ita* became an especially disruptive phenomenon, the impacts of which rippled through human social worlds. Restlessness could make humans sick: headaches, stomachaches, or feelings of unease were generally attributed to being *phiña* (angry) or *rinigasqa* (frustrated, from the Spanish *reniego*), both states of annoyance and agitation considered to result from wandering animals. The inability to confine one's animals to their designated pastures was also cited as a moral failure, and the herder was accused of being lazy (*qhilla*), selfish (*mich'a*), or disobedient (*mana kasukuqchu*). When I asked another herder why she thought there was conflict in the community, for example, she identified the failure of community members to *hark'ay* their animals well as the central issue: "us obedient (*kasukuq*) people *hark'ay* [our animals]. The careless (*mana kasukuqchu*) people do not." These tensions and typifications would inevitably erupt at the following month's assembly.

Hierarchy and Rupture

With animals, a little bit of *k'ita* wasn't necessarily a bad thing. Hierarchy and difference are essential to the social fabric of Andean multispecies communities. Relationships between landscapes, humans, and animals are profoundly asymmetrical: *pukara* (spatially located social entities, and the focus of chapter 3) are more powerful than humans, while humans are more powerful than domesticated animals and objects. What binds humans, animals, and places together is not a shared humanity, but rather the alterity of animals and landscapes is a central feature of their relationships with humans and that which animates the practices between them. Critically, places, animals, and objects are not considered nonhuman persons. Rather, the Andean world is constituted by "relationships between a diversity of beings and entities that coexist without having a human reference as something central" (Bugallo 2016, 116). As Peter Gose has described it, nonhuman beings like *pukara* are "semi-social," characterized by elements of wildness that resist human control (2018). Domestication is necessarily incomplete, because this alterity is vital and productive. Mountains, for example, can harness meteorological resources and distribute life-giving substances through ecological networks. While mountains are brought into human webs of sociality, the expectation is that it is only partial—people "neither expect nor want full success" (Gose 2018, 495).

Here I extend Gose's application of the "semi-social" from mountains to include animals, following the lead of Francisco Pazzarelli's *partepastor* ("semi-herder") (2020). There were expectations of restlessness built into the relationships between humans and herd animals. As Pazzarelli articulates, much of the daily work of herding involves "minimizing the wild parts" of the herd, but *never fully* (2020, 90). The herders expect resistance—which Pazzarelli characterizes in terms of *excesses*—from their herd animals. Alterity, after all, is generative: whether the being is a mountain, animal, or plant.[9] Herders *do* seek control over herd animals, but it is always only partial. They also trust and expect that the animals will act according to their intuitive volition. Under ideal conditions, this allows the herd to traverse the pasture peacefully, making their own way to their preferred grasses. However, under drought conditions, this untamed alterity becomes dangerous. As Pazzarelli noted in herding communities in northwest Argentina, an animal's wild excesses can start to spread and "infect" others in the herd (2020, 90). As I noticed in Chillca, this infectious restlessness extended even further beyond the herd, troubling broader social worlds.

When Concepción's animals wandered precariously toward the high ridges of Antapata valley, they touched upon the hard boundary between communities. If they crossed over, they were likely to get lost or captured by herders in the neighboring community, which would lead to a tense discussion at the community assembly and potentially a hefty fine. Even if they didn't cross that boundary, they were liable to get mixed up with her neighbor's herds in Antapata. While people were often resistant to raise their complaints in person, bimonthly sectoral gatherings provided a formal platform for critique. Every other month, herders in each sector would gather to evaluate the communal alpaca herd in the presence of the alpaca committee. Lingering at the edges of the herd's enclosure, community members would stand to face the alpaca committee while reciting lengthy diatribes against a careless neighbor. The accused herder would likewise stand and offer a formal rebuttal. The alpaca committee typically settled these arguments with a verbal warning, unless the charge was serious enough to be brought to the community assembly. In the most egregious cases—when an animal has repeatedly escaped into reserved pastures—the offending animal would be captured and slaughtered.

These arguments weren't soon forgotten. In a case where an animal had been slaughtered, the dispute lived on in community lore for years, providing an explanation for why two families were no longer speaking to each other, or participated only begrudgingly in shared herding responsibilities or reciprocal labor exchanges. At the community level, these tensions snowballed into broader discussions about the feasibility of living in a commons, which I'll speak to in a later chapter. Even the loss of a single animal was traumatic in ways that rippled throughout the family as well as their herd. Separating one animal from the herd was a delicate matter: when culling or selling off an animal, herders often took care to snip a lock of wool from the departing animal in order to tie it onto the back of another. This served to keep the *animu*—the vital life force that permeates all beings—in the herd. Wandering animals—especially those that could be captured or even slaughtered—were a condemnation of the herder, for failing to take care of the herd and allowing for the dispersal of *animu*. Not only did herders face the judgment of their neighbors, they also risked roping the broader community into lengthy disputes. Furthermore, they made themselves vulnerable to the wrath of other agentive and powerful beings in the landscapes, the *pukara*.

Bringing the Animals Home

The harsh brightness of the midday melted into the golden hours of the late afternoon. A chorus of distant whistles emanating from the three valleys of Antapata signaled that the herds were moving home. The animals ambled downhill along the well-worn paths as we collected stragglers from the ridge. By the time the herds all made it back to Antapata, the valley slipped into the liquid heaviness of early evening as the sun disappeared into the horizon. With the animals in their pens and the *puñuna*, the herders rushed into their homes to light the evening's fire. This hour, *phiru ura*, was full of trickery and danger—in the darkness, shapes began to morph and dissolve, and *kundinadus* and *kukuchi* roamed the hills. The air began to feel thick and heavy, the landscape almost oceanic in quality. Xavier Ricard Lanata, a French-Peruvian anthropologist who lived in the neighboring community of Phinaya, wrote of the marine qualities of the high Andes as they slipped into evening, drawing comparison to his childhood summers on the Peruvian coast:

> Beneath a sky both material and liquid, the mountaintops, crowned in snowy peaks, appeared as rocky submarines, full of niches from which some monster of the deep, an unseen and sly sentry, could emerge at any moment. And while I was drowning in the immensity of this imaginary waterscape—lifted up by some titanesque wave to over 5000 meters above sea-level—I seemed to find the echo of the marine memories of my childhood, as if the massif of Ausangate and the Peruvian coastal desert had maintained, always, a secret and mysterious correspondence. (2007, 385)

I similarly felt the tugs of my more distant island home in Maine, perhaps never more so than when the Andean gulls squawked on the pampa in the wet season, or a group of brightly clad tourists appeared on the other side of the valley on the Ausangate trek as if transported directly from Acadia National Park. That place felt much more distant to me now, as I tucked into the pile of blankets on the raised stone platform of Concepción's hut. Concepción crouched next to the fire, while her husband Julio, recently returned from his work as a porter on the Ausangate trek, settled into a corner and quietly plucked the strings of his small bandurria guitar. Concepción lit a candle—"Winas nuchis, siñurita"—and set a kettle of tea to boil. Recounting the day's work, she rubbed at her temples. "The sheep are giving birth in vain (*yanqapaq*)," she told Julio. If she brought the newborns to the Combapata market this Sunday, she could sell them for ten soles each. Julio was reluctant, but Concepción persisted. The frustration of chasing the herd had left her with a headache, and she was exhausted. "I'm no good for walking" (*mana puriyta valinichu*), she often told me—between her age and the increasingly restless animals, she couldn't keep up as well as she used to. She worried constantly that she'd fall ill—who would take care of the animals then?

Concepción ate four large bowls of soup that night, each time tipping the empty bowl to show me, amused at the depth of her own hunger. Julio played a few chords of an old song Concepción had written, and in the quiet of the late evening, she sang a few lines that harkened back to when she was a young woman and restlessness had almost caused her to wander, before she married Julio, had children, and become entrenched in the social world of Chillca:

Hinaya ripuchun, nispa niwaqtinqa	"Let her go," they'll say about me
Hinaya pasachun, nispa niwaqtinqa	"Let her go," they'll say about me
Wichaypas uraypas ripukapunaypaq	So that I'd go away, ascending and descending
Uraypas wichaypas pasakapunaypaq	So that I'd leave, descending and ascending
Rasunta mamay niwaran	My mother told me the reason
Rasunta taytay niwaran	My father told me the reason
Nuqaña mayta ripuqtiyqa	Where I must be going
Maypiraq kallin kallincha	Along which roads
Maypiraq wasin wasincha	In which neighborhoods

Rasunta taytay niwaran	My father told me the reason
Rasunta mamay niwaran	My mother told me the reason
Nuqaña mana kallaqtiyqa	Where I mustn't be going
Maypiraq wasin wasincha	In which neighborhoods
Maypiraq kallin kallincha	Along which roads

The hut settled into quiet, and the animals were silent on the *puñuna*. The day's herding would begin again in the morning.

CHAPTER TWO

Women's Work

CHILLCA LLAQTA (CHILLCA TOWN)—SUNG BY SONIA
HUAMAN (CONCEPCIÓN'S GRANDDAUGHTER)

Chillcapata llaqtayqa	My town Chillca
Ima munayta llanllashan	How lovely it is sprouting
Chillcapata llaqtayqa	My town Chillca
Ima munayta phallchishan	How lovely it is blooming
Chayhinallataq nuqapas	And just like that, I also
T'ikachahina wiñani	Grow like a little flower
Chayhinallataq nuqapas	And just like that, I also
Ima munayta wiñani	I am quite like my town itself
T'ikachahina wiñani	How lovely I grow
Llaqtay kikichan kashani	Like a little flower I grow

Mirelia's Haircutting

In the wavering light of our headlamps, Mirelia's face was still, her lips
parted in a deep sleep. Wrapped in blankets in her mother's arms, she
didn't wake—even as we approached her, one by one, and snipped off her
tiny braids with a pair of dull scissors.

Earlier in the evening, we had gathered in the warm, dark interior
of Mario and Maritza's house. Mario was Concepción's youngest son,
and I was especially close with his wife, Maritza, and their two-year-old
daughter Mirelia. As Mirelia's godparents, my husband and I were served
heaping plates of guinea pig and potatoes as the other attendees slowly
arrived. Concepción and Julio arrived with Mirelia's six-year-old cousin
Yuort, and Mario's uncle Julian came by soon after, bringing with him a
couple of young men who had just been passing through town but were
now inescapably roped into the evening's festivities. One of them was the

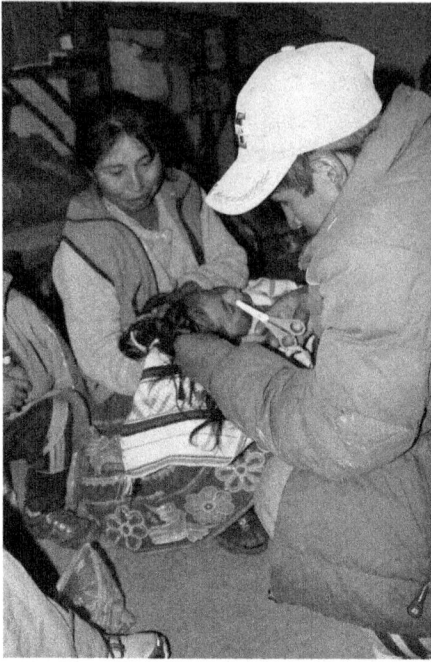

FIGURE 7 Mirelia's *chukcha rutukuy* (hair-cutting ceremony). Photo by author.

husband of Mario's cousin, but the other had no immediate family connection. They seemed uneasy at first, sheepishly settling down in the corner of the room, but as soon as Julio strummed a few chords on his bandurria, the mood lightened, and they joined in the lively conversation. Just as the conversation reached a fervent crescendo, Concepción stepped in. "*Chaylla*, that's enough talking." With a giggle, she continued, "The American *padrinu* doesn't know what you're saying." Julio put down the bandurria. "*Intindichiy*, help him understand," she instructed Julian, who held the position of the evening's secretary and was translating from Quechua to Spanish for the benefit of my husband. He began:

> Our *costumbre* is always like this, from [the time of] our ancestors. When a boy or girl is born, from the body of their mother, we are all born naked, no? All we have are the hairs on our heads. In the past, this represented the only inheritance of the boy or girl, just their little hairs . . . Today we continue cultivating this [tradition] . . . [The haircutting] is an inheritance that the child will have in his or her life. When we cut the hair, the first person to cut is the *padrino* or the *madrina* of the child, and after this, one contributes with whatever they feel in their heart—it isn't an obligation, one can put a large or small sum, because even if it is small, it is the blessing of the lord (*la bendición del señor*).

Mario passed a bottle of beer and a small glass around, and Concepción brought out a plastic bag of coca leaves. She uttered a soft *phukuy*, and Julio again picked up the bandurria, playing a few chords to lead us back into conversation.

On the table in front of Mirelia sat a small round cake, decorated in a thick layer of fluffy neon-green icing and the words *Feliz Día Mirelia*. Beside it lay a woven cloth folded in fourths to serve as the *misa*, the base upon which the ritual items rested: a dried ear of corn, a shallow bowl holding a pair of scissors adorned with an orange ribbon, and a notebook. My husband and I placed two coins in the shallow bowl as the seed, a reproductive pair, to beckon further contributions. Then, one by one, each person in the room crouched alongside a sleeping Mirelia, extending a single braid from the crown of her head and snipping it across the middle. When it was my turn, I placed the small braid in the bowl on the table, along with a crisp folded bill. Mirelia's grandmother and grandfather plucked a kernel from the corn husk and placed it in the bowl along with the braid, with an announcement to the secretary: *hina papay, chinacha alpakacha kanqa.* There will be an alpaca, a female. Six-year-old Yuort was invited to contribute, much to his delight, and gleefully offered a female sheep. Maritza then made a generous offering to her daughter, depositing a corn kernel and the promise of a horse. As the night sunk into a dark stillness, we made two more turns around the circle, after each of which we rested to toast one another with the tall bottle of beer, make jokes, and listen to the steady rhythm of Julio's bandurria.

The haircutting ceremony (*chukcha rutukuy*) has a long history in the Andes.[1] Typically performed when the child is around two years old, it marks the first step in their transition from a child to an adult. As Julian explained to us before the ceremony:

> When we cut her hair, in the days that follow she will change back to her other self. Sometimes this hair that she's had since she was little, it is betraying her and [that's why] she's being a little stubborn. Our ancestors always said: this child needs her hair cut, because the hair is spoiling her. So, when we cut it, the child will behave like her other self. She'll begin to act more grown up, she won't be mischievous any longer. It's this hair that makes her a child.

Marking her transformation from a stubborn child into a more developed social being, the haircutting ceremony also enters a child into a formal set of relations with people, animals, objects, and increasingly, the cash economy, tethering her to a series of reproductive and generative futures. The selection of godparents for the ceremony is key: parents almost always choose godparents from among the comparatively wealthy members of the community or from nearby towns or cities. The offerings made by the godparents are traditionally reproductive animals: young, female, or uncastrated male sheep, alpacas, llamas, cows, or horses. The gift is not merely the animal itself but also the animal's reproductive future, given with the intent of helping the child grow their own herd over their lifetime. It was readily acknowledged that in this case, as Mirelia's godparents, we wouldn't be able to offer her the traditional gift of a reproductive animal since we had none ourselves. Instead, cash was acceptable, along with the promise to contribute to her studies later in life and the hope that some of our luck (*swirti*) as "professionals" would transfer to her.

At the end of the evening, Julian wrote out the contract for Mirelia's haircutting ceremony:

Chillca, April 30, 2016

Document of Commitment:

In the residence of Mario H. and wife Maritza T. in the Community of Chillca, of the District of Pitumarca, of the Province of Canchis, Region Cusco. At 9:00 p.m. on the night of the 30th day of the month of April of the 2016, the family of Mario and Maritza gathered with the intention of the girl Mirelia's haircutting, in which the godfather and godmother of the girl Mirelia are the *señorita* Allison and husband Nikolas from the USA, with whom all those present accompanied in the event of the girl's haircutting. Afterwards, Mr. Nikolas and wife Allison began [the ceremony], with the following:

    1. Nikolas and Allison—cash

    2. Julio—one female alpaca

    3. Concepción—one female alpaca

    4. Julian—one female sheep

    5. Mario—one female alpaca

    6. Maritza—one horse

    7. Yuort—one female sheep

Although Mirelia was too young then to understand much of what occurred that evening as she slept, as she grew older, she would be told about the animals she was given. Everyone remembered the animals they received at their haircutting ceremony (called *chukchaq uywan*; literally "the hair's animal"). The animals were either delivered to their parents' herd or kept in another relative's herd until the child came of age. Children watched their animals grow in the herds of their parents and nearest relatives. At six years old, Mirelia's cousin Yuort had four sheep and two alpacas in Concepción's herd, the offspring of the single alpaca and sheep she gave him at his haircutting. When we were out herding, he pointed them out excitedly along with those of his big sister Karla, who was given one alpaca and two sheep from Concepción's sister, and at eight years old had two alpacas, one of which was pregnant, and five sheep. By the time a child was in their late teens and early twenties, their animals would have reproduced enough for them to have a respectable starter herd. Both men and women inherited and were gifted animals at their *chukcha rutuy*, and as they grew into young adults, their herds grew with them, such that by the time they separated from the household of their parents, they did so with full social standing, and a full herd.

As a herder entered adulthood, they would also have learned the knowledge and skills necessary to maintain their herd through their interactions with their family and community. This process of becoming a herder emerged from these situated relationships between people, animals, and landscapes in Chillca. The relationship of "mutual rearing" (*crianza mutua*) between humans and animals was first recorded by anthropologist Félix Palacios Ríos in 1977, during whose fieldwork in Chichillapi, Peru, a herder told him: "We raise the animals, and the animals raise us" ("Nosotros criamos al ganado y el ganado nos cria a nosotros") (Palacios Ríos 1977, 58; Bugallo and Tomasi 2012). At the center of these processes are practices of care through which beings—both humans and animals—are "fed, protected, disciplined, and made useful" (Allen 2016, 333), or, in the words of philosopher Vinciane Despret, "rendered capable" (Despret 2008, 127). Herders learned to bring their animals to the most nutritious pastures, and the animals then transformed those pastures into wool, meat, and dung, and alerted the herder to any changes in the health of the grasslands. The process of *uyway* involved not only feeding one another but also socializing one another: nurturing and compelling both humans and animals into full social beings, in all their relational interconnectivity. This rearing was continuously enacted from one generation to the next. As Denise Arnold noted in Qaqachaka, Bolivia, "Andean herders do not recognise a historically defined process of domestication that finally ended," rather, "in each generation, herd animals must be reintroduced into the human domain, *generally by the women herders*, by singing to them, instructing them in speech, and wrapping them in beautiful weavings" (Arnold 2022, 63).

This chapter explores this mutual rearing as women's work. Women in Chillca did the work of socializing animals through the daily practices of caring for their animals, cultivating their own senses, and participating in a network of rearing and regeneration, of *uyway*, that extended beyond their own herd and into the broader community.[2] Not only did young herders learn how to work with animals, but they also learned how to mobilize the material and social resources that reproduced relationships of mutual care across human and animal collectives. Animals were central to this process, both materially and socially. Through inheritance at crucial life stages like their first haircutting, as well as other forms of gifting, sale, and exchange, women configured their relationships to one another and undertook the practices necessary to establish themselves as good herders *and* fully social persons. In other words, the circulation of herd animals and herding labor created, maintained, and reconfigured bonds of social relatedness between humans, herds, and landscapes in Chillca, and it was through those broader networks of obligation (and related practices of feeding and cohabitation) that individuals themselves came into full social being.

There was obviously a lot of skill involved in this process, but there was also some luck (*swirti*, from the Spanish *suerte*). Indeed, *swirti* is inseparable from skill in the Andes. It is not passively acquired—rather, luck must be cultivated, nurtured, and strengthened (Göbel 1997). And, as Denise Arnold elaborated in her work in Bolivia, the cultivation of *swirti* is likewise women's work: *swirti* "refers to a female herder's ability to transform animals from the hills into family herd animals" (2022, 79). In the pages that follow, I describe how skill and *swirti* are cultivated relationally through the material, social, sensory, and affective practices through which women raise their animals, build their communities, care for their landscapes, and thereby cultivate themselves as social beings. I unfold the development of herding skill throughout a herder's life, beginning with her initial inheritance of herd animals during her childhood. I describe the series of exchanges through which herders establish, sustain, extend—and in some cases, sever—the ties that constitute their social lives. A keen attention to these practices yields insight into how women like Concepción have generated livable futures for themselves and their communities. It also prompts us to ask how these futures might be reconfigured in shifting socioeconomic conditions, as different possibilities are afforded to women in Chillca, like Mirelia.

Cultivating Skill

In the year I lived in Chillca, I watched as Mirelia became a herder. My field recordings are peppered with her voice calling me from a distance: "Allison, *hakusun!* Let's go!" As a fellow apprentice to this work, I was learning to watch the animals alongside her, and I was often tasked with her care while her mother ran after a restless herd. Her mother Maritza and I had quickly become friends during my first few months in Chillca, and while she was keen to show me how to watch animals, she was also happy to have a second pair of hands to watch Mirelia if she needed to pursue her herd. And so, I'd often sit and play with Mirelia in the pasture: building *kanchas* out of rocks, bundling stuffed animals into her *unkhuña* to carry on her back, and making up new *waynu* lyrics, "haqay wichaypi, munayukurayki . . ."

Becoming a herder was a process of "enskillment" (Ingold 2000) that was inextricably embedded in and emergent from the broader socioenvironmental landscape in Chillca. It began early in a child's life, and continued as they grew, watched, and learned from others within a situated network of animals, humans, and lands. A young herder's enskillment wasn't a tacit accumulation of knowledge, but rather a progressive attunement through repeated sensorial engagement with the world: a herder learned to sense, evaluate, and respond to their social world in ways that shaped them—literally—into the role of *michiq* (Ingold 2000, 416). All herders began as novices or apprentices, following in the footsteps of their human and animal elders within the sociosensory *taskscape* that was the pasture. As Tim Ingold has described it, "The novice watches, feels or listens to the movement of the expert, and seeks—through repeated trials—to bring his [*sic*] own bodily movements into line with those of his attention so as to achieve the kind of rhythmic adjustment of perception and action that lies at the heart of fluent performance" (2000, 141).

For a young herder, play was a central method of learning. On quiet afternoons, Mirelia and I would sit in the pasture and play games together: telling riddles and jokes, twisting yarn into elaborate shapes with our fingers, "herding" dried beans into their corral, and collecting and assembling plants into a small garden. When we were herding with Mirelia's older cousins, they'd recite the names of the plants we'd gathered: *yawar chunka, q'ara phuña* (soft like rabbit ears), *rumi unqu*, and *yuraq nipla* (lichen-like, tucked into the cracks of rocks). Some to gather for tea, some for medicine, and some to make soft pastures for our bean-animals. In one game, Mirelia's cousins counted the leaves of *q'upi q'upi*, a star-shaped, mat-forming grass—one, two, three, four, *huk, iskay, kimsa, tawa*—and whoever had the most leaves on their stem won. There were

FIGURE 8 A child playing games in the pasture. Photo by author.

many *q'upi q'upi* with two to three leaves, Mirelia's cousin Brisayda told me, but if you could find one with four or more, you were sure to win. Knowing this grass, as it turned out, was centrally important to marking the transition between seasons. The appearance of *q'upi q'upi* (*azorella biloba*)—especially those plants with abundant leaves—was a welcome sign that the wet season was returning.

Another afternoon, I would hear Mirelia's mother and her sister, Aniseta, discussing the distribution of *q'upi q'upi* in the high pastures. Aniseta tilted her head sharply to the pasture and observed, "The *q'upi q'upi* looks good (*munaylla*), no? It's plentiful (*sumaqta daliyamushan*)." Maritza nodded in agreement but also responded, "Ch'umpipayashan," the pasture is turning brown, much drier this year than it was last year. She worried about the lack of rainfall. "What will we do? The hail hasn't come yet. Last year it had come already (*dalinyalla*), right? By a month ago (*killallanña*), right?" Aniseta responded that it was only one month until *Santus*, All Saint's Day, and the community would gather and shear the alpacas shortly thereafter. Calibrating to these calendar events, the two sisters noted that the rains were precariously late. Indeed, in the weeks following that conversation, Maritza, Aniseta, and their extended families all stayed in their dry-season pastures for a few more weeks, waiting until the returning rains had replenished the grasses on the valley floor below.

When children played games in the pasture, they were learning how to see the landscape with the "skilled vision" of a herder's eye (Grasseni 2004). Learning to herd constituted a training of visual, physical, and vocal practice as well as a cultivation of appropriate moral orientations and relational networks. As Christina Grasseni has articulated in her work with cattle herders in the Alps (2009a; 2009b), skill emerges in the pastoralist encounter as "a privileged locus of identity-construction, as a complex of aesthetic involvement and moral stances, of strategies of belonging and expert practices" (Grasseni 2009a, 1). These skills were invaluable: nearly every decision made at the household, sector, and community level in Chillca relied upon the observations women made during their daily lived experience with animals in the pasture, and the conversations they shared with their fellow herders. As Mirelia grew along with her herd, she'd come to recognize and identify a range of grass types, often through playing games or telling riddles. She would hone a wide and varied repertoire of whistles and vocalizations with which she'd communicate with her animals. She'd learn to crack a whip and use her *wark'a* to fling a rock at an animal with alarming accuracy.

She'd also learn how to identify individual animals and evaluate herd health just by sweeping her eyes over her herd from a distance. Training her gaze softly over the animals and the landscape in one, the herder could use the distribution of individual animals and their distinctive features to determine the precise location, dispersion, and direction of movement of the herd. Even with multiple herds in a single valley, the herder could easily pick out her own animals: individual animals were often marked (with red clay markings [*taku*], colored ear tassels [*q'aytu*], or colorful plastic bags [*pullu*] tied into the wool of newly acquired animals). Even in the absence of these markings, a herder could easily identify their own and other people's herds from a vast distance. As the shape of each herd shifted over the hours, the herder's soft visual attention to certain key individuals—the young brown-coated male (*chumpi tuwi*) or the spotted adolescent female (*muru malta*)—gave her a sense of the boundaries, density, and directionality of the herd's movement.

This daily practice of scanning the herd always struck me, having grown up in coastal Maine, as remarkably similar to the soft gaze that people use when scanning the sea surface. The softly unfocused eye could evaluate the general state of the ocean, judging its energy and movement in the subtle differences of color and texture undulating on the surface, and honing in on any anomalies, disturbances, or inconsistencies: the slick head of a seal breaking the surface; a smooth patch hinting at the presence of a diving animal; bubbles emerging from the hidden, dark depths. Similarly, when a herder softly swept her eyes over the undulating herd, the shifting bodies of the animals gave her a sense of the well-being of the herd—perhaps calm and content, or forlorn and sullen, or agitated and restless. From that slightly detached vantage point, the herder could pick out the subtlest changes in herd dynamics and make inferences about the physical and emotional states of the individual animals as well as the herd as a whole.

Skilled vision is central to pastoralist work as one component of a "multi-sensory practice, where looking is coordinated with skilled movement, with rapidly changing points of view, or with other senses, such as touch" (Grasseni 2009a, 79). In this ecological model of perception, visual practices are inextricable from a broader multisensorial engagement with landscape. Grasseni's description of vision is similar to the Quechua concept of *sut'i*, which I defined in the introduction of this book as relatively equivalent to the Spanish *al aire* ("in the air"; revealed, discovered, laid bare). Although *al aire* could conceivably refer to traces that are left in the air as smells, or travel as sounds, its usage refers almost exclusively to the visibility of phenomena. I heard a range of scenarios in which the concept of trace (*sut'i*) expressed past, present, and future: a person's face appeared sad, telling of their misfortune ("they've been robbed," *sut'i kashan suwasqa*); an alpaca's belly was hanging low, indicating that the animal was pregnant (*sut'i kashan wiksa urayashanña*); or rain clouds loomed over a distant hill, signaling that rain was soon to come (*sut'i kashan pararinqa*). Ben Orlove similarly noted that herders in the neighboring community of Phinaya expressed the visible markers of glacial melt as being *sut'i*, which he translated as *a la vista*, literally "in plain sight." These visible markers were contrasted with "other processes and features that might require specialized knowledge or apparatuses to detect" (2009, 141). When something was *sut'i*, it was obvious, clear, and true, and it could easily be confirmed through observation by those with visual perception.

However, sensory experiences are heavily socialized, and a young herder had to be *taught* to see: to attune her eye and develop skilled vision (Bourdieu 1984; Mauss 1979 [1934]). It was through this "education of attention" that herders learned how to pick out the most salient features of their herd animals and make sense of them, in order to both evaluate their herd and communicate about their animals to other people (Grasseni 2009a, 78). Knowing how to both *see* and *describe* a herd was crucial: when Maritza patiently taught me all this, she said, "You've got to learn it all, everything, about alpacas." Otherwise, how was I expected to learn anything else about living in Chillca?

Seeing Like a Herder

There was an extensive, hierarchical lexicon of animal features that herders used to identify herd animals in Chillca. The foremost identifying feature was the animal's coat, described by texture, color, and pattern.[3] In his work in southeastern Peru in the 1960s, Flores Ochoa (1986) documented three primary hues: white (*yuraq*), saturated color (*kulur*), and black (*yana*), with a total of nineteen tones falling within the overall range. In Chillca, I found there to be a similar distribution, with the most common colors described as white (*yuraq, blanku*); camel or yellow (*parinu, ilifi, amarillu, q'illu*); gray (*uqi*); brown (*chumpi*); and black (*yana*), with gradations within each. While animals in the *majada*, the community herd, were only identified according to the three categories relevant to wool sale (white [*blanku*], color [*kulur*], or camel/yellow [*ilifi*]), in a family herd the animals were often named in greater detail, either as a particular shade (for example, *puka chumpi* or *winu* to describe a reddish brown, *khurus* for a grayish-brown, or *wik'uña* for a vicuña-colored animal), or with reference to the pattern of their coat.

Of the mixed-coat animals, coat patterns ranged from solid to spotted, with any number of variations between. *Alqa* described an alpaca with a coat of two colors, and the corresponding term for *alqa* among llamas was *paru* or *anti*. Alpacas and llamas with contrasting colors on the top and bottom halves of their body were *siwara*, with the top color noted (i.e., *yuraq siwara* for an animal with a white top half). Distinctive coat patterns, such as contrasting limbs, snout, face, tail, and so forth, were also named: *makitu* described an animal with contrasting limbs, with the body color noted (i.e., *yuraq makitu* for a white alpaca with colored limbs). An alpaca with a contrasting snout was *simillu*, with the color of the snout noted (i.e., *yana simillu* for a black snout). A llama or alpaca with a white face was *qiqara*, with the body color noted (i.e., *yana qiqara* for a black alpaca with white face). If the color extended past the ears to the nape, the animal was *ch'añu*. If the color extended down to the mid-neck, the animal became *qhillwa* or *mayu suthu*. A spotted animal was *muru* or *chikchi*. An animal with a patch on the side of its body was *ananta*, with the base color noted (i.e., *yuraq ananta* for a white alpaca with black spot). Markings on the hindquarters were *kasla*, possibly from the Spanish word *calza* (Flores Ochoa 1968, 144).

Distinctive patterns that resembled the markings of another animal, most often a bird, earned the alpaca the name of that animal. An alpaca with a differently colored rump or tail was called *wayllata* after the Andean goose (*Neochen melanopter*), while a stripe around the neck made the alpaca *kuntur* (*Vultur gryphus*). A white alpaca with a dark saddlelike marking on its back earned the name *chullumpi*, after the pied-billed or white-tufted grebe (*Podilymbus podiceps; Rollandia rolland*). A white alpaca with a black head extending down to the mid-throat was *qhillwa*, after the Andean duck (*Oxyura ferruginea*), and an animal with large spots was called *usqhullu*, after the Andean cat (*Leopardus jacobita*).[4] Knowing all these features in great detail allowed a herder to immediately recognize and differentiate animals in their own herd and identify them to others. This skill was critical, without which, as Maritza noted, a person would be unable to do the basic collaborative work of herding in a multi-herd sector.[5]

Finally, a variety of genetic variations rendered certain individuals in the alpaca herd especially distinctive. A small percentage of the herd population had phenotypic abnormalities in eye color, ear size, jaw shape, tail size, or foot bone morphology. One of the more common variations was polydactylism, which occurs in approximately 1 percent of the alpaca population. These animals were called *p'arqa*. Another common variation was lighter eye pigmentation, making the eyes appear blue or light gray. These alpacas were called either *qusi* or *misti ñawi*. Instead of

FIGURE 9 An example of alpaca phenotypic variation: a *mut'u* alpaca with stunted ears. Photo by author.

the usual upright, triangular ears, alpacas could also be born with floppy ears (*laphi* or *lakaku*), small folded ears (*chunu*), or no external ears at all (*mut'u*). Alpacas with short, stunted noses were called *thuta*, while alpacas and llamas with protruding lower jaws and prognostic teeth were *q'achu*. A stunted tail carried the name *withu*.

While a herder would not actively seek to purchase an alpaca with these features at the market, they were often a cherished part of the herd and were viewed with affection, amusement, and even admiration. Some of these phenotypic variations, however, were less desirable. Maritza remarked that blue-eyed alpacas (*q'usi*; *misti ñawi*) were not ideal because they didn't pasture well: they wandered off, or lost their young, which she attributed to their poor vision. In contrast, other features were considered "lucky," in that they generated *swirti*. Polydactyl alpacas (*p'arqa*), in particular, were considered good luck (*bwina swirti*). Having a polydactyl animal brought *swirti* to the herd as a whole, compelling it to multiply. Mario and Maritza didn't have a polydactyl alpaca in their herd at that time, but they'd welcome the possibility—"because then you'll have more animals [overall]," Mario said. Maggie Bolton likewise noted in her work among herders in Bolivia that the notion of polydactylism as a "generative prototype" is widespread throughout the Andes: unusual animals "represent the herd synecdochally and embody requests for more llamas to powerful beings" like landscapes beings (*pukara*) (M. Bolton 2006, 544).

Identifying animals and their unique features therefore constituted an affective and sensory practice of cultivating *swirti* in the herd. Again, *swirti* here is not equivalent to the idea of "luck"; rather, it is an expansive concept that "concerns a multitude of events, situation, and beings, but at the same time it cannot be isolated from specific contexts" (Bugallo and Vilca 2011, 36). It is an intersubjective, generative force that is cultivated through the relationships of care between beings (Arnold and Yapita 2006, 233–34). It is what enables beings—human, animal, and landscape—to be successful in their relationships and activities (Pazzarelli 2020, 89). It is deeply enmeshed with *animu*, the life force that circulates across all living beings. As Lucila Bugallo and Mario Vilca clarify, to have luck is to "to somehow have access to the *animu* of animals and plants, through the relationship of affinity, and thus be able to influence it," compelling reproduction and continuity (2011, 37). *Swirti*, however, was fickle and fluctuating. It had to be captured, transmitted, and recreated through practice. Maintaining *swirti* in a herd therefore involved protecting individual herd animals—including those that served as generative prototypes—as an integral part of the herd, as well as other practices of cultivation and circulation, like tying the wool of a departed animal back into the herd itself.

Reading the emotional states of animals was a related skill, one that likewise contributed to the affective work of cultivating *swirti*. I became familiar with the observation of animal contentment, or "happiness" (*kusisqa*), when I first began asking not about alpacas, but about grasses. I was interested in knowing which types of grass were preferred for alpacas. The most common response I received from herders in the pasture was that a certain type of grass was best because "the alpacas like it" (*munanku*). They would gesture to their animals and invite me to observe how happy (*kusi*) or content (*llaqhi*) they were. One could tell that the alpacas liked certain grasses, like *q'upi q'upi*, by observing how they ate it with dedicated focus, twitching their ears in joy. These were the traces, *sut'i*, of happiness.[6] For herders, helping the animals find their favored pastures increased the animals' happiness, thereby maintaining the *swirti* of the herd-household in its entirety. Indeed, the "well-behaved unity" of a contented herd, and the well-fed bodies of the animals themselves, could be read as testament to the *swirti* that the herder shared with their herd (Pazzarelli 2020, 89). Conversely, if animals couldn't find joy in their current pastures, their emotionality signaled to the herders that it was time to move. The traces of restlessness, interpreted through their bodily agitation and discontented wandering, made evident the animal's lack of *kusisqa*. And diminished happiness meant diminished *swirti*, threatening the generative possibilities of both the herder and her herd.

Speaking Like a Herder

I cherished the mornings and afternoons when I tended to Mirelia in the pasture—or rather, she tended to me, as two-year-olds are known to do. Her uncle Julian called her "Mamacha Saltapakuq," Little Miss Leapfrog, an appropriate moniker for a precocious toddler who always kept her whip handy in case some sheep needed wrangling. Over the year I spent with her, her language capacities were emerging and flourishing, and she was starting to put together who her interlocutors were. One point of delight, in her earliest months of speaking, was how she would use species-directed utterances in charming, if not yet accurate, ways. She'd make us all laugh each time she shouted an utterance reserved for dogs—"Pasay suwaq!" ("Shoo, thief!")—at people who got too close or tried to share her snacks. In the first months I was in Chillca, she often made a sweet *tsk tsk tsk* noise at me, a sound used to demonstrate affection toward children, puppies, *crías*, and lambs. Eventually her utterances reoriented to their appropriate addressees and became cheekier: she's relish in the opportunity to hurl a "pasay karahu!" (shoo, bastard!) at an errant dog, and she began using more complicated, multi-interlocutor utterances like *wuqchiy* (see chapter 1).

Speaking like a herder was an essential learned practice. As Mary Weismantel noticed in her work among families in the Ecuadorian highlands, social reproduction is not only a physical process through which families feed, clothe, and care for their children but also "*linguistic*: the words people use to talk to and about one another are part of the accumulated history through which relationships are established" (1995, 695). As a young herder grew up in Chillca, she was not only fed, clothed, and cared for by other women herders, but she was also learning to talk like them, with them, and about them. Young children could often be heard practicing their herder-speak with their relatives and friends, exchanging play conversations in which they shouted, "*Hakusun*, let's go!" or "Let's round them up!" and practiced their roles as kin and neighbors, learning to ask for help with the herd and offering food in return: "Let's play here, I'll share my bread."[7] Mirelia frequently practiced her herder-speak with her mother and grandmother, referring to fictional sheep in similar ways that she had heard other women do:

MIRELIA: Mama, I'm asking you a favor (*valikamushayki*). Over there . . .
    my sheep . . .
MARITZA: Your sheep, you lost it?
CONCEPCIÓN: My sheep . . .
MARITZA: I don't see your sheep. Ask your grandmother, *awir*, let's see?
CONCEPCIÓN: What is it, *awir*?
MARITZA: She says she lost her sheep.
CONCEPCIÓN: Oh, what a bad sheep . . .

FIGURE 10 Mirelia and her herding whip. Photo by author.

In just this short conversation, Mirelia was practicing an important form of herder-speak. First, she engaged in the collective animal-location that often initiates conversations between women in the pasture, making observations about where their animals are, what they are doing, and— perhaps most importantly—complaining about them. These discourses of animal-based complaint were a fundamental component of Quechua herder conversation, as the phatic expressions with which herders created openings for social engagement when they came upon other herders in the field. More broadly, talking about animals was a discursive practice that entered a young herder into crucial relationships with other women in her social world. Although men also talked about animals (with other men as well as women), animal-speak was considered the domain of women (*warmirimay*, "women's talk"). I was once told by a group of women sitting on the outside of a conversation among men that women didn't "meddle" (*mitiy*, from Spanish *meterse*) in men's conversations or vice versa, clarifying that women talked about their families and animals (*wawanmanta*, *qharinmanta*, *uywanmanta*), while men talked about their travels or experiences (*purisqanmanta*, *vidanmanta*). At that time, there was a general association of men with outward mobility, and women with situated networks of care. On more than one occasion, I heard women chastise their husbands for "just sitting there like a little woman" instead of going out to monitor the llamas or to check on the potato farms.[8]

But this type of talk also produced reciprocal action: in that short conversation between Mirelia, her mother, and her grandmother, Mirelia imitated the initiation of a reciprocal labor exchange, *valikamuy*, referencing a common social practice in which women asked one another to watch their animals with the expectation that the favor will be returned at a later date.[9] Reciprocal labor exchanges are a central feature of classic Andean ethnography, particularly in relation to the concept of *ayni*—the overarching ethic of generalized reciprocity and cooperation that undergirds economic, social, and political life in Andean rural communities (Allen 1988; Brush 1977; Mayer 2002; Alberti and Mayer 1974; Mannheim 1986; Van Vleet 2008a; Leinaweaver 2009). Accounts of *ayni*-in-practice were initially rooted in the exchanges of agricultural labor and house-raising, the central labor of which is performed by men. Thus, accounts of Andean reciprocal exchanges initially focused on men's work, such that it was once typified as "formal male reciprocity" (Wilhoit 2017, 6). Women's reciprocal labor was often subsumed under the informal, kin-based reciprocal cooperation of the household (Brush 1977). However, there are many examples of women also exchanging labor under contracts of *ayni* (Babb 2018; Leinaweaver 2005; Paerregaard 2012; Seligmann 1993; Van Vleet 2008b; Weismantel 1988; Wilhoit 2017).

In Chillca, women herders participated in multiple, overlapping forms of labor exchange throughout the year, in which they distributed and circulated animal labor and care among a network of neighbors and kin. On a daily basis, women watched the animals of their mothers, sisters, mothers-in-law, sisters-in-law, and neighbors, freeing up time for them to run errands, go to the market, or visit relatives in other sectors or communities. These labor exchanges were managed almost exclusively by women, and could be more or less formal: a more formal request was referred to as *valikuy* (to ask, petition, contract), while a spontaneous request was *ingaray* (from the Spanish *encargar*, to entrust).[10] The practice of *valikuy* was always made in advance: at least one day ahead if the herder's labor was needed just for one day, or far in advance if the herder was needed for multiple days. When the request was made of family members or neighbors, there was a tacit understanding that the person making the request would return the favor another day. If the contract was made with someone with whom the herder could not reciprocate (e.g., a person without animals, or someone from a distant community), then payment of some kind was required.

These labor exchanges were so common that my fieldnotes were peppered with them. In one entry, I noted how Maritza initiated an exchange with an older woman from a neighboring community, who had stayed the previous night with us and watched Maritza's animals for the day. As she departed that morning, Maritza was already planning her next request:

> *Maritza paid the older woman 5 soles to herd her sheep for the day, and gave her* wilma *(wool),* muraya *(freeze-dried potato), and* ucha *(alpaca dung) when she left this morning. She will come back in November (the 11th) to herd for 2 days while we go to a festival. Maritza will pay her 15 soles. This weekend we'll go to Japura to visit Martiza's mother, so she will ask [her neighbor] and pay her 5 soles for the day or ask one of the [neighboring] kids.*

Taking care of herd animals was a collaborative effort that created bonds between people, building collaborative networks of animal care and herd management (Bugallo and Tomasi 2012, 210). In both the daily care of the animals, as well as the exchange practices around selling, buying, trading, or redistributing labor, herders reproduced their relationships with one another. Even in toddlerhood, Mirelia was beginning to understand the importance of exchange as a social practice, something I noted in other contexts as well. Once, I had a solar lantern stolen from my yard, and Mirelia told me, "Don't be sad; I'll sell an alpaca and buy you another one." Before she had even reached her third birthday, she was already verbally indexing different forms of exchange through which animals, labor, goods, and cash were circulated in the interest of cultivating contentment, *kusisqa*. She also recognized how the transfer of food was at the heart of these exchanges, and always invited her playmates and kin to share bread with her. Indeed, it was tacitly understood that the person making the request of their neighbor always did so with food—a bowl of soup, some roasted corn or broad beans, a few boiled potatoes or chunks of meat.

Knowing how to initiate these exchanges was a learned practice, in which verbal strategy was especially key: asking, imploring, and joking in just the right ways to be convincing and to avoid offense. Maritza and Concepción were especially gifted in this regard. Once, I watched in amusement as the two of them employed their best efforts to convince an older widower from a neighboring hamlet to herd their animals for a few days while they attended a festival. Inviting him in from the cold to share a hot bowl of soup, they jokingly offered to help him find a new bride if he agreed to herd: *Hinallaaa, favor!*—Please! *Yuyarisaykipuni*—I'll always remember you (return the favor), *T'inkata apamushayki*—I've brought you a gift of alcohol to toast! *Payakunatapas qhawanayki!*—you've got to watch [admire] the old ladies too! Eventually after much back-and-forth, they finally informed me that he wasn't interested in herding, just in chasing the old ladies. Despite their best efforts, he declined, and the search for another herder began anew.

FIGURE 11 Preparing food for the *valikuq*. Photo by author.

While *valikuy* required a bit more planning and strategy, *ingaray* (from the Spanish *encargar*, to entrust) was always a last-minute request, typically made in haste. The herder entrusted their animals to a neighbor for a few hours, up to a day, as they were rushing out to complete an errand, with the implicit or voiced promise that they would watch the person's animals another day ("kuidapusayki huq punchayta"). This sort of exchange was only possible between two individuals with a close social relationship: mother and daughter, sisters, or neighbors who had lived alongside each other and participated in labor exchanges for years. It didn't involve a transfer of cash or goods. Once when I asked Maritza whether she would pay her mother-in-law to watch her animals, she laughed uproariously. It would be unthinkable to pay your female relative to help you herd. *Ingaray* was effective only as an instantiation of *ayni*, with the assumption of reciprocal return. However, *ayni* also had its limits. When I inquired if a man from a distant sector was practicing *ayni* by helping Mario's grandmother repair her roof, Mario responded no, and clarified the family relation: "That's her son-in-law; he lives with my aunt Carmen. Since he lives with her daughter, he has to help. If she was from another family, then yes, she would have to return the favor, saying '*aynita kutichipunay*,' or she would have to pay him."[11]

Learning how to distinguish and engage in these forms of reciprocal obligation was an essential herding skill, and a central component of a herder's social world. While these requests and exchanges of herding labor were an everyday occurrence, they were especially nerve-racking for a young woman new to a particular sector or community. And indeed, most younger women in Chillca *were* new to the community at a certain moment in time, given that young couples in Chillca almost always resided in the husband's natal sector, unless they petitioned to live elsewhere.[12] While this residence pattern, common in the Andes, is referred to as patrilocality, women in Chillca described it in notably women-centric terms: "The *qhachun* lives alongside her husband's mother" (*qhariq mamanpa ladonpi tiyan qhachun*). Before a woman became a herder (*michiq*) in Chillca, therefore, she first had to prove herself as a *qhachun* (daughter-in-law).

Being a daughter-in-law was a notoriously uncomfortable role to occupy. There is even a potato variety in the Peruvian Andes that references this tense social moment in a woman's life. Called "that which makes the *qhachun* cry" (*qhachun waqachiy*), it is especially difficult to peel, causing the embarrassment of the *qhachun* desperate to impress her new in-laws. In addition to being separated from her family, a *qhachun* is in a subordinate position to her female in-laws, and lingering tensions can erupt into conflict and even violence (Van Vleet 2008b). While relationships between daughters-in-law and mothers-in-law are especially tense, newly married women also struggle to navigate relationships and obligations with their female neighbors. Krista Van Vleet noted in Bolivia that the amount of labor this entails can be overwhelming: "at the same time that a young wife is working for her mother-in-law, she is also trying to establish more reciprocal labor exchange relationships with other women in the community" (2008a, 569). This requires an initial imbalance, as the young woman struggles to prove to her female neighbors and affines that she can pull her weight.

In Chillca, young women talked often about the difficulties inherent in occupying the category of *qhachun*. There was a formal process, known as *qhachun riqsichiy* ("meeting the daughter-in-law"), in which young women were ceremoniously presented to the community assembly by their new in-laws. In February 2016 I watched as a young woman was introduced to the community after marrying into the sector of Chimpa Chillca. Her new husband and his mother brought an offering of food (chicken and a pallet of soda) and briefly spoke on her behalf. They promised to help her learn to herd the community's animals, specifically the *majada*, the community herd, the care of which would fall under their household in the coming year. She likewise echoed these commitments in a tentative voice, her hands clasped and her gaze respectfully lowered to the floor. The *junta directiva* replied with recommendations: live in harmony with your family and your neighbors, and herd the animals well. While the *qhachun riqsichiy* was notoriously intimidating, it didn't get easier from there. There was the constant scrutiny of being watched and evaluated by your in-laws, and women were often subjected to various forms of ridicule: men might tease them, and other women might refuse to greet them or offer them food. A new daughter-in-law had to learn to initiate and sustain the various relational threads that made up her social world before she could cultivate the vital networks of care through which she established both material and social well-being in the community.

I often asked Concepción, in the evenings as she and her neighbors brought the animals in from the pasture, what made a woman a "good herder" (*allin michiq*). In those moments, ducking through the darkened doorway, Concepción might complain bitterly about one neighbor or another that wasn't pulling her weight. She happily gossiped with me when I asked who was or was *not* a good herder: one young woman in particular was considered lazy (*qhilla*), and too forlorn. This woman was a recent *qhachun* who had just moved to the community with her young husband. Eighteen years old and living away from home for the first time in her life, she was desperately homesick and would often run away to her mother's home down the valley, leaving her animals with neighbors. The work of exchanging herding labor fell to her husband and father-in-law. In contrast, Maritza and her sister Aniseta were both considered good herders by the older women in the sector. They were both considered *viva*, alert and active: they were watchful of their animals, making sure they never escaped into neighboring sectors or into the potato fields down below. Most importantly, they helped often with the animals of their neighbors and in-laws, regularly taking them out to pasture alongside their own herds. To be fair, they had been there longer than the other young woman and had learned how to be good herders and good kinswomen over time. Concepción conceded that perhaps, over the years, the newest herder would learn how to cultivate these relationships like the other *qhachun* in the sector had before her.

Of course, all this was on Mario and Maritza's minds as they raised Mirelia. They wanted Mirelia to be in a good position before she herself moved to another sector of Chillca, or to another community. By giving her animals, teaching her how to care for them and to build relationships through that care, they were helping to cultivate her *swirti* as a herder. But they were also initiating and cultivating other forms of *swirti*. In her haircutting ceremony that opened this chapter, Mario and Maritza were also bringing Mirelia into connection with the kind of *swirti* that circulated among *profesionales*, people with titled careers. This type of *swirti* wasn't incompatible with the kinds that were generated within the pasture, corral, and herd-household. Indeed, as Francisco Pazzarelli writes, *swirti* has to be understood in a more generalized sense, as a "force that links [a person] within the framework of fertile relationships . . . people can be lucky in business, in animal management, in agriculture or in mining" (2020, 89; Göbel 1997). People can, and increasingly do, cultivate various forms of *swirti* to generate potential futures.

Picturing *Michiq* Futures

In Mario and Maritza's house in Chillca's town center, there was a particular photograph that always caught my attention. It was a large family portrait of Mario, Maritza, and Mirelia, but unlike the other photos tacked to the painted adobe wall, it held a central position in a thick and glossy plastic frame. On closer inspection, it became clear it was a composite image in which their faces had been grafted onto generic bodies: Mario's wore a suit, Maritza's a starched blouse and cardigan, and Mirelia's a white christening gown. Mario had commissioned the portrait from a studio in the regional city of Sicuani, and the images had been lifted from their national identity cards. Mario's expression was severe, and Maritza had a knitted brow, her chin tilted downward and away from the camera as if she were looking into the sun. Mirelia gazed wide-eyed into the camera, caught in a flash of confusion. While their faces held expression and movement, the bodies were oddly flat, reminiscent of the photo stand-ins at fairgrounds.

These portraits were popular commissions in Sicuani, and they seemed to capture a glimpse of the aspirations of Mario and Maritza's generation. Like many other couples their age, Mario and Maritza spoke often about the future that they envisioned for themselves, and for their children. They specified that they only wanted two children so that they could invest in their education and raise them to be *profesionales*. The word was a direct cognate for the English "professional," and indeed it encapsulated many of the same connotations of professionalism: suits, ties, briefcases, and starched cardigans, as well as titles that carried prestige, like doctors, lawyers, and engineers.

It was evident for future generations in Chillca that a young woman's well-being might not be solely tied to her skilled vision as a herder, or to her accumulation and circulation of animals and animal-based labor. Indeed, for Mirelia and other young girls her age, her parents envisioned multiple potential futures. In Mirelia's *chukcha rutukuy*, these potentialities were invited into the ritual and made present through the disproportionate inclusion of cash, and the fact that the central ritual participants—my husband and I, the *madrina* and *padrino*—were not livestock-rich individuals, but foreign researchers who might transfer some of our *swirti* as *profesionales*. While Mario and Maritza still considered the accumulation of animals important for their daughter's future, they also envisioned themselves selling many of those animals in exchange for her enrollment in formalized education in the cities of Sicuani or Cusco.

The animals themselves were also changing: due to state-sponsored breeding programs, solid white animals were becoming more desirable, and herders noted that there are fewer color or mixed-coat animals than in previous decades. The sensory practices of seeing, naming, and describing animal appearance—knowledge that Maritza insisted I know in its entirety—were necessarily shifting.[13] Through novel practices of attunement, new futures were being rendered possible, in which one's luck emanated not only from their relationships to their animals but also from connections to foreign researchers, wealthy *compadres*, and the cash economy. The following chapters explore these potentialities, and their imaginations, in greater depth.

CHILLCA LLAQTA (CONTINUED)

Ausangati q'uchaman rumichalla chhanqasqay	Having thrown a pebble in Ausangate lake
Ausangati q'uchaman rumichalla wikch'usqay	Having tossed a pebble in Ausangate lake
Maytaq kunankamari kutiramusqankichu	And (until now), where have you been coming back to?
Maytaq kunankamari vueltaramusqankichu	And (until now), where have you been returning to?
Kutiramusqankichu	Have you come back?
Chayhinallataq	And like that,
Taytamamay maytaq kutimushanchu	To where are my parents coming back?
Chayhinallataq	Just like that
Mamataytay maytaq wiltamushanchu	To where are my parents returning?
Sapachallay sulachallay	All alone, all on my own

Kay llaqtapi tarikuni	I find myself this town
Kay llaqtapi rikukuni	I see myself in this town
Kay llaqtapi rikukuni	I see myself in this town
Pipas kashachun	Whomever accompanies me,
Maypis kashachun	And wherever I may be,
Kay waynuypiraq tusuylla tusuyusaq	I will still just dance, dance this *waynu*
Pipas kashachun	Whomever accompanies me,
Maypis kashachun	And wherever I may be,
Kay waynuypiraq takiylla takiyusaq	I will still just sing, sing this *waynu*

CHAPTER THREE

Shifting Landscapes

A REMEDY FOR RESTLESSNESS
Ucha (Alpaca dung)
Zapallu ruru (Dried pumpkin seed)
Runaq chukchan (Human hair)
Ch'illpi (Tuber peels or grain husks)
Hankay (Toasted corn)

Line the base of a metal pan with alpaca dung coals from the hearth. Sprinkle a handful of pumpkin seeds on top (can be mixed with tuber peels, grain husks, or toasted corn, if available). Add a tightly wound ball of your own hair. Let burn lightly until the mixture releases smoke. Fan softly to extinguish the flames, and place in the threshold of the sheep's pen. Leave overnight until the contents are fully consumed.

In the morning, long after the smell of burnt hair and seeds had dissipated in the night's chill, Concepción and I made fry-bread next to the fire, scraping the sticky dough from our fingers with a knife. In a pot on the stovetop, the remains of an aborted lamb boiled softly beneath a gray foam. As we dropped the flattened circles of dough into the sizzling alpaca fat, I asked Concepción about the medicinal pot burning in the sheep's pen. The pumpkin seeds, she explained, were so the sheep would eat peacefully (*llaqhi mikhunanpaq*). She reached out and swept her hand across a dried pile of potato skins. "These too, all of this, *ch'illpikuna, hankaykuna*"—she patted it softly for emphasis—"this stored food, it all roots low (*urallamanpi tirukun*); it doesn't take to the hillsides but stays below." The pumpkin seeds and dried corn she had brought up the previous month from a town down the valley, and the potatoes came from her own farms on the valley floor.

FIGURE 12 A remedy for restlessness. Photo by author.

She rested the tip of her finger on a pumpkin seed: "the pumpkin, it just sits there on the ground, peacefully (*llaqhi*); it doesn't go anywhere," and with a nod, "that's why I burn it." Just as a gourd or a tuber is grounded, the sheep too will become grounded. They'll stay to the valley floors instead of running up to the hilltops, where they feed on the grass types that are preferable for alpacas and llamas. "And the hair?" I asked. The hair was harder to explain. "It's medicine, *hampiy*," she said, "for craziness, *mullu unquypaq*." I had been told many times by women in the community to collect and burn the hairs that escaped from my braids, or else the wind would carry them off and I'd go mad. It seemed that burning one's hair could also protect one's own animals from suffering the same. When malevolent winds blew through the corrals at night, the smell of burning hair held them off, preventing the winds from making the animals restless.

While chapters 1 and 2 focused on communicative and sensorial practices between humans and animals, this chapter focuses on the relationships between humans and a sentient landscape. The practice of *q'apachiy* ("to make smoke") is one example of what Mario Blaser and Marisol de la Cadena have called, drawing upon the work of Martin Heidegger, "worlding" practices (Blaser 2013; de la Cadena 2015, 200). *Q'apachiy* is a communicative and material practice that mediates across humans, animals, and landscapes to (re)produce predictable states within the shared "matrix of animated substance" that is Andean life (Allen 1997, 75). It falls within a recognizable category of restorative practices in the Andes, in which the qualities and essences of one entity are made consumable through a variety of processes (burning [*kanay, q'apachiy*], steeping in a tonic or tea, burying, blowing on the breath [*phukuy*], or allowing to rot [*ismupuy*]) in order to regulate and sustain hierarchical relations between animals, humans, places, and other forms of sentient life. Not only do these practices bring the world and its participants into being, but they also shape that world into a *desired* world: in this remedy for restlessness, for example, the medium of smoke or scent compels the essence of one entity (grounded tubers, gourds, and human hair) to be transferred to another (sheep), to compel different behavior.[1]

While many of these actions and logics could be integrated into what has been defined as "ritual practice" in Andean communities, they were also a part of daily, routine life for herders like Concepción. Every morning when she went out with the animals, she prepared a *phukuy* to keep herself and the herd healthy. Once she had settled the herd somewhere, she'd take her plastic bag of coca leaves, stashed in the folds of her shawl, and set it on her skirt as she was seated on the ground. She'd open the bag wide and search through, gently moving the leaves from one side of the bag to the other, finding three that were perfectly shaped. Laying the leaves on top of one another, she'd grasp them with the thumb and index finger of her right hand. With her gaze to the hilltops, she'd recite the names of the surrounding places, and ask for protection for her herd, herself, and sometimes me:

Phhiiiuuu . . .	[Blowing on leaves]
Apu K'illukunka Machula	Apu K'illukunka Machula
Apu Llusquchu Machula	Apu Llusquchu Machula
Ama kunanqa unquchinkichu	Don't make her sick now
Phhiiiuuuu—kay gringachata!	[Blowing sound]—this dear *gringa*!
Qhalilla purinqa	She will walk healthy

Kallpata valurta qunki apukuna   Give us strength, courage, *apu*
Ama laqʼachinkichu!   Don't make her slip!

By completing the *phukuy* every day, Concepción kept the relationships between herself and surrounding places active: saying their names, transferring the essence of her coca leaves to them, and ensuring that she and her animals would be protected from misfortune. As she explained:

> [I do the *phukuy*] for my animals, or I say, "don't make my house sick." If not, you might get sick, if you didn't *phukuy*. That's why I do it. You could get sick, you could trip—you'd roll right down that hill! Like that time you slipped over there, that's why. Every day. For my weaving too.

With the herd calm, and her *gringa* safely posted on the hillside, Concepción could then soften her attention, or turn to the weaving in her lap, trusting that a state of calm had been enacted.

That these worlding practices—*qʼapachiy* and *phukuy*—are deeply intertwined both materially and symbolically with the routine practices of daily life directs our attention toward the subtle ways that Quechua people reaffirm critical relationalities during times of transformative change. It is especially important to notice these daily practices, given that "formalized" ritual contexts—those set apart from daily life and adhering to a ritual calendar, for example—are indeed becoming less common throughout the southeastern Peruvian Andes. This change can suggest an ontological rupture, or a sense that preexisting cosmologies may be "broken" or lost in a time of rapid social, ecological, and climatological change (Paerregaard 2014; Cometti 2020). However, I would caution against such a fatalistic interpretation, although the evidence of rupture does raise an important set of questions: as Marieke Winchell writes, "seeing relations to other-than-humans as contingent upon action introduces new questions of their *disruption, weakening, or attenuation* in conditions where devotion is impossible or newly unappealing" (2023, 614, emphasis mine). Indeed, reciprocal relationships and the worlds they create are dependent upon both the material existence of entities and the actions of people, both of which have been put into question under changing social and material conditions.

Practices like *q'apachiy* and *phukuy* were still very much active in 2015, as were the *pukara* and *apu* to which they were directed. This suggests that we must, as Winchell proposes, "reframe ontology from questions of a stable, discrete sphere of meaning or materiality to an ethnographic problem of how people strive to uphold ties through which other-than-human relations are sustained, or not" (2023, 622). By "dwelling in the dissolve" (Alaimo 2016), we can turn our attention to the intentional—and, at times, improvisational—practices of being-in-relation through which people in Chillca both maintained and reconfigured their lives in a shifting terrain.

People and *Pukara*

There were many places in Antapata that evoked strong memories for Concepción: the rock that she used to ride like a horse when she was a little girl; the windblock her grandfather built on the windy ridges behind her home; the tufted knoll where she collected duck eggs; the shallow caves where her brothers would try to trap condors by luring them with chunks of meat. She told me about these places one day while we were herding her mother's animals up into a high glacial valley. The audio recorder in my right palm caught her words between the squelching of our footsteps in the wetlands. Walking along the river from her home in Antapata to the glacial pastures of Uqi Kancha, Concepción narrated her own history as deeply intertwined with the landscape unfolding before us: "Nuqaykuq llapapaq, Rojo"—"It's ours, all of it, the Rojo family." Each sector of Chillca was associated with a particular family, and the Rojos were rooted most deeply in the herding hamlets of Antapata and Uqi Kancha. Concepción carried the surname Rojo from both her mother's and father's side—Concepción Rojo Rojo—and she rooted herself very firmly and definitively in this place.

The alpacas ambled along ahead of us, following the well-worn paths that crossed the hillsides: tracings of the comings and goings of people and animals for generations. Interspersed with her narrative, Concepción called out to her animals, or paused to pluck a medicinal herb from under a rock, tucking it into the folds of her shawl: *maycha llucha* for kindling, *sutuma* for headaches and memory loss, *tikllaywarmi* for the kidneys, and thick clumps of *ch'uku* for wounds. As she went along, she made subtle alterations to the path beneath us, removing scattered rocks that could injure or scare the animals. In some places, I noticed that little steps have been carved out of the hillside. Too small for humans, they had been carved by herders to ease their alpacas' steps.

Descending slightly into the valley of Uqi Kancha, Ausangate loomed ahead, strikingly white against the blue sky. Each smaller peak, ridge, knoll, hillock, flat place, lake, and hillside also had a name: Stone Door (Qaqa Punku), Two Lake Plateau (Iskay Qucha Pata), Sun-Play Peak (Inti Pukllana Punta), Duck Plateau (Qhillwa Pata), Candlelight Peak (Vilachiy Punta). Concepción felt a particular affinity for a few places: Palumani, a wide, ochre-red hillock on the southern ridge of the valley; and Warmi Saya, a knoll shaped like a rising woman. In the *waynus* she performed in regional festivals, these places were prominent orienting figures:

Palumani urqutaqa	On Palumani mountain
Warmi saya q'asataqa	On Warmi Saya pass
Yana phuyu wasayamun	Dark clouds pass over
Aqarapi chakichayuq	[I'm] walking in the frozen dew
Iphu para chakichayuq	[I'm] walking in the mist
Chay phuyuq chawpichallanpi	In the midst of those clouds
Chay rit'iq k'anchallapi	In the brightness of that snow
Maris, maris waqayunay	Why, oh why, must I cry
Waqayuspa puriyunay	Crying, I must go on

It was peaceful herding in the high glacial valleys of Antapata, where the wide swaths of wetland provided nourishing cushion plants for the alpacas. However, the abundance of glacial water could also be dangerous: she pointed out the watery holes in the pampa and islands of floating grass. She had to be vigilant and watch the young animals closely up here, and she always checked the pools before she returned home at night. As we moved closer to the glacier, the pools gradually expanded into deep, eerily green lakes. Her paternal grandfather used to tell her stories about the giant serpent, Liun Amaru, who lived in one of deepest lakes, Q'umir Qucha. When she was a child, she and her little sister and their friends would play around the edges of Q'umir Qucha, scaring themselves by calling out to the serpent, "Amaruuu, Amaruuuu!" She once saw the lake swallow up an entire horse. These lakes took humans too. Not immediately, but eventually: if you fell into a lake and managed to escape, you'd still die years later. As Concepción told me, she was the only one of her group of friends who played around the lake to survive to advanced adulthood. "Llapan pukllamasi wañun, sapa, unitu, sulu kashani," she said. "All of my playmates died; I'm all alone, one, solo, just me." One time when they were playing, her little sister Nikolasa slipped and fell into the lake, and although they were able to pull her out at the time, the lake claimed her years later by deploying a fatal lightning strike.

Thus, while Palumani and Warmi Saya are familiar and comforting interlocutors, Concepción avoided the ridge of Tuqlla Pata, across the valley, where splintered spalls of rock marked the repeated contact of lightning and stone. Tuqlla Pata loomed as a reminder of the unstable nature of relations between the humans and other beings that inhabited and animated this place. It was there, a decade earlier, that Concepción's sister Nikolasa and her infant daughter were caught in a late-afternoon

FIGURE 13 The mountain of Ausangate above Uqi Kancha with Palumani (hill) visible on the left, and Warmi Saya (knoll) on the right. Photo by author.

lightning storm with a neighbor and her two small children. When the two women didn't come home in the evening, neighbors found the only survivor, a six-year-old boy, trembling in a storage house. He led them to the spot on Tuqlla Pata ridge where a single lightning strike had made contact with the earth. "Icha ñañachayta mikhupunpascha chay q'ucha, chaypischa wañuran aswanta"—Concepción told me—maybe, even decades later, the lake did eat her sister after all.

For Concepción, her own history and that of her family was inextricably embedded and emergent within the landscapes of Antapata and Uqi Kancha. Her grandfather's struggle to reclaim his land from the haciendas; her childhood, adolescence, and adulthood; her marriage with Julio and the births of their children; the death of her sister. All were moments that emerged from a shared history with the places and beings of this locality. Particular beings of significance, like Warmi Saya, Palumani, Q'umir Qucha, and Tuqlla Pata, were crucial nexuses of the lived and *living* topography in which Concepción located herself and her family (Basso 1996). By recounting stories and songs about these places, she oriented them within a network of topographical relationships that were at once social and spatial. When Concepción asserted, "It's ours, all of it, the Rojo family," her claim was at once legal and ontological: the land belonged to the Rojo family, but it also *was* the Rojo family.

The landscape features themselves were also living: Warmi Saya, Palumani, Q'umir Qucha, and Tuqlla Pata were themselves social beings in many of the same ways that human persons were. They had names, were gendered, and carried complex social histories that defined their material qualities, temperaments, and the relationships between them and the humans in their company. They experienced joy and pain, felt anger and exacted revenge, and became hungry and demanded to be fed. Looming over them, Ausangate stood as the most powerful *apu*, followed in rank by the smaller, less-potent topographic features at his feet. Like humans, these places also cared for animals: the vicuña (an undomesticated cousin to the llama and alpaca) were considered their herd animals, the *wisk'acha* (*vizcacha*, small rabbitlike rodents) their horses, and foxes their dogs. They also cared for humans and the humans' herd animals: when they were pleased, they protected humans and animals from misfortune, bad luck, and malevolent spirits and essences. When they were perturbed, they deployed their weapons: hail, thunder, and lightning. The very conditions of life and the circumstances of death were enabled through the relationships that people had with the places that surrounded and enveloped them. At times, these relationships were reciprocal; at other times, they were predatory (Przytomska-La Civita 2020). Which modality—generous or rapacious—depended on the conduct of the humans in their midst.

In the literature on Andean ontologies, these places are typically represented as earth beings or *tirakuna* (de la Cadena 2015); place persons or place kin (*lugares parientes*) (Salas Carreño 2016; 2019), and places (Allen 1988). In Chillca, the term used most often to describe the spatially located social entities with which humans shared their lives was *pukara*, which overlapped conceptually with the term *apu*: the main difference being one of scale (*apu* are larger, more powerful social beings than *pukara*). The relationship between humans and *pukara* was co-constitutive, a mutual emergence of humans and places through their continuous social, material, and communicative engagement with one another. Concepción's son, Mario, and his wife Maritza made this practice-based relationship clear to me. One late evening, at their home in Uqi Kancha, I asked them to explain who and what the *pukara* were:

ALLISON: Who are the *pukara*?

MARIO (in Spanish): It's the earth (*tierra*). *Pukara*, for example, the *pukara* K'illu . . .

MARITZA [interrupting, in Quechua]: We serve them like this [holds out a bowl of food], like that. The mountains, we serve them nicely. That's *pukara*.

MARIO: It's said Ausangate is *pukara*.

MARITZA: Yes.

ALLISON: So, it's similar to an *apu*?

MARIO: In Quechua, they say *pukara*, like the *apu*.

MARITZA: People serve them. How could they not, right? The *pukara* have to be respected, right, so they serve them [holds out the bowl again].

ALLISON: Are all *pukara* similar to *apu*? Or are some different?

MARITZA: They're the same, *apu*, *pukara*, the same.

ALLISON: And other places (*lugares*) can be *apu* too?

MARITZA: Always. The people serve the mountains. Like how we would serve Ch'uma [nearby mountain], like that.

ALLISON: Is Llusquchu Q'uchu a *pukara*?

MARITZA: *Pukara.*
ALLISON: And Illachiy?
MARIO AND MARITZA: Illachiy too.
MARIO: They have names, right?

While dictionaries often translate *pukara* as a "fortress," "hole to burn offerings," or a "mountain deity," its usage was much more complicated. The term *pukara* is used throughout the Ausangate region, and was likewise encountered on the north slopes of Ausangate by Marisol de la Cadena, who recounted the difficulty of its translation in the book *Earth Beings* (2015). When de la Cadena asked her central interlocutor, Nazario, to explain *pukara* to her, he responded with frustration: "*Pukara* is just *pukara*" (2015, 29), adding that, as de la Cadena recounts, "whatever I wrote on my paper, it was not going to be *pukara*; it was going to be something else" (108). As I likewise discovered in my fieldwork, it was necessary to pursue "communication without commensurability," and accept that any translation of *pukara* would never capture what this social being was and did (2015, 27). What Mario and Maritza were urging me to understand was that *pukara*—like all social beings in the Andes—were defined not by their form but by the practices that sustained them and brought them into being.

In other words, that which defined *pukara* was not its status as a particular type of entity—whether it was a mountain, wetland, or herding place—but the social relations that animated it. *Pukara* had names, Mario reminded me, which was at once indicative of their status as social beings, and a condition for the productive practices that defined them. Their names transformed them into addressees and interlocutors, as anthropologist Guillermo Salas has written, thereby "allowing humans to address them and offer them food" (Salas Carreño 2016, 822). Maritza repeatedly demonstrated this aspect of their identity by holding out a bowl of food in front of me: people did not serve *pukara* because they were *pukara*; rather, *pukara* were *pukara* because people *served* them, thereby endowing them, like all social beings, with substance and vitality through the circulation of food (Salas Carreño 2016). And *pukara*, in return, offered the conditions of life for humans and animals. They provided vital substances in the form of water and grasses, offered protection from misfortune, and enabled the reproduction of herd animals.

Much has been written about the principle of *reciprocity* as the predominant organizing ethic of relationality in the Andes, through which
social beings like humans and mountains are drawn into bonds of obligation with one another through practices of active cohabitation, con-
substantiation, and collaborative labor (Alberti and Mayer 1974; Bolin
1998; Mayer 2002). It bears noting that earlier studies of this ethic of
reciprocity, and the expression of *ayni* in the Quechua and Aymara languages, were often laden with associations of harmony or balance, and
"imbued with a certain nostalgia and idealism" (Arnold 2022, 58). In
conversation with Quechua peoples, however, it has become apparent
that reciprocity—much like care—contains elements of dependence and
autonomy, and nurture as well as predation (Arnold 2022; Bugallo 2020;
Lema 2014; Przytomska-La Civita 2020).[2] Modalities and practices of
ambivalence, antagonism, and violence are also products of—and, importantly, productive of—human-animal relations (Abbink 2003; Das
2013; Dave 2014; Govindrajan 2015a; 2018; Rivera Andía 2005), as well
as kin relations more broadly (Carsten 2013; Van Vleet 2008a; 2008b).
Or, as anthropologist Radhika Govindrajan has written in her work on
human-animal relationships in India's Central Himalayas, "mutuality and
connection do not imply on an erasure of difference or hierarchy," but in
fact often rely upon it (2018, 4). This asymmetry between social beings
like humans, mountains, animals, and objects lends weight to the moral
obligations between them, and it also colors the affective qualities of
these relationships—with fear as well as admiration.

Mario explained it in this way: *pukara* were not intrinsically bad or
good, but they could do good or bad things depending on the quality of
their relationships with the people in their sphere. This relationship often
originated with the birth of a child. "When a baby is born, for example,"
Mario began, arranging the cups on the table in front of us into a triangle:

MARIO: Let's say this is Ausangate *apu*, this is Ch'uma *pukara*, this is K'illu
   pukara—when a child is born, the *pukara* wait, and then one of them
   traps [the baby] like this, *poom*, and takes it. People say this is why, when
   a baby is sick or has *malviento*, the healers look at him and say "*chay
   chaymi hapisqasunki, chay gastilluyki,*" your *gastillu* has caught you.[3]
ALLISON: Are all [*gastillu*] bad, or no?
MARIO: Some of them can be bad.

ALLISON: But, aren't some *pukara* good?

MARITZA: Not good, they're the same. But people serve them, right, maybe doing a *phukuy* like *phiiuuu* [mimes blowing on coca leaves], then they might be good.

Proactive action, like *phukuy*, *q'apachiy*, or offering food could compel *pukara* to be good, to prevent them from leveling misfortune against the people and animals in their midst. However, as I began asking more and more questions about *pukara*, it became evident that these proactive actions were increasingly rare—with varying interpretations of what consequences lay ahead.

Dwindling Offerings

The first of August was one of the most important dates on the formal ritual calendar, when the earth was considered "open," and relationships between place persons and humans were at their closest—and most tense and fragile—point. Late in the evening of July 31, 2015, Julio, Concepción, and I gathered in their dry-season home in Antapata to prepare the year's *dispachu*. In the dark, Julio laid out a shawl (*lliklla*) on the floor of the hut, placing a smaller carrying cloth (*unkhuña*) in the center, covered with a piece of rectangular white paper and a soft, white layer of synthetic wool anchored by beads of camelid fat. Concepción rummaged through one of the many plastic bags stored between the rocks of the hut wall and handed Julio small paper envelopes, the contents of which he evaluated and then poured delicately onto the open paper: beads of various colors around the edges of the paper, broad beans and garbanzo beans placed in the four corners, small silver-plastic replicas of animals (sorting through them to find the right ones: a condor, llama, alpaca), and then sweetened ash (*llift'a*, typically consumed with coca), yellow confetti, rice, and incense, all poured into a mound at the center. Meanwhile, Concepción carefully sorted her coca in the folds of her skirt to find the best leaves, handing them to Julio as he formed them into neat groups of three (called a *k'intu*), organized gently between the fingers of his left hand and held together with a small bead of vicuña fat.

With each *k'intu*, he identified a place within the surrounding landscape, performed a short *phukuy* in which he recited the name of the place, blew softly on the *k'intu*, and gently placed the coca in the center of the *dispachu*. On this particular night, Julio offered the *k'intus* in a particular order: Ausangate was always first, followed by the places in which the Rojo family resided and the places where they herded. The practice of naming places in the correct order was a collaborative effort, and as the *k'intus* dwindled, Concepción reminded Julio of which places he needed to name next: the surrounding rivers, springs, and waterfalls; the valley floors where their corrals and potato farms were located; and other significant landscape features, including Palumani and Warmi Saya. With the *k'intus* resting in the center of the bundle, we passed around the *hallpuna*, a small envelope of coca made from lambskin, and chewed coca together (*hallpanakuy*).

As midnight approached, we bundled ourselves in blankets and emerged from the smoky hut into the piercing clear cold. Julio had prepared a small fire in the corner of the enclosure where the sheep slept in tight clusters. He placed the folded paper *dispachu* onto the glowing embers, packing the walls of the small firepit around it. He sprinkled alcohol from a wooden cup (*q'iru*) on both the *dispachu* and the surrounding herd, and with a final flick of *kañiwa* onto the fire, he repeated Ausangate's name as the flames began to consume the edges of the *dispachu*. We watched in silence as the coils of smoke dissipated into the air. Minutes later, Concepción announced that the lambskin bags were hungry for more coca, and we went back inside to fill them.

Julio was considered especially qualified to perform the yearly *dispachu*, given his status as a *paqu*, a traditional healer whose services are often called upon for healing, ritual practice, and divination. Regardless, that evening, Concepción monitored him with a watchful eye, periodically correcting him when she believed him to be doing something wrong: "Mana yuyarisqakunapaq churankichu, aynallanpuni," she reprimanded him. "You're not placing things like you're supposed to; it's always [done] like this." I noted how Concepción and Julio would pause to dig through plastic bags, rummaging for various essential components of the ritual that had gone missing over the years and muttering half-amused and half-irritated to themselves ("*Anis, anis*, where in the world is the *anis*?"). At one point, they realized that they'd left a crucial bottle of wine back in the town center, but it was too late to retrieve it.

It became obvious quite quickly during the time I lived in Chillca that, although people wanted me to witness what they referred to as their "customs" (*kustunri*, from Spanish *costumbre*), many of these practices were no longer regular occurrences. In my first few months in Chillca, Concepción and Julio spoke enthusiastically about my participation in their yearly rituals—particularly the *dispachu* in August, and also the practice of sprinkling chicha (maize beer) over the herd (*ch'allay*, *anqusay*) around Carnival in February—always telling me how they would do it so that I could see it (*rikunaykipaq*). When I asked them about the last time they had sprinkled chicha on the herd, however, they responded that it must have been about four years ago when the other anthropologist was there. A young Japanese anthropologist lived in Chillca in 2011 and he had been especially interested in ritual practice. Especially in my first few months in Chillca, he was a helpful point of reference as we all made sense of one another and our now intimately shared lives. But his previous presence in Chillca also meant that people had expectations about what kinds of practices I might be especially interested in witnessing.

Many of these conversations about my ritual education arose around early February 2016, in the weeks leading up to the major holidays surrounding Carnival. *Carnavales* was a central ritual time of the year, in which people from surrounding communities would gather to celebrate with drinking and dancing, while marking their animals' ears and sprinkling chicha over them as a blessing for the year to come. During *carnavales* in 2016, Concepción was especially enthusiastic about showing me the *kustunri*, even if it caused some confusion on the part of her children and grandchildren. Once I asked Concepción when they were planning to *ch'allay* the herd, and she simply said "Soon," but her six-year-old grandson asked what it meant to *ch'allay*, causing her to become momentarily embarrassed. She laughed slightly, and didn't answer, turning her attention to the pot she was washing. Another time she told her daughter Vilma that she was going to sprinkle chicha on the herd, to which her daughter responded, irritated, "what for?" Vilma reminded her that there more important tasks: she had to finish sewing borders on the skirts and beads on the hats that her daughter and granddaughter would wear during the *danzas* in the central plaza.

After we had completed the *dispachu* in August, Concepción and Julio admitted that ritual practices of communication between humans and landscapes were increasingly rare. It was around midnight by that time, and as the *dispachu* smoked lightly in the pen outside we sipped a tincture of lavender and alcohol to ward off the cold. Concepción and Julio reminisced about how things used to be. They recounted how all the families in the area participated on August first, coming together to drink, dance, and share coca through the night, the hillsides twinkling with the little fires of other families preparing their *dispachus*. Not anymore, Julio noted, "because of the evangelicals (*irmanukuna*), it doesn't happen." They likewise noted that the materiality of the *dispachu* had changed. In the past, they would search for *inqas* (small stone amulets shaped like animals) hidden in the mountainside, which they used to incorporate into their *dispachus*. These had been replaced by plastic animal figurines like the ones they had selected that day: "Now, the evangelicals have changed people's minds (*chay umanta suwapun* [lit. 'stolen their heads']). Sellers come and we buy [figurines] . . . [people] don't pick up *inqa* anymore."

While Peru is a predominantly Catholic country, the presence of Protestantism—particularly North American Evangelical Protestantism—rose substantially in the late twentieth century, especially in the countryside surrounding Cusco. The central evangelical church in Chillca was the Iglesia Evangélica Maranata, which was first established in the city of Puerto Maldonado through the Swiss Mission of Evangelical Cooperation (Misión Suiza de Cooperación Evangélica) in the 1970s. Following the Interoceanic Highway from Puerto Maldonado up to the highlands of Cusco, the Maranatha church established a congregation in the town of T'inki on the northern slopes of Ausangate in the 1980s, which was later established as a regional center (Iglesia Zonal) that by 2015 coordinated fifty local churches in the districts of Carhuayo, Ocongate, and Marcapata, and trained pastors in the nearby town of Ocongate.[4] In 2016 the community of Chillca completed the construction of their own Maranatha church with the assistance of church leaders from Ocongate.

Catholicism, by virtue of its five-hundred-year history in the Andes, has been so deeply entangled with Indigenous ritual practices in Chillca that calling someone "Catholic" was another way of saying they practiced many of the traditional forms of human-landscape communication. The Maranatha faith, however, was felt as a distinctly new and different presence, one that was in many ways incongruent with existing social and ritual practice in Chillca. These fractures were expressed in terms of differences in character and morality: Catholics often typified Maranatha as selfish (*maqlla, mich'a*) and obsessed with the accumulation of money. They considered domestic disputes, divorces, and family separations unique to Maranatha families, even though these were seemingly equal occurrences among the Catholic population. Even Concepción was incredulous that her own family members had converted to the Maranatha faith. When I asked if she herself ever considered converting, she responded "No, they wouldn't be able to trick me (*mana ingañanmanchu*), it [would be] a betrayal (*traysiun*)! God would punish me (*castigawanman Dius*), I couldn't do it." Maranata community members, on the other hand, maligned Catholics in the community for being sinful in their drinking and dancing, and regarded practices such as the *dispachu, phukuy, q'apachiy*, and the chewing of coca as the work of the devil.

In the same conversation in which they explained *pukara* to me, Mario and Maritza confirmed that many people no longer believed in *pukara*, and fewer people knew how to serve them. "It's all changing with religion [*rilihiun*]," Maritza said:

ALLISON: So, people don't believe in *pukara*?
MARITZA: That's right, they don't believe.
ALLISON: Do you two believe?
MARITZA: Not anymore.
MARIO: I don't believe anymore either.
MARITZA: People did those things in vain (*gustullapaq*), it's said now.
ALLISON: And you don't *phukuy* with coca anymore?
MARITZA: No.

At this point in the conversation, Maritza turned to Mario and, giggling, recounted a time when the Japanese anthropologist was living in Chillca and they sprinkled chicha on the herd with Mario's sister, Vilma:

MARITZA [to Mario, laughing]: [Remember when] we danced with your sister Vilma?
MARIO: Where?

MARITZA: Over there, in Chillca Q'asapi.

MARIO: What were we doing?

MARITZA: Sprinkling chicha on the alpacas. [Remember] we were sprinkling chicha? He [the Japanese anthropologist] made us sprinkle chicha.
You all threw grain too. And the schoolteachers came over, right.

MARIO: And then?

MARITZA: For no good reason [*yanqapuni*], we were just messing around
doing that stuff, right?

MARIO: Of course.

MARITZA: Then we marked the animals [*taku*], made them drink chicha,
all that. We weren't messing around with [the *taku*] though, we did that
in an orderly way.

Mario and Maritza, along with many other young couples in Chillca, had
converted to evangelicalism a few years prior with the arrival of the Maranatha church in Chillca. For Mario, it was the sermons that captured
his attention. Upon attending his first service, he was moved to tears by
the stories of people who were visited by angels or heard divine voices
and were compelled to change their ways. "It changed my heart," he said,
citing how becoming Maranatha compelled him to stop drinking alcohol,
a habit that he had picked up in his youth while working wage labor in
the lowland mines. For Maritza, she had followed in the path of her older
sister, Aniseta, who had married into the community of Chillca first and
was now a close neighbor. The Maranatha church had provided another
source of comfort and solidarity for them as they adjusted to living in a
new community. Neither Mario nor Maritza practiced the "old ways," but
I also noted that they maintained a quiet respect in the presence of those
who did. I'd come to understand that their lack of "belief" (*creencia*) in
the *pukara* reflected a cessation of practice, but not an ontological denial.
Even without their acknowledgement, the *pukara* were still there, always
watching the community of Chillca.

Topographies of Blame

The breakdown of reciprocal relations between human and nonhuman
beings brought a crucial question to the foreground. If social beings
were brought into existence through reciprocal engagement, then would

the inverse be true: did the disappearance of communicative practice lead to the disappearance of the entity itself? Indeed, this is a question that has been grappled with throughout the Andes. The pace of rapid glacier retreat in the late twentieth and early twenty-first centuries brought to bear ontological questions about the association of glacial ice with the social power of *apu* and other landscape beings. If *apu* were losing their glaciers, or "their white ponchos" as Inge Bolin wrote (2001), did this mean they were "los[ing] their power" (2009, 232) becoming ill, or even dying?[5] When the communicative practices of reciprocal engagement—feeding, naming, speaking—began to slip, it seemed logical that the entities themselves would also fall out of being, losing both their substance and their subjectivity. And yet I noticed an odd tension in Chillca: even though it was widely acknowledged that people were failing to engage in reciprocal practice with *pukara*, they still admitted that the *pukara* were alive—and in many cases, they were not weakened but rather emboldened by their abandonment. Even for evangelical community members that viewed communicative practice with skepticism and even scorn, *pukara* still existed and impinged upon human life in powerful ways.

Concepción's in-law Virginia, a woman of eighty-one years old who identified as Catholic, spoke with me at length about the waning communication between humans and *pukara*. I visited her one morning to see her prized foal that had been born a few weeks before. On the pampa beside the meandering Q'inqu River, she described to me how *pukara* and *apu* used to talk to humans through the medium of a ritual healer (*altumisayuq*):

> In the old times, the *pukara* were like humans. They talked, they came to visit us. There was an *altumisayuq*, and the *altumisayuq* would talk with Cinco Machula Icchunayuq [a nearby place], and also with the *apu* from down the valley, Poma, back then. Sayri [another place] also talked. All these *pukara* talked. In those times, we made offerings to the *apu* when they came. People served the *apu* so that the animals would reproduce. We played music and made offerings to the *apu*, and the animals reproduced. That's how we lived . . .
>
> . . . My father used to beckon the *pukara* with the *altumisayuq* and they would come, just like people would. They all had names. They always talked, the *pukara*: saying "my name is this, my name is that." The

mountains would talk to us. They'd speak in Spanish, and also in *runasimi*, Quechua.

The *pukara* communicated in the very languages spoken by humans in the area, but not all humans could hear or understand them. The *altumisayuq* was a critical mediator of these communicative practices, often voicing or otherwise facilitating the verbal engagement of the *pukara* with their human interlocutors. The loss of reciprocal practice between *pukara* and humans was made evident in the disappearance of the role of the *altumisayuq*, and the loss of verbal communication, resulting in the silence of the *pukara*:

> VIRGINIA: Back then we used to make offerings to the earth (*tira*) here, now the earth isn't remembered (*mana yuyarisqachu*). Now there are no offerings whatsoever. It's just forgotten, lost (*wikch'usqallaña*) . . . My father used to call the *altumisayuq* and he'd come. Now there are no *altumisayuq*.
> ALLISON: Why not?
> VIRGINIA: It's over now, that was just in the past.
> ALLISON: And the *pukara*, they don't talk anymore?
> VIRGINIA: Not now, they don't say anything. The *pukara* are still living, in August they're alive. [But] now there are no offerings. Nobody prepares offerings.

While the *pukara* had fallen silent, they hadn't disappeared. Virginia went on to clarify that not only were the *pukara* very much present but in fact they were angered by the lack of reciprocal interaction—particularly the lack of offerings—from humans. Like many Catholics, Virginia attributed recent increases in human and animal illness and climatic changes (especially the increase in hail) to the loss of these communicative practices between people and *pukara*.[6] She explained further:

> VIRGINIA: And the hail (*chikchi*) that beats down—in the past, it didn't kill animals or people. Now, since people don't remember [the *pukara*], it kills people and animals. *Chikchi*.
> ALLISON: Ah, *chikchi* comes from the *pukara*?

VIRGINIA: Of course, the kind of hail that explodes, that's from the *pukara*. It's always been like that; the hail comes down like bullets (*balas*).

ALLISON: Bullets?!

VIRGINIA: Its hail, its bullets. The *pukara*'s bullets are what are beating down (*t'uqashan*), right? Just like that. In the past, [the *pukara*] didn't harm animals, they didn't harm (*hap'iy* [lit. to grab]) people, because offerings were made. Now people don't make offerings, so the hail harms people and animals . . . Now because everyone is evangelical (*irmanullan kapun*), they don't make offerings anymore. In the past, they made offerings. On Santiago, we made offerings with fire (*sankay*) to the *pukara* so we could have animals. Now we don't do that. So, [that's why] there are fewer animals.

Of course, followers of the Maranatha faith attempted to correct for this interpretation. Their own interpretations of climatological changes were likewise rooted in logics of reciprocal communicative practices. However, while Catholics focused on social relations with the *pukara*,

FIGURE 14 Virginia and her horses. Photo by author.

evangelicals were attentive to their relationships with God. They all agreed that the origin of misfortune was human disobedience, and that the remedy was the initiation of reciprocal communicative practice. However, the interlocutors had changed: for evangelicals, the primary interlocutor was not an earth being, but God, and the appropriate communicative channel was prayer. Climatic changes were not indicative of a breakdown of communication between humans and *pukara*, but were potentially *the result* of these encounters. When I mentioned Virginia's explanation of *pukara* to Mario and Maritza, for example, they agreed that when they were younger and considered themselves Catholic, they too had lived in fear of the wrath of *pukara* and served them diligently alongside their parents. Yet when I asked if they were still afraid of the *pukara*, they paused before responding uneasily:

MARIO: Of course, I'm still afraid.

MARITZA: Me too, I'm afraid of them. People say they're alive. The mountains are still alive, right? They protect us from hail, people *phukuy* with *llift'a* [sweetened ash], saying *phiiiuuu* . . .

Then their conversation became quieter as they spoke directly to one another:

MARIO: [That was] to Satan though.

MARITZA: Of course, that's just what they say, right?

MARIO [quietly in Spanish]: The Bible says it clearly: "I'm in the air, in the water," [switches to Quechua] "Also in the soil," it says. We served him [Satan] too often.

MARITZA: If we're faithful to God, then hail won't hurt us, that's what they say, right?

MARIO: Mm-hm.

I could feel the tension and equivocation in their words, the way they were actively trying to reconcile their fears with the teachings of their faith. According to the Maranatha faith, communicative practices with *pukara* were useless at best and dangerous at worst. It was, rather, the failure to be faithful to God—by abstaining from prayer, or engaging in "sinful" practices such as drinking, chewing coca, or serving Satan through ritual practice with *pukara*—that led to misfortune. The appropriate remedy, in this case, was the demonstration of fealty to God through sanctioned religious practice. And yet other Maranatha community members expressed that climatic changes were part of the inevitable, foretold progression of the Second Coming of Christ and the approaching end-of-times and were therefore unaffected by human intervention. The greater concern was in preparing oneself for the Second Coming. As one herder, an older woman who had recently converted to the Maranatha faith, told me:

> The climate is going crazy [*muyupushan*]. And why? God's word says so, right? 'For your sins, the rainy season will become the dry season, and the dry season will become the rainy season,' he said. It was said, like this, in God's word: 'This is the punishment for your sins, I gave you a good harvest, the months and the seasons in their time,' he said. When I was a child, we enjoyed the dry season in the harvest months, everything in its time. Now it has changed. All of us people, in our sins, we have caused [these changes] through God's anger. One day, He will return.

Secular interpretations of climatic changes have likewise rooted climatic events in changing human material and communicative practices, a widespread sentiment that Anders Burman has called the "moral meteorology of the Andes" (2017).[7] Changing communicative practice— the failure to acknowledge *pukara* with ritual offerings, like Virginia warned—was one way to enact meteorological rage. Human moral failure was indexed by changing materialities, specifically the presence of pollution: there was a strong association between climate change and *kuntaminasiun* in the form of smoke (*q'usñi*, from factories and cars) and trash (*basura*, largely plastics). On the radio, trash was a common topic of discussion, and reports of high levels of *kuntaminasiun* in the cities of Cusco and Lima gave people in Chillca the sense that urban spaces were especially polluted. Many people expressed fears that *kuntaminasiun* had reached Chillca and was making people and their animals sick. Concepción noted a rise in diarrheal illnesses among her animals, which she attributed to pollution:

ALLISON: Are there more illnesses now than before?

CONCEPCIÓN: Uh huh, there's more. Before there were few. There wasn't much diarrhea back then, now there is.

ALLISON: Why?

CONCEPCIÓN: *Kuntaminasiun*, right? When I was a child we didn't see as much diarrhea, and it wasn't as difficult to treat the [sick] animals.

ALLISON: What kind of *kuntaminasiun* is there?

CONCEPCIÓN: It comes from those things . . . it comes in the smoke— from the factories. From people. In the past there were few factories. It's because of that.

Walking along the main road in Chillca, Concepción would decry trash that had been tossed from a passing car: "Look at this. They toss trash, these people of bad conscience (*mala fe*), and then they leave. Stupid people." Trash was also a source of consternation at the monthly assemblies, and municipal trash collection initiatives. Every two months the municipality designated a woman in the community to pick up litter in the town center on Mondays, Wednesdays, and Fridays, for a small sum. Donning a long, skirted blue coat bearing the municipal emblem and plastic white boots, she strolled throughout the center of Chillca with a plastic bag collecting the bottles, cans, plastic bags, and other bits of trash that scattered along the edges of the main road, plaza, school, health post, and community assembly hall. Sometimes the owner of the town store would join her, and together they would note the amount of trash, remarking back and forth: "Too much *basura*, *plastiku*, too much *kuntaminasiun!*"

The rising levels of *kuntaminasiun* were also linked to the rapid snowmelt on the surrounding peaks: Another herder, who worked as a caretaker at one of the tourist lodges on the outer edges of the community, spoke at length about this problem when I visited him:

[The snow] is disappearing. As time goes on, there is more of this, umm, what's it called? Plastic, litter, corrugated tin. All of that is polluting the environment, making [the snow] melt. [The peaks] are bald now. In the past, there wasn't any of that plastic or rubber, nothing like that. The mountains were normal, they retained snow. Now they are being contaminated and

it's melting the snows. Sometimes the trash gets all the way up that distant
Vila [mountain]. The tourists go climbing on Vila, and as they climb they
make the snows melt even more, until the mountain is bald. [The tourists]
throw trash, they are polluting as they come through.

In particular, he noted, the reflective qualities of novel substances like
corrugated tin caused "embarrassment" or shame to the mountains, scaring them and causing them to retreat or melt:

> The highways are coming [to the *alturas*], bringing more *kuntaminasiun*
> to the snowy peaks. With the arrival of cars, the snows are melting. The
> reflection of things like corrugated tin, like a mirror, it embarrasses (*p'in-
> qaspas*) the snow and makes it melt (*chulluchipun rit'itapas*).[8]

The paradox in many of these explanations is that they imply Quechua
peoples may blame themselves and their abandonment of reciprocal
practices for climate change—which it appears they do, in part (Burman
2017; Salas Carreño 2021). However, read another way, many of these
explanations also offer a powerful and "radical critique of fossil-fueled
capitalism" that aligns with environmental justice perspectives (Burman
2017, 924; Salas Carreño 2021, 64). While people in Chillca placed some
blame on their own actions for causing climatic changes, they also recognized the disproportionate responsibility of other people: those that built
factories, highways, and drove cars, and particularly those people that
came to Chillca and tossed trash in their landscapes, without any recognition for the beings—human, animal, and landscape—that lived there.
Marieke Winchell has likewise noted in Sarahuayto, Bolivia, that discourses around *kuntaminasiun* have linked processes of environmental
degradation and disrespect to the longer histories of land dispossession
and extractive economies wrought by settler colonialism (Winchell 2023,
618). In Chillca, people were encountering the traces of a reconfiguration
of social and material relationships across the landscape, evident in the
accumulation of trash as well as the disappearance of snow, water, *inqa*,
and *dispachu*. And as certain entities and essences became present and
others slipped away, relationships between social beings in Chillca were
becoming less predictable, stable, and generative.

Worlding and Reworlding

By the time I arrived in 2015, and despite the earnest efforts of my hosts to show me their *kustunri*, many of the customs and communicative practices that once held humans and landscapes together—in particular, the practices through which humans served *pukara*—had fallen away for many people. *Pukara* still dwelled in Chillca, but the changing quality of the relationship between humans and places indicated a general instability in the world: a restlessness of both relations and matter. It was a broader socioecological instability and unpredictability that yearned, and in fact demanded—sometimes violently—to be mitigated. While some herders continued to turn their attentions to the *pukara*, others enacted their relationality with other entities: God, the Peruvian state, NGOs, and other powerful social entities.

I was initially surprised that Concepción didn't express worry or distress over the loss of communicative practice, like her in-law Virginia did. She was far more fretful about other things, such as the well-being of her children—which, importantly, she did not tie to their performance of ritual practice as many herders used to, but rather to their performance in wage labor and the sale of animal goods. Her own efforts were increasingly turned toward cultivating other relationships and other modes of luck (*swirti*) through material exchange, communicative acts, and other efforts that would contribute to her children's continued health and prosperity in the future.

What I witnessed in Chillca in 2015 was not a collapsing ontology, but rather a shift in practices that mobilized a plurality of social actors: some old, some new, but all inextricably implicated in the process of sustaining life in the high Andes.[9] As Anders Burman has written, worlding is not "a solipsistic activity; rather, other powerful actors—be they transnational corporations, states, or ancestral beings . . .—are indeed active in the sociophysical formation of lifeworlds" (2017, 931). Even with the changes wrought by glacial retreat and global climate change, we likewise can't presuppose a rupture in the future, but rather must acknowledge the continued "mutual confirmation and unfoldment of relational existences and beings" among a plurality of social beings (Burman 2017, 931). Worlding practices like *q'apachiy* and *phukuy* were not holdovers from a long-gone time, but intentional and purposeful practices that were wielded for contemporary aims. People in Chillca sustained their relationality with *pukara* through *q'apachiy* and *phukuy*, and they also brought into being new relationships that mobilized their connections to the cash economy, the international wool market, formalized education systems, and regimes of private property. All the while, they reflected on these varied practices and social relations with ambivalence, uncertainty, and tentative hope.

And these new practices of relation didn't negate but rather creatively reconfigured people's relationship to their landscape. When I revisited Concepción after enclosure happened years later, in 2023, I noted with relief that her parcel of land included Illachiy, her beloved valley and *uqhu*. She would continue to *phukuy*, sending her wishes of health and good fortune to Ausangate, Palumani, and Warmi Saya. She would continue to sing her *waynus*, stitching her concerns, sorrows, and longings lyrically into the landscape. And, at the same time, she would dutifully erect the fence that marked the boundaries of her landholding from that of her neighbors. Instead of a refusal of capitalistic interpretations of property and resources, Concepción enacted a strategic accommodation and creative re-fashioning of them in her daily practice, weaving a multiplicity of relations to continually shape her world into her desired rendering.

AUSANGATIMAN PHUYU TIYAYUN (CLOUDS SETTLE
ON AUSANGATE)
Ausangatiman
Phuyu tiyayun qunqaylla
Llaqtay urquta
Phuyu muyumun wayrantin
Chaypa chawpinpi puriyushani nuqaqa
Así es mi vida, así es mi suerte soltero

Haqay chinpa Ausangatiman phuyu tiyayamun
Imaraq viday? Hayk'araq swirtiy?

Haqay urquta
Kuntur muyumun phuyuntin

Llaqtay urquta
Kuntur muyumun wayrantin
Chayllatapis qhawawaqmá chulitu
Chayllatapis qhawawaqmá ingratu

Imallamantaq purishanri, nirani
Hayk'allamantaq hamushanri, nirani
Alpacaytaña mikhuruspa hamusqa
Uwihaytaña mikhuruspa hamusqa

Yanqallanpaqcha ganadira karani
Yanqallanpaqcha alpakira karani
Imanasaqtaq kunanpachari chulitu
Hayk'anasaqtaq kunanpachari ingratu

Imanasaqtaq kunanpachari turachay
Hayk'anasaqtaq kunanpachari ñañachay
Mamataytaycha ripuy, niwanqa turachay
Taytamamaycha pasay, niwanqa ñañachay

On Ausangate
The clouds suddenly settle
My mountain town
Is encircled in clouds and wind
I am walking in the middle of it
That is my life, that is my lonely luck

The clouds settle before me on Ausangate
What of my life? What of my luck?

On yonder mountain
Condors circle in the clouds
Over my mountain town
The condor circles in the wind
Just like that you'd watch me, *cholito*
Just like that you'd watch me, ungrateful one

Where, oh where is he walking, I said
When, oh when is he coming, I said
Only my alpaca, grazing, has come
Only my sheep, grazing, has come

Perhaps in vain I was a herder
Perhaps in vain I was an alpaquera
Whatever will I do now, *cholito*
However will I be now, ungrateful one

Whatever will I do now, brother
However will I be now, sister
Go home to mother and father, my brother will tell me
Get home to mother and father, my sister will tell me

CHAPTER FOUR

Commoning Futures

Ausangatita qhawarinkichu	Do you gaze upon Ausangate?
Llaqtay lumata qhawarinkichu	Do you gaze upon the hills of my town?
Yanayarintaq yuraqyarintaq	Through black and white
Wayrarimuntaq phuyurimuntaq	Through the winds and clouds
Chayhinallataq nuqapas kani	Just like this, so am I
Así lo mismo nuqapas kani	Just the same, so am I
Ripusaq nini	I'll leave, I say
Pasasaq nini	I'll go, I say
Karu llaqtata ripusaq nini	I'll leave to a faraway town, I say
Ripushaniñan, pasashaniñan	I'm already leaving, I'm already going
Ripushaniñan, pasashaniñan	I'm already leaving, I'm already going
Llaqtamasiypa waqachiwasqan	My fellow townspeople having made me cry
Llaqtamasiypa chiqnikuwasqan	My fellow townspeople having spited me

The Community Assembly

At the community general assembly, a familiar scene emerged: two herd-ers stood to face the community leaders and argued bitterly about whose alpacas had been crossing which sectoral boundaries. Community mem-bers distractedly conversed with one another in the background, the men slumping in their plastic chairs and the women huddling tightly against the wall to ward off the evening chill as the sun set outside. These types of arguments were a regular feature of community assemblies, and they were considered a necessary, if onerous, part of living within a communal land tenure system. Finally, a young man rose to his feet and raised the issue of dividing the community into private landholdings (*parcelas*). Unsurprisingly, it was José Luis who broached the issue: a wiry man with a toothy smirk and a voice perpetually lilting toward playful humor, José Luis was well-known for his brash and often provocative commentary at public forums. His seriousness regarding this matter was made palpable by his punctuated pleas for his compatriots' attention: "Compañeros," he pleaded through the rowdy back-and-forth of the herders' argument, "Compañeros, su atención por favor . . ." José Luis was widely respected as an educated city-dweller who split his time between Chillca and Pitumarca, achieving the kind of mobility and professional status that many in the community desired for their children. His argumentation slipped between Spanish and Quechua and was grounded in claims to legal knowledge, which he marked by repeatedly hedging his remarks with the qualifier *legalmente*. Although parcelization had come up many times before, this time it led to a lengthy discussion that continued well into the evening before the community leadership tabled the issue for further discussion and a community-wide vote the following month.

�֞

Chillca was a community in transition when I arrived in 2015. The *comunidad campesina* of Chillca had operated under a communal land tenure system since the dissolution of the three major haciendas in the area following the Peruvian agrarian reform of 1969. Over the past decades since, the steady growth of Chillca's population had placed greater pressure on the pasture and led to increasingly tense encounters between neighbors, and between herders and a community leadership that periodically sought to exert limitations on herd sizes. By 2015, restlessness permeated the community, and many of Chillca's residents felt increasingly discontented with the current situation. The constant squabbles with neighbors were burdensome, and often hurtful, as Concepción attested in the song that opens and closes this chapter: *llaqtamasiypa waqachiwasqanta, chiqnikuwasqan, sufrichiwasqanta*; neighbors made each other cry, spite, suffer.

The entanglements of Chillca had shifted, allowing for novel possibilities of reconfiguration. More of Chillca's residents sought seasonal wage labor opportunities in mining and tourism, and herders wanted to tap into a growing luxury alpaca wool market. Many people wanted to spend less time and effort on transhuman herding and the associated tasks of

FIGURE 15 The community assembly. Photo by author.

communal land tenure management, and they found the frequent communal work requirements burdensome. People in Chillca envisioned a more lucrative future with improved herds, intensified fiber production, and more time to devote to other forms of income, without the surveillance and judgement of their neighbors. In short, many people in Chillca envisioned improved (*mejorado*) futures for themselves, their alpacas, and their land, and imagined these futures to be attainable through a parcelized land tenure system.

In the introduction, I framed this book as "the prelude to the breakdown of the commons." Indeed, only a few years after I left in 2016, the community of Chillca would decide to dissolve their communal land—the pastoral commons—into privately owned parcels. This chapter documents the final rumblings before the fragmentation and reconfiguration of Chillca's landscape and community. However, I also want to challenge the latent finality or inevitably that the framing of *preluding* might suggest. This requires shifting our understanding of Chillca's "commons" as merely the property or pasture, to recognizing continued practices of *commoning*, or "more-than-human, contingent relations-in-the-making that result in collective practices of production, exchange, and living with the world" that existed long before, and well after, the creation of a communal land management system (Nightingale 2019, 18). Rather than a simple story of enclosure, what emerged in 2015 was a set of strategic practices of future-making and interpretations of property regimes through which people in Chillca imagined, articulated, and curated their idealized versions of themselves, their children, their animals, and their community as a whole.

When people in Chillca imagined the future of parcelization, their imaginations were not immaterial musings of what could be, but were powerfully actualized in the present through human, animal, and landscape bodies. Furthermore, these practices were not "solipsistic" (Burman 2017, 931) but engaged a multitude of other entities and actors and interpolated with powerful and enduring narratives in Peru. In particular, the futures that people in Chillca sought in 2015 drew upon widely recognizable cultural ideologies of *mejoramiento* (improvement): in addition to producing *mejorado* animals that fetched higher prices for their wool, people in Chillca envisioned *mejorado* versions of themselves as savvy livestock producers and educated professionals (*profesionales*). These "better versions" that herders imagined were crafted in partnership with development initiatives aimed at the rural poor and shaped in the images promoted by the Peruvian state, neoliberal development agencies, and international wool markets. And there were many points of conflict and contestation: there were generational differences that made the discussion of Chillca's future painfully fraught, especially for herders of Concepción's generation. These discussions brought to the surface the limits of living in community, of confronting and cultivating a future together, in the face of transformative change.

Living in Community

Many of the conversations around what it meant to live and work *en comunidad* emerged during communal work events (*faina*). When Chillca became a *comunidad campesina* in 1985, the people of Chillca established a cooperative system of land and resource management, well-documented through the Peruvian Andes, in which heads-of-household were incorporated as members (*comuneros*) of the *comunidad campesina* through a process of registration (*empadronar*).[1] Once someone became *empadronado*, it was their responsibility to participate in the community assemblies as well as the communal work events. It was a significant time commitment: in addition to the monthly assembly, which lasted from nine in the morning well into the evening (and sometimes into the next day), *comuneros* were required to attend multiple *faina* work events each month. Then, there were the other required administrative tasks such as serving on the community governing board or subcommittees and participating in holidays and school events. There was also the maintenance and harvest of the community potato plot: planting in September and October, harvesting in May and June, and processing freeze-dried potatoes (*chuñu, muraya*) in July and August.

Most of the *faina* work events were related to maintenance of the communal alpaca herd, the *majada*. There were medicating events (*hampiy faina*) every two months, in which communities members administered vitamins, medications, and vaccinations to the herds; the *tuwi taqay* in January, when the weaned alpacas (*tuwi*) were separated from the female herd and relocated; and multiday shearing events in November throughout the community. The *hampiy fainas*, given their regularity, were a regular touchpoint for members of each sector to come together to collaboratively assess the health of the herds and grasslands, discuss community business, and mediate any conflicts between herd-households. The herders would gather the animals into a corral and, before the medicating would even begin, they would often sit for hours along the stone walls of the corral sharing food and conversation.

As an observer, the *hampiy faina* struck me as a place of beginnings and ends, a moment to recalibrate and commit to the collective work of regenerating the herds as well as the community as a collective. The herders would check to see how many animals were gestating, either by observing their bellies or placing their hand on the distended abdomen of a pregnant alpaca to feel the fetus protruding, round and hard as a knuckle. The young alpacas would be marked with ear tassels (*q'aytu*) or clay (*taku*). Sometimes, an older nonreproductive female animal was selected from the herd to be slaughtered and eaten by the gathered herders. The food was plentiful: multiple rounds of soup and roasted meat, and always plenty of chicha. A younger member of the sector would dutifully refill the glasses of their elders, the older women often taking their time to sip from the communal cup, not to be rushed, as a young man waited patiently, bottle in hand, to refill it.

Especially in the transition between seasons, the *hampiy faina* were critical moments of collaborative decision-making. The herders' predictions of when they would migrate had to be recalibrated constantly, and their schedules were continuously delayed or augmented depending on a variety of factors: house construction, reciprocal labor obligations, school responsibilities, illness and injury, disputes with neighbors, agricultural schedules and community work events, among others. At the *hampiy faina*, the sector decided which herd-households would migrate and when. The alpaca committee always attended these events and served as the mediating presence when the discussions inevitably veered into conflict around who had access to preferential pastures, or whose animals were wandering over community boundaries.

I caught up with José Luis a couple of months after the assembly, as he rode his motorcycle up to a *hampiy faina* at the town's edge. The reverberations of the previous assembly still echoed throughout the community, and we both knew that the topic of parcelization would inevitably come up at the *hampiy faina*. Patting the dust from his leather jacket, he elaborated on his initial suggestion that the community move toward parcelizing: "Now that we are living *en comunidad*, we can't improve. *No podemos mejorar pe.*" He explained,

> It's a bit of a problem. [A person] wants to do this, he wants to do that. Then he says I can't, [my neighbor] won't let me do it. So, there are problems. But, if there were a parcel—it's just for me (*es para mi es*). It's more productive (*productivo*).

He continued with an analogy: "It's like, in the city for example, this is your property, your house, and you pay for what's yours every year, through your earnings (*por lo que has vivido*), right?" I would hear this analogy again, many times, among those who advocated for the creation of parcels. Many of the people who made this argument had property down the valley in Pitumarca, where they had built small houses on sectioned lots. In their opinion, subdividing land in Chillca would compel others to embark on new forms of accumulation and improvement, similar to those available in larger towns and cities. Another young man would use a nearly identical analogy a short time later when I asked his opinion on parcels:

> A *parcela* is like . . . in a town you have your lot, right? Your house. You worry about your house, how you're going to fix it up. You worry about the space you have; you improve upon it. By your own will (*a la voluntad que tienes*) you go about working for what you want.

A reference to will (*voluntad*) and responsibility (*responsabilidad*) echoed throughout these explanations. The term *voluntad* is multivalent, and in many usages it can be interpreted as one's "social volition," or ability to contribute to the broader social community in which one lives (Paerregaard 2015, 52). And yet the *voluntad* expressed in these conversations seemed to hinge in a different direction, referencing a kind of self-realization that would emerge through the attainment of a private property. Discussions of land parcelization reflected an emphasis on individual responsibility, and the cultivation of individualistic qualities (ambition, self-promotion, economic rationality) as part of a broader process of improvement. According to those in favor of enclosure, the current land tenure configuration was a hindrance to this subject formation—it prevented people from cultivating *responsabilidad*.

José Luis gestured to the surrounding landscape to make this point, presenting the bare and rocky patches on the surrounding hillsides as evidence. He reimagined these neglected patches of pasture as privately owned parcels. If it were his own property, he said, it would be his responsibility to take care of it:

> This [rockfall] is delaying the growth of the pasture. Let's say, if this were my *parcela* here, then I would collect all [of the rocks] and build an enclosure over there. That's where I would seed pasture. It wouldn't be like it is now. I would also bring in water from other places. This would be my responsibility alone.

Proper pasture maintenance, for José Luis and others, involved investing in irrigation, enclosures, and seeding improved grass varieties. All these techniques and products were available through regional training workshops. Citing the current rates of pasture decline, he continued, "Us owners (*dwiñus*) would irrigate what is ours (*prupiuykuta*) . . . [living communally] who will irrigate? Nobody irrigates, so the wind quickly blows [the grass] bare." Living in a commons land tenure system, "who cares [about the grass]—nobody! No one gives it a thought. This is the future of the community."

As I described briefly in the introduction, before Peru's agrarian reform most of Chillca's land was occupied by three large haciendas and a smaller private landholding. After the agrarian reform, the Peruvian state held title to those lands until the community of Chillca became a *comunidad campesina* in 1985. Much of the initial land retitling process in Chillca occurred during the late 1980s and early 1990s, overlapping with the "alpaca boom" that saw greater interest and investment in the modernization and mechanization of the alpaca industry (Browman 1983; Dong et al. 2011; Orlove 1977a; 1982; Postigo, Young, and Crews 2008). The community was targeted by a multitude of lawyers and engi-

FIGURE 16 The *majada* (community alpaca herd) and the communal pastures. Photo by author.

neers that overcharged them for hastily done retitling services that had to be continually revised in the years since.

Following the agrarian reform, many of Chillca's residents that had previously fled the area during the hacienda period—including Concepción's family, who had lived in Quispicanchis between the late 1960s and early 1980s—returned and established households in their natal lands.[2] Selected community members were then tasked with initiating the land-retitling process. This included Concepción's late father, whose descendants recall his many lengthy and laborious trips to Lima to file the paperwork necessary to reclaim his family's territory of Antapata—lands that the family maintains were purchased by the hacendado under false pretenses for an *arroba* of coca. It was during this initial process of retitling that the community established sectoral boundaries corresponding to historical family claims. The sectoral management of pasture was also established at this time, although it wasn't subject to central management by the community governing structure until some years later.

In 2015 the land tenure system in Chillca resembled a fairly widespread system of mixed property rights in the Andes (Damonte et al. 2016). In general, land tenure regimes can be understood as institutional configurations that articulate "bundles of rights" with regard to the access and use of land by individuals and groups within a specific territory (Schlager and Ostrom 1992). Two such bundles of rights include (1) the rights to access the land and obtain resources within it ("operational rights") and (2) the right to define *future* operational rights in terms of how, when, where, and who will access those resources, and if they are available for transfer or sale ("collective choice rights"). In Chillca, the operational rights were largely held at the sectoral level, such that the families that resided within each sector established who had access to the pasture within those boundaries, and who was able to utilize the resources therein. However, these were subject to oversight by the broader community governing structure. In other words, the community governing structure held many of the collective choice rights, with ultimate decision-making over future operational rights in each sector. However, in the simplest terms, both bundles of rights were shared in coordination between the sector- and community-levels of management.

The general trend in land tenure change in Peru in the past fifty years has favored a transition toward privatized land tenure systems in which operational rights (who has access to the land and the resources within it) and collective choice rights (the right to define how, when, where, and who will have access in the future, and if transfer or sale is allowed) are both held at the household level. A similar "parcel" system is also widespread: a land tenure system in which operational rights and some collective choice rights are held by the household, but the ability to sell or lease rights to property remain under the control of the community governing structure (Casaverde 1985; Sendón 2008). The system that people in Chillca were debating in 2015, while referred to as a "parcel" system, actually more closely resembled that of the privatized model in which both operational and collective choice rights were held at the household level, such that each family had ultimate control over both the present and future usage of their land-holding, including its future sale or lease.

As herders in Chillca contemplated the transition from a communal land tenure to a parcel system, there were familiar echoes of the classic "tragedy of the commons" argument: that common pool resources would invariably be exploited by opportunistic individuals in the community (Hardin 1968). Many of the disputes in Chillca originated in accusations of selfishness, leveled at herders who had disproportionately large herds, or who had partitioned areas of land for unapproved corrals. Indeed, the dispute that initiated the December assembly discussion involved a herder who had nearly four hundred alpacas—four times the average herd size— and whose animals often spilled over into neighboring pastures. Other alpaca-rich herders were accused of neglecting their community work requirements by failing to attend assemblies or participate in *fainas*, or buying their way out of community responsibilities by paying the fine rather than attending. Others argued that herd-wealthy individuals should be required to participate even more than other community members due to their disproportionate pasture consumption. People who took advantage of the communal pasturelands were widely considered to be acting selfishly: "Some people have lots of animals, and they're taking advantage (*están aprovechando*) because they don't think of the [other] *comuneros*, they only think of themselves," one young man told me, implicating one individual in particular who had 240 sheep.

Of course, Garrett Hardin's assertion that "freedom in a commons brings ruin to all" (1968, 1244) has led to many decades of rebuttals, many of which critique the cynical portrayal of humans as purely rational economic actors, and instead provide pertinent examples of successful, sustainable, long-term common-pool resource management.[3] But this distrust of individual opportunism within a commons land configuration still loomed large for many in Chillca. When it came to herd sizes, the community governing board (*junta directiva*) was the linchpin that held the system together, and its members repeatedly attempted to place limitations. Initially, they targeted the larger animals: horses were reduced to two per family, and cows were banned entirely in the early 2000s. In 2015 the community leaders attempted to impose a reduction of sheep by limiting herd sizes to fifty sheep per household. These efforts were met with resistance by community members, largely on the grounds that the reduction deadlines (originally planned for February, and then November) did not account for fluctuations in the price of sheep's meat. Regardless, many in the community critiqued this resistance as yet another example of the desire to exploit the commons for personal gain.

Many people in Chillca claimed that herders would be *more* responsible and conscientious land users when the land belonged to them alone. Indeed, there was a core tension in the arguments around land tenure change: individualism was complicating the social contracts that undergirded the commons, but these same social contracts were also restricting individualistic pursuits in ways that prevented improvement. Those in favor of parcels argued that the absence of community oversight would compel herders to regulate their own behavior more effectively. When I asked Mario, for example, if he thought that the Chillca governing board should restrict sheep further, he immediately pivoted toward an appeal to parcels:

> I don't know, but hopefully in ten years from now there will be *parcelas*. When there are *parcelas*, if each family member has two hundred or one hundred sheep, that wouldn't [be in their] interest . . . if they gave you this [parcel] and you raise a hundred sheep or two hundred alpacas, and the pasture doesn't withstand it, where else [would you go]? Everything would die. People would *have* to be responsible.

Furthermore, rather than espouse the virtues of communal living, many argued that it was burdensome, and they didn't necessarily fault the herders that could buy their way out of community labor. Those in favor of parcelization saw the work of community living—especially the *fainas* and other labor obligations—as a significant barrier to their own improvement. It prevented them from devoting their time to other pursuits, or amassing cash wealth through wage labor. People made comparisons to surrounding communities that had parcelized or privatized land tenure and suggested that living *en comunidad* was preventing them from "advancing," getting ahead or moving forward like these other communities had done. One young woman referenced her relatives living on the other side of Ausangate:

> They say [parcelization] is good. They dedicate themselves to lots of different ent things. People [over there] are knowledgeable, more awake (*dispirtu*) than [the people that live] on this side. They devote themselves to trout fishing, *artesenía*, making woven borders for skirts on machines, everything. Not here, people just watch alpacas . . . they have not yet attained other ambitions.

She was not the only one to contrast the people who devoted their time to other income-providing pursuits against those who just "watched alpacas" in terms of their industriousness (*ambisiun*) and acuity (*dispirtu*). Per this argument, freedom from the time-consuming responsibilities and discomforts of communal living would allow for greater individual industriousness—and, as a result, the ability to cultivate improved futures for their animals, their children, themselves, and perhaps the community as a whole.

Beautiful Animals

What did it mean to produce improved futures for animals, or rather, "improved animals"? This question loomed large in the weeks before the major animal market, which took place in mid-January of every year in the nearby town of Pampamarka. As the date approached, people talked excitedly about the animals they were going to purchase and speculated what their neighbors might buy, and families began scrutinizing their own herds and selecting individual animals to sell. Most of the community travelled to the market together, packing into the caravan of cattle trucks that arrived for the occasion. The market was busiest on the day the alpacas were sold. A large crowd descended onto a wide field where the animals were gathered in pens, surrounded by a ring of brightly colored trucks. Families and neighbors meandered together through the thick crowds, gravitating toward the vendors they knew best or the animals that were drawing the most attention.

Among the swirling crowd at each vendor, a central performance would begin: the family member deemed the most knowledgeable about alpaca fiber (an uncle who served on the alpaca committee, for example) would designate the finest alpaca in each pen, parting the animal's wool and assessing the density and sheen of the fiber at its root. The finest alpaca would then become the metric from which to evaluate the relative quality of other animals, and to calibrate the price for the medium-range alpaca they were more likely to buy. Once an animal had been settled upon—a process that could take hours of deliberation and discussion—cash would finally exchange hands. While both men and women were always involved in the purchase of animals, they took different roles:

FIGURE 17 Preparing for the alpaca market. Photo by author.

men would typically position themselves, physically and dialogically, at the center of the exchange as the seller and the buyer. Women would typically position themselves slightly outside of the conversation, either slightly behind or to the side of the transaction. This isn't to suggest, however, that women were not active participants: they typically held the money, and would often direct the interaction, commenting on both the animal and the price. They would suggest questions for the buyer to ask, or simply shout them from outside the transaction. But there was an order to things: men could buy animals without their female kin present (the purchase already agreed upon ahead of time), but women rarely did such an exchange without men present. Oftentimes, mothers would have their sons come to help them purchase animals. Mario usually helped Concepción, who was worried that she had "bad luck" (*mala swirti*) with financial transactions, since she didn't perform them as often as Julio or Mario. She feared she wouldn't be given a fair price or that the animal would be of poor quality, or even bring *mala swirti* itself.

Fiber was of central and definitive importance in the selection of an alpaca. Wool, after all, was the primary source of income for families in Chillca. Alpaca fiber was sheared and sold once a year in November. Until 2015, the wool was sold to middlemen from Pitumarca, but herders complained that the prices were low: in 2015 wool was selling for 12 soles/lb. for white *suri*, 8 soles/lb. for white *wakaya*, and 5 soles/lb. for *wakaya* of another color (brown, grey, black, or tan). In November 2015 the community entered into an agreement (*acopio*) with a wool consortium that utilized a direct export system, thus cutting out the usual chain of middlemen and promising the community more money. The wool was sorted into classes: white *wakaya* wool of average quality sold for 10–11 soles/lb., while finer quality white *wakaya* wool sold for 12–13 soles/lb. However, families could also choose to continue to sell their fiber in bulk (unsorted by color and texture) for 9.5 soles/lb., which was judged to be an agreeable price and often the easiest option.

More than the income, however, animal fiber was a powerful marker of prestige. It transformed herders into "wool producers" and tethered them to a distinguished national brand—literally, Marca Perú. A branding campaign designed in part by the US-based luxury advertising firm, McCann-Erickson, and PromPerú (the agency within the Ministry of Foreign Trade and Tourism that is tasked with promoting "the Peruvian image") Marca Perú was best known for its 2011 viral campaign launch video in which a bus carrying their geoglyph-inspired logo traveled to Peru, Nebraska, to tout Peruvian music, food, clothing, dance, and cultural heritage. It has since grown to encompass the "Alpaca del Perú" brand, which promotes the alpaca as "the treasure of the Andes" that "Peruvians have protected for thousands of years." The image of the Indigenous herder is central to the promotion of alpaca fiber, and Quechua and Aymara herders are widely celebrated on the Alpaca del Perú website not only for their "good management of the herd," but also their inextricable, kinship-like bond to their animals: they "love and care for their alpacas as if they were their children" and "respect these animals and acknowledge the sustenance they provide as if they were their parents" (Alpaca del Perú 2023).

In Peru, producing improved alpacas has become an issue of national concern. As Maggie Bolton noted in Bolivia with the llama, since the 1990s the symbolic ownership of these animals "has slipped discursively from herders to the wider nation," rendering the project of the species' care and improvement a national endeavor (M. Bolton 2006, 534). Alpacas have long been at the center of Peruvian efforts of improvement, efforts that have often aided in dispossessing Indigenous peoples from their lands and knowledges. For example, it was the expansion of the international wool market in the 1860s that initially drove the spread of haciendas into Indigenous pastoralist territories (Orlove 1977b; 1985). After the agrarian reform, state-sponsored breeding programs progressively integrated with poverty-alleviation development initiatives to promote breeding management programs in rural communities (Valdivia Corrales 2013). These efforts converged with Peru's rebranding efforts in the 2010s, through which Peru sought to distinguish itself in the national market for its privileged access to this "exclusive and highly prized fiber" (Alpaca del Perú 2023). Now, municipal and regional governments partner with development organizations like Heifer International to promote alpaca breeding throughout the highlands.

Livestock improvement programs have always involved multiple forms of negotiation and accommodation between Indigenous knowledges and elite scientific "expertise" regarding animal improvement, although the metrics have typically favored elite registers. The most pervasive shift has occurred in the curation of the "ideal" alpaca, whose image has been progressively co-opted by national and international economic interests. As noted in chapter 3, while distinctive features like spotted coats, folded or missing ears, blue eyes, or polydactylism may be charming and even desirable features in a herd, they are selected against in national breeding programs. Besides fine fiber, alpaca breeding directives specify that the animal's eyes should be clear, bright, and black; the teeth should be straight and free from wear; the ears should be upright and the appropriate shape and size; the tail should be thick and wooly; and the overall size and stature of the animals should be "well-formed" (*bien formado*). Development programs disseminate these metrics through documents and workshops that meticulously demarcate an alpaca's most desirable features, and they reinforce their importance by awarding cash prizes and dramatically large ribbons to herders and their show animals in regional competition circuits.

One nongovernmental organization, Pachamama Raymi, was an especially prominent player in Chillca in 2015. This Cusco-based NGO spearheaded multiple development initiatives in Chillca and surrounding communities based on a development methodology established in the 1980s under the Rural Development Program PRODERM and financed by the Dutch Cooperation and the European Commission. A central feature of their methodology was the use of competitions or contests between families and communities as a form of incentivization, in which the winners were awarded a cash prize. As is the case in many global developmentalist projects in Peru, Pachamama Raymi espoused the neoliberal tenets of competition, ambition, and self-promotion as necessary components of the project of *mejoramiento* (Hirsch 2022). In 2015–2016, Pachamama Raymi held a major competition in Chillca centered around the "genetic improvement" (*mejoramiento genético*) of alpacas, culminating in a regional livestock competition.

It wasn't the first livestock competition Chillca had participated in, and Pachamama Raymi was just one of many programs in Chillca. The traces of previous developmental efforts could be found throughout herder's homes, often in the form of dusty and worn training manuals stuffed behind beds or in cracks in the stone walls. Tucked behind Concepción's cupboard, I came across one document from a workshop called the "Improvement of the Competitiveness of Producers of Alpacas and Llamas of the District of Pitumarca," part of a thirty-three-month de-

FIGURE 18 Preparing alpaca wool for sale. Photo by author.

velopment project implemented between 2012 and 2014 by the district municipality of Pitumarca in partnership with Heifer International. The stated goals of the program were to "improve the living conditions of the alpaca producers in the face of climate change" through managing animal breeding and genetic quality, cultivating improved pasture varieties, and increasing access to the international wool market. Most families in Chillca had a copy of this document in their home, and some had diligently referred to it, as evidenced by their extensive notes and markings throughout the pamphlet.[4]

In these development initiatives, the adoption of material practices was explicitly framed as the personal responsibility of the herder. Pamphlets provided recommendations for shearing, breeding, calving, and registering individual animals, along with photos of herders weighing, marking, tagging, medicating, and weaning *crías* and *tuwis*. They provided templates for the herders' own self-evaluation: extensive charts and tables that prompted them to keep detailed records of the selection, breeding, calving, weaning, culling, and general health of their alpacas.

In the letter that opened the Heifer International document, for example, the mayor at the time wrote to his "high Andean brothers and sisters" who "work tirelessly to genetically improve the production and productivity of alpaca breeding," urging them to take advantage of the document and handle it with responsibility. This message was reiterated throughout the pamphlet: "This material should be used with *great responsibility and honesty*, because the misuse of this booklet will not serve as an instrument for the better management and success of the producer." As a point of emphasis, the pamphlet included a photo of an emaciated alpaca corpse with the caption "lack of attention will bring consequences."

Thus, while herders may be celebrated by Marca Perú as the "knowledge-keepers" of alpaca genetics, increasingly the expert parameters of animal physiology established by development organizations have taken precedence over those of the herders. Even though these programs come and go, their metrics of the ideal alpaca inform the purchases herders make at local markets and set the aspirational expectations for the breeding studs that herders would purchase if they were to acquire more income. Herders in Chillca aspired to buy studs like those they had seen in Puno, where long-standing breeding programs produced high-quality studs valued between 10,000 and 20,000 soles (approximately $3,500 to $10,000 USD at the time). The community governing board typically purchased two of these studs every year or two for the community herd. Although families usually settled for less expensive studs in regional markets such as Combapata and Pampamarka, they envisioned being able to purchase animals that reflected the highest quality standards of animal breeding. As one young man excitedly told me, "In my case I'm going to buy an alpaca with 10,000 soles, 20,000 soles. I'm going to buy a good animal because I'm going to put it with my animals." His boast trailed off, however, as he reflected on the complications of buying stud males in a commons system: "But it's also going to [mate] with other people's animals, and it won't be possible to improve." Gesturing toward his herd, he said wistfully, "When [the wool] is fine it's beautiful, like cotton. This is where we want to get. When you have your own *parcela*, your stud can't go to another place, to [mate with] other animals. Since it is yours, only in your own [herd] will there be the most beautiful animals [*bonitos animales*]."

Those in favor of *parcelas* argued that the commons system of land tenure was a deterrent to breed improvement: the constant mixing between neighboring herds in the communal pasture rendered a household's attempts to selectively pair reproductive animals ineffective. One man in his midforties, Teodoro, who had a small herd of thirty alpacas, dreamed of buying better studs as a means of "getting ahead" (*supirasiun*, from Spanish *superar*, to overcome):

> In the community, raising alpacas and sheep, there isn't improvement (*mihuramintu*). Because they are mixing, [the animal] purchased by one person is mixing with that of their neighbor, so one can't get ahead (*mana kanchu supirasiun*) . . . But in a parcel, you would tend to your improved alpaca and it wouldn't mix. That's what I'd like.

For those in favor of parcels, this future—one with *bonitos animales*, and *animales de calidad*—felt frustratingly out of reach. It was easy to feel impatient, anxious, restless. There was work to be done, prestige to be had.

And there was the promise of cash. Herders spoke in very practical terms about the income they could gain through selling *mejorado* alpaca fiber. When I then asked what they would do with that money, the answer was, overwhelmingly, that they would invest it in their children—and in their children's education, specifically. Florentina (the woman with relatives on the other, more "*despierto*" side of the mountain) told me: "I would sell [the wool] so that I could send my children to study. They [on the other side of the mountain] study, we don't have any *profesionales* here. In your country they produce *profesionales*, right? Here no." Children in Chillca represented the future: they were "figurations," as Claudia Castañeda writes, entities in the making whose potentialities allowed for the cultivation of not only their own individual futures, but for the "making of worlds more generally" (Castañeda 2002, 1). In many communities throughout the Andes, people's hopes for the future have been articulated through the aspirational narratives they bestow upon their children (Leinaweaver 2008, 60). In that sense, Chillca was no different.

Cultivating Subjects

Much like cultivating *bonitos animales* had become an issue of national concern in Peru, educating children was likewise a national project. In

2015, the municipal government initiated an early childhood development project in Chillca in collaboration with several international gov-
ernmental and nongovernmental organizations, including Pachamama Raymi as well as the Korean International Cooperation Agency
(KOICA). Similar to the Pachamama Raymi alpaca genetics program,
a key aspect of this initiative involved using contests and cash prizes
as incentives. In this case, the competition focused on children, whose
height, weight, and attendance to a play center were documented and
compared across the participating communities of Chillca, Ananiso, and
Pampachiri. When the center opened in November 2015, the community
healthworker implored parents to invest in the program, telling them,
"Our children walk forward [into the future]. *Manaña wawanchis nu-
qanchishinañachu kanan*, let our children not be like us anymore—[let
them be] better than us, *mejor que nosotros*."

Through developmental initiatives aimed at the rural poor, the Peruvian state has articulated clear visions of what improvement looks like,
and they have urged new models of subject formation in partnership with
international NGOs and development programs that have been critiqued
as "racism in disguise" (Leinaweaver 2008, 64). It was no coincidence,
for example, that ideologies of improvement in Chillca were articulated
through the Spanish-language concepts of *superación* or *mejoramiento*,
embedded in Quechua speech as *supirasiun* and *mihuramintu*. In Peru,
Spanish is the language of social, political, and economic power, and
is inextricably linked with developmentalist narratives of progress, improvement, and upward mobility (Mannheim 1991). Aspirational narratives in the Andes have historically been tethered to a racial geography
that assumes the superiority of urban whiteness: in these models, one
must shed the markers of indigeneity (dress, speech, diet, habitus, and
geography) in order to improve their standing and livelihood (Drinot
2011; de la Cadena 2005; Hill 2013; Weismantel 1988; Whitten 1981).
These efforts often hinged around labor, transforming Indigenous workers into entrepreneurial-minded producers of raw goods like agricultural
products and alpaca fiber for the glossy, national branding campaigns
selling Peruvian cuisine and luxury fashions (Drinot 2011; García 2021;
Hirsch 2022).[5]

The developmental emphasis on training and education—to become
a competitive wool producer, or to hone a career as a *profesional*—

emerged from a broader history of social improvement in Peru that has deep racial undertones. Along with church campaigns that promoted "clean-living" and abstention from alcohol, sanitation efforts aimed at bathroom construction and trash collection, and housing initiatives that emphasized the creation of improved homes with painted exteriors, metal cookstoves, and gendered bedrooms, the training workshops and education efforts in Chillca were aimed at not only improving living conditions but changing subjectivities, "by educating desires and configuring habits, aspirations and beliefs" (Li 2007, 5). And, as anthropologist Eric Hirsch has noted, these efforts have been particularly successful in grounding developmental goals in appeals to personal responsibility, positioning practices of "individual self-realization" as a necessary and central component of broader developmental growth (Hirsch 2022, 125). When development workers urged parents that their children would be "better than us," *mejor que nosotros*, they were recruiting them into a familiar project oriented around neoliberal tenets (competition, individualization, economic rationality, etc.), encouraging a model of the idealized human subject as an autonomous, self-directed, entrepreneurial agent (D. Harvey 2005, 42; Escobar 2011; Ferguson 1994). This would allow their children to live "better" lives: lives in which they could navigate urban centers, elite institutions, and the market economy in particular ways.[6]

This wasn't a simple story of erasure, however. Even though their imaginations of "better" futures sought to align human and animal bodies with the idealized types that were, indeed, shaped in the image—or at least the imagination—of those in power, people in Chillca were not striving to transform their children into wealthy urbanites. Many wanted their children to go to the cities and study, speak Spanish and English, and become professionals—but many people also wanted them to come back to Chillca and continue working with alpacas. Education was considered the essential key to *mejoramiento*—not just for the children but for the community as a whole. If children were given the opportunity to complete their education and become *profesionales*, they would return to contribute to the overall well-being of the entire community.

At one general assembly, the president of the community reiterated the importance of childhood development programs, stating, "more than anything this is for the children, this work is part of education."

He posed a rhetorical question to the assembly: "Why is it our children aren't going to university, or to institute, *compañeros*? And why
don't we have *profesionales, compañeros*? For a lack of [attendance to
the program] we don't have *profesionales*. Think about it, *compañeros*."
He implored those present to take responsibility for the success of the
program, adding "the children will become good *profesionales*, they'll
be good lawyers, doctors, and that is how Chillca will be for us, *compañeros*, we are going to get out of poverty and all the [other] bad things,
compañeros. Isn't that right?"[7]

The notion that these children would return to Chillca and improve
upon the community represented, for many, the end-goal of parcelization, and by extension, *mejoramiento*. Dividing the land, selling animals,
and sending children away to study—in other words fragmenting and
then reconfiguring the various components of Chillca—would ultimately lead to the improvement of its entirety. It was perhaps here that
the notion of *voluntad*, of *responsabilidad*, retained the nuances of "social volition" noted elsewhere in the Andes (Paerregaard 2015). While
deeply imbued with the tenets of individual self-promotion espoused by
neoliberal development initiatives, there remained an enduring sense of
commitment to Chillca: the place, the community, the idea.

A Common Future

Chillca held a public vote on parcelization in December 2015. Community members voted almost entirely in favor. The parcelization of Chillca's pastures would seem, at first glance, an open-and-shut case of
enclosure—however, as I'd find years later, there were enduring channels
of connection and creativity at work below the surface. The conversations
that I witnessed in 2015 already deviated from what one could consider
the "conventional" narrative of enclosure, in which encroaching capitalist
expansion inevitably leads to the collapse of the commons. That narrative lends itself to fatalistic and capitalocentric interpretations in which
the stakes are centered around a narrow interpretation of both the commons as "property," and access and control as "ownership" (Sato and Soto
Alarcón 2019). According to people in Chillca, rectifying troubled land relations always required creative practices that promoted grounding, stabi-

lizing, and rest, much like remedies for restlessness in other domains (like *q'apachiy, phukuy*) that soothed relational tension. Land tenure change was likewise a creative remedy for restlessness, through which they might avoid further tension and fracture between community members.

Although land tenure change in Chillca took on many of the legal, linguistic, and material practices of privatization, it still left opportunities for continued circulation and commoning, albeit through different modalities. I'd find that, when I returned to Chillca years later, people were still rotating their animals in the pasture and sharing critical knowledge, labor, and resources, but often in new ways that intersected with the cash economy and novel systems of rent, debt, and obligation. These tensions and contradictions expand our understanding of the "commons"—as many postcapitalistic community economists and feminist political ecologists have urged us to do—beyond material resources or property to consider "everyday practices, social relations, and spaces of creativity and social reproduction" (Clement et al. 2019, 2; Federici 2018; Gibson-Graham 2006; Linebaugh 2008; Shiva 2005).

Particularly when it comes to Indigenous land relations, and especially those that resemble conventional understandings of the commons, there is often an assumption that the fragmentation of the commons is an externally imposed process that leads to the collapse of Indigenous practices, relations, and institutions. This argument both perpetuates a simplification of Indigenous land relations and presupposes an irrevocable destruction of worlds, rather than drawing attention to enduring practices and creative reinterpretations (TallBear 2019). Instead of a simple story of refusal or acceptance of capitalism, a more nuanced perspective lends itself to, in the words of Chizu Sato and Jozelin María Soto Alarcón, "seeing how women and men are 'staying with the trouble' [. . .], how they *common* in the absence of a *commons* through practices of 'reappropriation, reconstruction, reinvention'" (Sato and Soto Alarcón 2019, 38–39).

Much of Chillca's story of commoning has yet to be told, but the vibrant and fraught conversations I witnessed in 2015 were yet another reminder that Chillca was not a community headed for collapse, erasure, or removal. As Joseph Weiss argued in his research on the Haida community of Old Massett, Canada, Indigenous practices of futurity deliberately resist the temporal logics of settler colonialism that have relegated Indigenous cultures to the past and thereby deny them a future (Weiss 2019; Fabian 2002). By engaging in practices of future-making—imagining, cultivating, and debating improved futures—Indigenous peoples "assert critical control over their pasts and their presents through the work of producing their futures" (Weiss 2019, 14). Future-oriented strategies are especially powerful in a time of climate change, when apocalyptic narratives portend the erasure, removal, or assimilation of climate-impacted peoples throughout the world.

At the same time, future-making practices likewise emerge within matrices of power and exclusion. Despite the "unanimous" support for parcelization in Chillca at the January 2016 assembly, many community members were privately skeptical or even opposed to the idea. In addition to those that were doubtful of the logistical viability of the project as a whole—particularly regarding the equitable division of land and water—many feared being removed from their lands. People preferred to subdivide the land by sector, so that families could remain where they lived. This was especially important for people like Concepción, who felt herself rooted inextricably in the lands of Antapata. Others were skeptical of other community members' motivations. Some argued that landowners would make decisions without considering the impacts those decisions would have on their neighbors. Others expressed fears that parcelization would open the community's lands to appropriation or exploitation by the Peruvian state or mining companies. However, there was also a small contingent of the community that felt favorable toward extractive industries, and a few community members who envisioned radically different uses for their lands: one young woman mentioned that she'd be interested in using dynamite to blow up the hillside behind her house and sell the rocks to construction companies, for example.

This is all to say that humans, herd animals, and landscapes didn't coexist in a harmonious network in Chillca in 2015, nor had they ever. For some people in Chillca, a life without the pastoral commons didn't seem feasible, while for others, it was the necessary way forward. While some lamented the loss of communicative practice with *pukara*, others saw it as the devil's work. And while some mourned the future loss of ties to the landscape, others wanted to take dynamite to the hillsides and sell the rocks for cash. In the futures that people imagined for themselves in

Chillca, current assemblages of humans-animals-landscapes were not always preferred—nor were they necessarily possible. Not everyone is interested—or included—in future-making in the same ways. As anthropologist Elizabeth Roberts has written, "entanglement is not always welcome, even in highly relational worlds. It depends on the how and the what and the when" (2017, 596).

Being Forgotten

In sum, imagined futures in Chillca were laden with ambivalence around the entwined fates of people, place, and animals. The topic of parcelization was especially troubling to members of the older generation, who felt uniquely left out of these future worlds. As one older man, Rosindo, said, "a life of herding is all we've known." He continued:

> I think [parcelization] would be sad (*tristi*). Because we have lived this life, I don't know other types of work, I only know herding animals and farming potatoes in the *chakra*, that's all I know. I haven't studied either. If I had studied, I could be living in a city, even just cleaning houses, but I don't know [this type of] work. I don't know how to read, only just a little . . . Parcelization wouldn't be good, because people haven't thought through it. I don't want it.

His fears went beyond his own prospects, however. As he worriedly told me, "I truly think this community will disappear (*tukupullanqataqcha*)." For his generation, it was a community for which they had fought so fiercely. He referenced the hacienda period during which people worked without pay for wealthy landowners and were subjected to routine abuse. In the years after the haciendas, Rosindo and other members of his generation had struggled to obtain titles for the land, often making arduous trips to the capital city of Lima to wade through expensive and humiliating bureaucratic procedures. By seeking parcelization, he argued, the younger generation was forgetting Chillca's land and its history. They'd already forgotten the names of Chillca's places, and they were forgetting the labor of the older generation who had reclaimed the community's land on behalf of the Indigenous families that had lived there for generations.

As Benjamin Orlove expressed in *Lines in the Water*, forgetting is a social act in the Andes, one that constitutes an intentional denial of coexistence, shared history, and social equality. The fear of being forgotten is a fear of being intentionally forsaken and abandoned by those who might view others as inferior. It is a reflection of people's "sense that they have been overlooked, that they are not merely at the bottom of an unequal and unjust social order, but have fallen out of this order altogether" (Orlove 2002, 13). Towns overlooked and neglected by their government are likewise described as forgotten (*pueblos olvidados* [Orlove 2002, 13]). Another elder voiced these fears by stating simply, "People will ask what happened to [the community of] Chillca."

Rosindo continued, "We worked day and night, we suffered so much. Now it's so tranquil, now the animals reproduce. [People] should thank the community for the lands. But in the time of parcels, it won't be like this. All the animals will die; all the land will disappear with the parcels." This fear that the fragmentation of land would lead to animal death and, ultimately, the end of Chillca, was grounded in a painful history of dispossession, racism, and settler colonialism through which relationships between Indigenous peoples, landscapes, and animals were forcibly severed in the Andes. And, as I've discussed in previous chapters, this fear was also grounded in a broader moral universe in which the fragmentation of one component leads to the unraveling of the entire entity. Or, as Rosindo described it, "When the land is divided, we won't have animals like before. It will all end (*tukukapunqa*)."

The broader community discussion around parcelization quickly stalled when it came time to discuss the dissolution of the alpaca herds. It was then that the stakes of parcelization came into sharp relief. Most of the community remained hesitant about getting rid of alpacas altogether, especially the community's shared alpaca herd, the *majada*. A future without animals wasn't quite imaginable yet. At least for that moment, they were still in this together, staying with the trouble. Even Concepción's song that opened this chapter concludes with her unable to leave her homeland: despite how angry her neighbors had made her, she just couldn't leave Chillca, whose lands and waters had nourished her, her animals, and her neighbors—holding them in troubled, ambivalent, restless relation to one another.

AUSANGATE (CONTINUED)

Pitumarquiñu sultiritucha
Pitumarquiñu sultiritucha
Llikllachaytapas hap'ikushaspas
Amurchallayta kutichipuway

Qaparit'i mayutari qhunchuntintachu tumarani
Ripuy pasay nishaspapas
Manalla ripuy atinaypaq
Manalla pasay atinaypaq

Qaparit'i unutari laq'intintachu uharani
Pasay ripuy nishaspapas
Manalla pasay atinaypaq
Manalla ripuy atinaypaq

Dear Pitumarca bachelor
Dear Pitumarca bachelor
Tugging on my little shawl
Return my little affections

Did I drink from the ice of Qaparit'i river?
So that, while saying "leave, go"
I just couldn't leave
I just couldn't go

Did I drink from the spring of Qaparit'i's waters?
So that, while saying "leave, go"
I just couldn't go
I just couldn't leave

CHAPTER FIVE

Life Change

BANDURRIAY (MY BANDURRIA)

Bandurriay waqayamuya	My bandurria, cry to me
Chay kunkaykiwan waqayamuya	With your throat, cry to me
Phinaya llaqtaq anivirsariunpaq	For Phinaya town's anniversary
Chillca llaqtaq fiyistachallanpaq	For Chillca's celebration
Kay waynuchalla takiyusqaytaq	Perhaps this little *waynu* that I've sung
Kay qinachalla takiyusqaytaq	Perhaps this little *qina* that I've sung
Llaqtaypa rikwirduchaypaq	Will be my little memento for my town
Wañuqtiy ripukapuqtiy	When I've died, when I've left
Tukayusqayqa takiyusqayqa	That which I've played, that which I've sung
Tukayusqayqa takiyusqayqa	That which I've played, that which I've sung
Llaqtaypa rikwirduchanpaq	May it be a little memento for my town
Wañuqtiy ripukapuqtiy	When I've died, when I've left . . .

Concepción's Illness

Early in the new year, I returned to Chillca from a short trip to the city. As I hopped off the cattle truck in the town center, I came across Concepción's mother, Emilia, as she was walking down from the high pastures of Uqi Kancha. In her early seventies, with a thick braid of jet-black hair down her back, Emilia was discerning and didn't suffer fools gladly. When I arrived in Chillca, she had less patience with me and was quick to brush me off when I couldn't do something right. But she had a sweet tooth, and I always brought her dried apricots from the market in Cusco. She eventually warmed to me, and I would spend nights at her home and mornings herding with her in the high valleys of Uqi Kancha. Like Mario and Maritza, she had recently converted to evangelicalism, and she'd sing religious songs in Quechua as we herded, and regularly admonished Concepción for chewing coca. I appreciated her candor—which meant if she was headed straight for me with something to say, I had better listen.

Emilia's tone was hurried. Gesturing toward the wetlands at the foot of Ausangate's icy peak, she urged me toward Concepción's home in Antapata. Concepción had told her she was dying. "You'd better go see her," she advised. Alarmed, I dropped my bags at the town store and hurried up the narrow path to the high pastures. The walk took about forty-five minutes when walking at a clip, and I arrived at Concepción's home breathless. She was seated on the stone threshold, her gaze trained on the animals meandering the hillsides. As I approached, she greeted me with a weak smile and told me, quite nonchalantly, that yes, she was dying. I asked how she knew, and she replied that she had felt it that morning, in the moment between sleep and wakefulness—a distinct wrenching, as if she were being pulled forcefully backward into a free fall. A tug that portended a detachment from this life into whatever came next.

I sat down at her feet to catch my breath and organize my thoughts. I hadn't noticed any symptoms of illness in our long days herding together, and I always interpreted her bounding strides alongside her animals as an indication of overall good health. "But . . . what are you dying *from*?" I asked. She described her symptoms to me: full-body aches, fatigue, headaches, chills, sensations of heat, and the sudden onset of sweating, light-headedness, and nausea. In the pause after describing her symptoms, she must have sensed my need for something more concrete, stable, commensurable to hold onto. She identified two health conditions: "lack of blood" (*pisi yawar*) and "life change" (*gambiu wida*). At least, that's what she had been diagnosed with at the local health post earlier that week. She had been sent home with instructions to add more meat to her diet and to visit the health clinic in Pitumarca for fortifying injections. From her descriptions of both the illnesses and their treatments, I realized that what she was describing overlapped conceptually with what I recognized as anemia ("lack of blood") and menopause ("life change"). However, her experience also exceeded those categories in crucial ways.

For example, as Concepción described her sensory experience, she also relayed a cascade of concerns: her alpacas were hungry and restless, her eldest son's prized llama had gone missing, and her two young grandchildren had been left by themselves while her daughter sought wage labor opportunities in the lowlands. *"Imanasaqmi*, what will I do?" she asked. That past week she had gone down to Pitumarca to watch her grandkids march in a school procession, and a fox had eaten one of her alpacas in Illachiy. She was in a rush and hadn't been able to contract another herder, and Julio had stayed in Pitumarca with the tips he earned from the Ausangate trek. It also snowed unexpectedly that past week in Antapata, so now half of the herd was down in Chillca, and the other half up in the hills. She was overwhelmed: her herd and her family members were scattered, and she was too tired to bring them back together. "I don't have the strength (*mana kallpay kanchu*)," she said. Concepción's affect changed from perfunctory to sorrowful, and it was clear that this sudden string of seemingly unrelated concerns was also constitutive of her ill-health, inextricably wrapped up in the ways that she felt herself to be dying.

In order to understand Concepción's illness, I propose we take as our starting point the Andean modes of relation explored in previous chapters, which posit inherent connections between landscapes, herds, and humans. It would be tempting, for example, to consider Concepción's health condition from the top down, as a cascading chain of causality: global climate change had altered hydrological profiles and patterns of seasonal rainfall in the Andes, leading to lower levels of moisture in grasslands and thus less edible biomass for the animals. Less grass had led to hungry sheep, which led to wandering sheep, which led to frustrated and exhausted herders. However, if left entangled, these connectivities prompt us to ponder how climate change, animal restlessness, *gambiu wida*, and *pisi yawar* are not only interrelated but mutually emergent within the same historical and material processes of socioecological disruption.[1] A disorienting shift has occurred across humans, animals, and the landscape at once: a progressive process of drying that pervades landscapes and bodies as they all undergo similar transformations within a broader planetary shift.

To that end, in this chapter, I again suggest we "take seriously, rather than metaphorically" the ways that women like Concepción have felt their bodies and lived experience as bundles of relation that are unraveling in the face of persistent drought, glacier retreat, and climate-forced migration (de la Cadena 2010, 361; Viveiros de Castro 2011). This is not an isolated premise: the intricate, vital, and fraught interconnections between human well-being and the environment is a fundamental tenet underlying environmental justice (Bullard 2000), environmentalism(s) of the poor (Nixon 2011; Martínez-Alier 2003), Indigenous ecological knowledge (Abram 1997; Gilio-Whitaker 2019; Hernandez 2022; Kimmerer 2015), and the "science of loss" (Adger et al. 2013; Barnett et al. 2016; Kirsch 2001). These perspectives are themselves indebted, as Sunaura Taylor rightfully asserts, to the marginalized, Indigenous, and poor communities who have "long exposed that human well-being is inseparable from the well-being of the land" (2024, 19). While there is increasing attention to the *somaterratic* qualities of human well-being (Albrecht et al. 2007, S95), its logics nevertheless continue to be housed in a Cartesian separation of mind, body, and landscape. The challenge often remains to analyze bodily, social, and environmental conditions as mutually emergent, rather than one (illness or grief) as the somatization of another (political instability or climate change).

In this chapter, I root the analysis within the socioecological conditions through which women in the Andes conceptualized their own state of health and well-being in broader landscapes. Key to this understanding is examining how disease categories like *pisi yawar* and *gambiu wida* are enacted or "made to cohere" through the material and semiotic practices of diagnostics and treatment (Mol 2002). Etiologies of illness, emotional disturbance, and physical maladies are inextricably interwoven with broader networks of relationality in the Andes: to be *well* is to be *in relation*. This state of well-being is troubled by the instability of entities and phenomena within the context of broader climatological shifts. Emplacing *gambiu wida* and *pisi yawar* within the logics and practices of restlessness—and its perils as well as its remedies—reveals the expansiveness of this troubling, of *k'ita*, across beings, relationships, and bodies. And, it also raises the question of how to heal, and to be well, in a fragmenting landscape.

Diagnosing the Body Fractal

Concepción informed me she was dying just before the herds of Antapata migrated back down to the Chillca valley floor in anticipation of the wet season. A key problem had emerged that month: the location of that year's potato farms, which were on a yearly rotation across four different locations in the community, overlapped with a large area of the wet-season pastures in Chillca center. Given that the herds would be arriving just as the first leafy sprouts of the potato plants were emerging, the herders would have to expend extra energy to keep their animals out of the farms. Instead, Concepción and Emilia would have to construct temporary homes in Yana Rumi (Black Rock) and Misk'i Pukyu (Sweet Spring), two locations just outside the town center. With this change in plans, they needed to push their seasonal migrations back even further, into late December and early January.

Herders throughout Chillca remarked that the increased intensity of heat, cold, wind, and rain over the past years had impacted both animal and human health. Periods of intense cold had caused stomachaches, diarrhea, and head colds, while periods of intense heat and sun had caused headaches, fever, and lethargy in both people and animals. Heat during the rainy season caused enterotoxaemia in sheep and alpaca, a gastrointestinal bacterial illness that led to anorexia, lethargy, recumbency, and the distended abdomen that gives the illness its name in Quechua

FIGURE 19 Administering medicine to a sick sheep. Photo by author.

(*wiksa punkiy*, "swollen belly"). Excessive precipitation also caused sodden corrals, leading to a cascade effect of illness: if a corral became too wet, it could split the animal's feet, give them worms, and increase their likelihood of developing gastrointestinal illness. And, of course, animal restlessness was producing a different kind of sickness. Herders were becoming sick with frustration (*rinyigu*, from the Spanish *reniego*), which produced headaches, stomachaches, and general feelings of unease and fatigue. There was a looming sense that the herds, humans, and wetlands in Antapata were at a breaking point, and the strains were starting to emerge across various bodies and beings.

There were many theories about what was happening to Concepción. We talked at length about it one morning with Mario, who had come by to install a sprinkler near Concepción's home in the hopes of simultaneously relieving some of the drought as well as his mother's worries. Lugging a hose across the river and up the hill toward Illachiy, Mario connected it with the canal he had dug the previous year, where he had embedded a hose beneath a moss overhang concealing a small spring in the hillside. As he connected the hoses, securing the two ends carefully with twisted plastic bags, he remarked, "Twenty years ago, this wasn't necessary." Back then, the valley floor of Antapata was an open pampa with plenty of pasture, parts of which, over time, had been divided into houses and enclosures. They'd been irrigating with sprinklers for about four years by that time, and herders were discussing ways to extend the existing networks of irrigation in anticipation of future droughts.

Concepción and I sat together in the doorway peeling *muraya*, while Mario worked on the sprinkler outside. While he cleared sand out of the hoses, we cut some carrots, onions, and potatoes for the soup. While he tinkered with the sprinkler head to get it to spin, Concepción found some dried llama stomach and broke it into small pieces to add to the boiling broth. As he got the sprinkler into the perfect spot, Concepción brought the sheep back to the corral, and the alpacas returned to the valley floor. Mario came to sit with us while we ate, and we talked about Concepción's health. "When I was younger, I didn't bundle up well enough," Concepción surmised, explaining that she often rushed out herding in the mornings without putting on the additional tiers of skirts and cardigans that allow herders to shed outer layers as they get soaked in rain or hail throughout the day. It was more complicated than "catching a cold," however. The issue as she described it was not the wetness or the coldness of the water, but rather *the process of drying* that had left her vulnerable. "My clothes got soaked, and [the water] passed from the clothes to my body," she continued, explaining the chain of events. "Then my body dried (*ch'akirapun*) as I walked, allowing the cold to get in (*chiri pasawan*)." This had left her with *chiri sufla*, or "cold infection," which was a generalized malady understood as the primary cause of bronchitis in high-elevation communities like Chillca, and also the root of other illnesses such as osteoporosis, arthritis, and even some cancers.

For Concepción, she continued to feel the impacts of this cold as a persistent ache in her waist in the evenings after she finished herding. In addition to the more recent symptoms of lightheadedness, lethargy, weakness, and ephemeral sensations of heat and nausea, it also contributed to her overall sense of discomfort and waning vitality, and the troubling feeling that she was no longer strong enough to care for her animals. "I don't have the strength (*mana kallpay kanchu*)," she repeated. "I'm no good for walking (*mana puriyta valinichu*)." When she returned home in the evenings, she often felt so tired from herding that she didn't have the strength to prepare the large pots of soup to feed herself, her children, and her neighbors. She was losing weight, which she noted every time she tied her skirts a bit tighter around her diminishing waist.

Her references to an inability to walk—"I'm no good for walking" (*mana puriyta valinichu*)—signaled this more expansive sense of illness and discomfort. In one sense, Concepción was speaking literally of her fatigue and her inability to keep up with her animals in the pasture. But she was also saying something more akin to "I can't go on." The verb *puriy*, while directly translatable to walking, more broadly "denotes a kinetic or dynamic form of existence," which all beings—humans, animals, and landscapes—can have (Mannheim 1998, 269). Its semantic range encompasses walking as well as traveling, functioning, and general well-being.[2] To be unable to *puriy* is to be unable to set into motion the various components of one's physical and social existence. For Concepción, the multivalence of *puriy* captured her sense of illness in its multiplicity: her inability to walk with and thereby feed her animals was deeply interwoven with her inability to feed herself, her kin, and neighbors. "Who would take care of the animals?" she often asked, contemplating the future impacts of her fatigue and illness. Who would be able to do the work of herding in her place, and with these animals she knew so well and with whom she worked so closely? It was no small feat to take on someone else's herd, even more so to have to divide it. This question, for her, encapsulated her deepest lingering fears about her own mortality.

Mario gently comforted her between bites of soup, telling her not to worry. But mostly he listened quietly and respectfully, creating a silent space for his mother's worries to unfold. Mario would tell me later that he wasn't too acutely concerned about his mother, and although he sympathized greatly with her discomfort and sadness, he thought his mother often dwelled on death in a way that was unnecessary. He was concerned about her symptoms, however, and mentioned that he had heard women going through *gambiu wida* could go into a fugue state (*phawaychariy*), a cyclical affliction that causes people to wander the hills without direction. Sometimes it gets better, he heard, but sometimes it can portend the end of life. He worried about it afflicting his mother, but he hadn't noticed any signs that told him this state was imminent. He was more immediately concerned about her spending too much money on questionable healing remedies: Concepción had gone to a healer recently in Combapata and purchased olive oil, copaiba oil capsules, and two herbal mixes, a purchase that Mario disagreed with. But she had decided to visit another healer anyway, and he insisted that this time I go along.

And so a few weeks later, Concepción and I climbed into the back of a cattle truck headed to the town of Combapata. As we descended down the valley, the air shifted from a dry icy cold to warm and humid, the road dipping into groves of eucalyptus trees and fields of corn and broad beans. When we finally reached the central square of Combapata, we clambered out of the back and stretched our tired legs, before making our way to see José, a local healer and owner of the local drugstore. José's shop was dimly lit, the dusty wooden shelves lined with herbs and tinctures in glass bottles, as well as plastic bottles bearing bright, commercialized labels with pictures of people smiling, grimacing, or clutching their stomachs. We quickly greeted José at the counter and took our seats on a wooden bench to wait for our turn. Her voice hushed beneath her hat and shawl, Concepción again described her illness to José: the headaches, fatigue, chills, and lightheadedness. José listened intently, nodding and consoling Concepción with a periodic "Ya, mamá, don't worry, mamá." She told him the health post worker had suggested she

FIGURE 20 Collecting medicinal herbs. Photo by author.

had *gambiu wida* and *pisi yawar*, and he nodded his head in agreement. "Everyone has anemia here," he said, looking in my direction. He recommended vitamins, a few tonics, and a fortifying injection.

Finding myself invited into the conversation, I took the opportunity to ask the healer about his interpretation of *chiri sufla*, and how the sensation of cold might contribute to her discomfort. I wanted to see if and how he connected Concepción's experience walking in the cold rain with *pisi yawar*, and discern why the discomfort seemed to have settled in her waist. "The cold gets to them (*les pasa el frío*)," he responded, referencing the people up the valley in Chillca, "and the body how it is—with such little blood, the little nutrition (*alimentación*) they have up there—the body breaks down (*se les decompone*)." He explained:

> Discomfort (*malestar*). Their bones and joints are hurting, so sometimes they feel discomfort. It affects the bronchi a bit too. It also affects their womb, sometimes that's why their waist hurts. The spine, the nerves . . . since it's a lack of vitamins—combined with the nerves, then with the

cold—[the body] becomes tense. [That's why] when they move their waist hurts. That's the result of the cold. That's why they need tonic, vitamins. Vitamins, especially, to increase the blood (*para que le aumente sangre*), and to strengthen the body a little.

José's analysis of Concepción's discomfort quickly expanded into an assessment of the general health of people living in high-elevation communities like Chillca. He immediately connected the issue of cold to a broader issue of malnutrition, specifically a lack of vitamins that he attributed to a lack of nutrient-dense foods. He then pivoted to bone and joint health—"What they really need up there," he suggested, lifting an index finger to emphasize his point, "is a doctor [who specializes] in bones, who can increase fluids to the joints. Because mainly [their bones] dry out (*se les seca el liquido*)."

> Mostly they suffer from their bones. Their bones and [the lack of] vitamins. It's like I say, there is only potato, *chuño* and meat, nothing more, there are no vegetables [up there]. Here in the town, we eat vegetables, we eat a variety of things, even fruit. Up there, there is is nothing to eat . . . Now, by age 40, they already suffer from a lack of fluid, from here in the knee. What is called osteoarthritis. Then the osteoarthritis wears on, they can no longer walk. So, before that [happens] you have to increase the liquid, give them vitamins. You have to control it.

In the space between Concepción's description of her own illness and the town healer's explanation, multiple processes of translation had taken place. Both she and the healer were pulling together the traces of illness and discomfort, tethering her bodily sensations to phenomena in the broader world and trying to find ways to make them cohere into something identifiable, manageable, treatable. But their attentions were drawn to different sensations and events, and while they both settled on the diagnoses of *pisi yawar* and *gambiu wida*, these conditions were multivalent. Their uses of the terms were not equivalent but *equivocations*, containing shades of one another but only in part (de la Cadena 2015, 27; Viveiros de Castro 2004).

José's assessment of Concepción's illness, for example, appealed to the broader sociopolitical assemblage that defines "malnutrition" in the

Andes. Although anemia is technically defined as a condition of low hemoglobin concentration or red blood cell count, it is utilized more generally in the Andes as a proxy for various forms of malnutrition, or "lack of vitamins." It was a looming area of concern and intervention in Chillca when I was there, and indeed throughout the Peruvian Andes. It eventually caught the attention of the Peruvian Ministerio de Salud, which pledged in 2017 to reduce anemia by half within four years. Most of these efforts were targeted toward young children and lactating mothers and revolved around the distribution of multimicronutrient powders (Mayca-Pérez et al. 2017; Brewer et al. 2020; Nureña 2023). The disease category of anemia and its treatment mobilized anxieties and stereotypes about what kinds of food people did or did not eat in the highlands, and referenced not just a lack of iron-rich foods, but foods deemed "healthy" more broadly, glossed as containing "vitamins" (fruits, vegetables, and other cultivated foods from the lowland regions). It was also based in assumptions about the marginality of the highlands due to the lack of agriculture in these ecosystems.[3]

In contrast, Concepción identified various strands of relation that were becoming distended and threadbare. Concepción's description of her illness immediately referenced her role as a caretaker, for both her dependent children as well as her animals. One of her most pressing concerns was, if she got sick or died, who would herd the animals? Who would take care of her grandchildren? The ability to caretake was especially salient in this context, where, like elsewhere in the Andes, health was calibrated to "one's ability to work and one's capacity to be productive" (Sax 2015, 51; Camino 1992). Productivity, in this sense, referred to one's ability to undertake crucial social and life-sustaining activities. Since many of these practices were gendered in Chillca, a woman's well-being was observed specifically in her ability to undertake practices like herding animals and cooking for family members. Illness, on the other hand, was evidenced in her inability to do so, as Concepción expressed in her admission about her fears for her children, and the fact that she was "no good for walking" with her animals.

There were some interesting areas of convergence in José and Concepción's analyses, however. They both revolved around ideas of vitality and productivity, and referenced the centrality of certain bodily substances, namely the volume of blood, fat, and synovial fluid. And their concerns specifically referenced practices of feeding and being fed. An especially salient feature of Concepción's illness was her feeling of weakness, and her inability to gain weight even when she was eating. While the weakness associated with anemia and iron deficiencies could also be linked to the inability to feed oneself, Concepción's experience of *pisi yawar* was more broadly reflective of her inability to feed others: to walk with her animals to the high pastures or to cook large soups to share with her neighboring kin. Life-sustaining practices, like herding animals and cooking for others, not only provided material sustenance for human and animal bodies but also constituted their social existence by bringing them into relation with others. Providing food and feeding others were inherently relational practices that sustain both corporeal and social well-being across collectives: it was a crucial practice as much for the person doing the feeding as the person being fed (Orr 2013, 695; Weismantel 1995, 695). The weakness that Concepción attributed to *pisi yawar* was likewise expansive, and brought to bear her multiple relationships and commitments to other social beings, both human and nonhuman. The restless alpacas, the missing llama, her wayward daughter, and her hungry grandchildren were all enmeshed in this condition of existential weakness, of her "lack of blood."

The focus on blood as a metric of well-being, rather than fat, seemed to be another translation, reflecting more recent biomedical logics and related understandings of "what constituted the life source" (Canessa 2000, 709, 718n4). Historically, fat had been widely understood throughout the Andes of Ecuador, Peru, and Bolivia as the source of bodily vitality—not only because it sustains the human body but also because it tethers human bodies to the landscape through circulatory flows. Fat is centrally important to ritual offerings like the *dispachu*: the beads of vicuña fat that Julio placed at the corners of the dispachu, and in between the *k'intu*, for example, would also be consumed by the *pukara*, who would then provide rains to the pastures, contributing to the accumulation of fat in both herd animals and humans. The absence of fat—visible in the shrinking bodies of herd animals or in the tightened skirt strings of herders—was troubling, not only for individual bodies but also for the broader networks of relation in which those bodies were located. Given that the networks of relation facilitated by fat are the "basis of legitimate social reproduction," the stories of predatory fat-stealing beings like *pishtaco, kharasiri,* or *ñakaq* have been particularly terrifying for Andean peoples, and have historically been linked to the broader traumas of settler colonialism and land dispossession (Canessa 2000, 706; Weismantel 2001).

The centrality of blood in Concepción's and José's interpretations of her illness also brought to bear the multitude of connections between Concepción's body, her community, and the broader landscape. The term for "anemia" in Quechua, *pisi yawar* (*pisi*: little, *yawar*: blood), referenced the overall *volume* of blood rather than the lack of one component (hemoglobin) and related specifically to a lack of flow. This circulatory notion of health was described by anthropologist Joseph Bastien as a "topographical-hydraulic model of physiology" (1985). In this model, human bodily health is directly analogous to environmental health, since the basic circulatory structure of both is the same: both human bodies and landscapes contain the same hydraulic system through which vital substances—water, air, blood, and fat—flow. When a person or landscape is healthy, these substances are easily dispersed and circulate without obstruction. Sickness is thus the hydraulic disruption of these vital channels through which "fluids that provide emotions, thoughts, nutrients, and lubricants" flow (Bastien 1985, 598). This hydraulic interpretation of health was reflected in some of the treatments for increasing blood in Chillca, such as drinking *chicha de cebada*, which increased blood volume (*yawarchata yapan*), and, crucially, was always consumed in the company of others—with the first sip offered to the *pukara*.

Although Bastien referred to the relationship between bodies and landscapes as "metaphor" (1978), it is evident that bodies and landscapes are mutually emergent in material as well as symbolic ways. This suggests that bodies and landscapes are, rather, as Francisco Pazzarelli and Veronica Lema have recently proposed, "fractal reflections" of one another (2024). Whether human, nonhuman, or landscape, the materiality of the body acts as "a kind of conduit," the porosity of which allows animating substances, essences, and entities to pass between them (Allen 1982, 193). In Concepción's experience of health and illness, the transfer of substances and essences from one body to another had both proactive and reactive therapeutic qualities. Daily practices of herding, feeding, making offerings, and caring for others were essentially proactive therapeutic practices through which social beings maintained their well-being. When there were disruptions—in the form of disease or distress—this required therapeutic actions that "[mobilized] botanical, animal, mineral and sound pharmacopoeia" across those porous channels that intersected human, animal, and landscape bodies (Ferrié 2018, 155–56). Concepción's remedy for restlessness that opened chapter 3 was one such kind of therapeutic practice that mediated across human, animal, and landscape bodies to regulate the harmful impacts of restlessness, for example.

This isn't to say that people didn't also integrate biomedical interventions into their healing practices. Later that year, Concepción prepared another treatment, this time for me. One afternoon, I became suddenly and deliriously sick: unable to eat or drink, my vision became foggy and my hearing was replaced with a dizzying ringing. My illness was attributed to the frustration of chasing restless animals. In a clay pot, Concepción prepared a base of alpaca dung coals, on top of which she placed cobweb and lavender, wafting the smoke onto my face and into my hands. She rolled a leafy herb, *ufway suru*, in her hand until it leaked a bright-green juice, which she dripped into my ears. Before she left to tend to the animals, she placed two additional treatments next to my pillow: two tablets each of paracetamol and loperamide from the local health post. It is unlikely she would have done the same for her own children: perhaps, as a foreign body, mine required different methods and relations of intervention. Eventually, when my illness became acute, Concepción urged me to return to Cusco, where doctors discovered a robust colony of *blastocystis* living in my gut and prescribed me with an antiprotozoal pill. While the antiprotozoal did eventually eradicate my unwelcome parasitic guests and alleviate my discomfort, it couldn't address the root of the problem: my frustration (*rinyigu*). For that, I'd have to return to Chillca and attempt to rectify the strained relationship with the restless sheep.

Accumulating Frustration

This wasn't the first time I had been struck with frustration: a few weeks before, I woke up with a stiff neck, which Concepción and Emilia quickly identified as the result of *rinyigu*. And although this sounded vaguely

FIGURE 21 A young herder wrangles an uncooperative llama. Photo by author.

equivalent to a familiar etiology—acute stress causing muscular aches and pains—it wasn't quite as simple as that. Rather, frustration had altered my body: specifically, the *accumulation* of frustration in my body had caused an overall weakness. It had made me more susceptible to malevolent winds, which were the more likely cause of my illness. Emilia explained to me that frustration had a material weight to it, and when it accumulated in your body, it could disrupt your bodily functions— including the volume and flow of blood and the adherence and distribution of fat—causing you to become vulnerable to sickness. This disruption could wreak havoc on not only the individual body but also the broader social collective in which it resides, particularly, the other beings that individual cares for, nurtures, and feeds.

Similar relational understandings of sickness etiology have been explored within the pathologies of fright sickness (*susto, mancharisqa*), nerves (*nervios*), mental illness, and conditions caused by bad winds (*malviento, machu wayra, uraña*) (Greenway 1998; Orr 2013). In order to make sense of disease categories like *susto* that don't map onto conventional biomedical diagnoses, researchers have instead drawn attention to how these diseases articulate the inherent interconnection of bodies, households, communities, and landscapes, such that illnesses are "less the isolated manifestation of pathological symptoms within an individual than . . . a disturbance in the social relationships of which the sufferer forms a part" (Orr 2013, 695). While emotions like *rinyigu* had a potent materiality that resided within an individual body, their etiology could be better understood as an emergent quality of broader "sociality and social relations rather than as natural internal biological states" (Tapias 2006, 403). Given this etiology, biomedicine is often insufficient in addressing these conditions because its logics do not extend to broader social collectives or landscapes, and its specialists do not typically have expertise in mobilizing substances and essences between social entities.

Concepción always articulated a broader socioecological collective in her description of her own illnesses, as well as mine. While restless animals were often to blame, the conversation inevitably drifted to family members, neighbors, the broader community, as well as the landscape and weather phenomena. In my case, my illness was also a consequence of my being far away from my family and my home. I told my friends in Chillca about my own remedy for homesickness: I kept a sachet of pine needles in my backpack, the scent of which reminded me of the forests of my home. But for my friends, this was an especially wise, if unintentional, remedy for keeping my strength and health intact in a new place. When traveling between places, bringing "stones, earth or food from the place left behind" was a protective measure, in which "the powers from the place left behind are seen to work protectively against the dangers found in new surroundings" (Ødegaard 2018, 340; 2011). I was not yet accustomed to the people, animals, and landscape of Chillca, and they were not yet accustomed to me, rendering me particular vulnerable. As Cecilie Ødegaard has written, "the question of 'knowing'" in the Andes is often, rather, "a question of relating, through the interchange or flow of substances" (2018, 341). Having a piece of my home—and particularly, its scent—was considered an effective way of remaining healthy until I could come to know, and relate, with the Chillca landscape.

Even José, the healer, was quick to expand his description of Concepción's illness to implicate a broader collective. He did so by imploring that I make human health a central area of my study. "You have to study everything," he suggested. "Why do [people in Chillca] live fewer years? Why did the ancients live longer? They didn't know disease." I asked if he had any theories about the rising rates of illness he reported among the local population. He returned to the topic of food and linked it to the increase in pollution, plastics, and factories: "the food before was natural, well matured [*bien madurado*]. Now the diet . . . what they sow, the potatoes, aren't well ripened and, with all the pollution, it's poor [quality]. [The pollution] affects the plants; they don't mature as they should. That's why [people] no longer live like their grandparents. They're not strong anymore."

Both Jose's and Concepción's understanding of health—although articulated in different ways—emphasized the social and relational entanglements of human well-being. Indeed, anthropological approaches to illnesses like *susto* have likewise contextualized individual health within broader sociopolitical contexts in Latin America, such as general poverty in pre-Columbian and contemporary communities in Mexico (Mysyk 1998); structural adjustment reforms and associated poverty in Bolivia (Tapias 2006; 2015); and droughts and the lack of irrigation infrastructure in northeast Brazil (Rebhun 1994). This approach to understanding health as relational is reflective more broadly of critical medical anthropological approaches to structural violence and social suffering (Farmer 1996; 2004; 2009; Kleinman 1989; Scheper-Hughes 1993). Likewise, in Peru, the solution would need to be structural, as José continued. He critiqued the short-term medical campaigns that often visited places like Chillca: "They bring doctors. The doctor just looks at them. You have osteoarthritis, you have this, etc. That's not enough, *pe*. They must get to the root of the problem (*le den en el clavo, pe*)." He continued, this time implicating himself and his townspeople in his assessment: "We are practically surviving *no más pe*, as you see, like animals, *no más pe*. That's what we do. We go out, we wake up, [saying] 'what do I do, what do I do to look out for my belly?' You fill your belly in the afternoon and go to sleep. On to the next day."

Concepción's analysis wasn't quite as stark as José's, to which she listened with quiet deference and contemplation. She demurred when I asked her later that afternoon whether she agreed with him. Her priority was finding our ride back home—a cattle truck that would take us up the valley, back to the high pastures, where we could bring the animals in for the night and prepare the evening's meal.

✳

I reflected on our trip home that we had not talked about *gambiu wida* with the healer. I suspected that, because that *gambiu wida* was a condition specific to women, Concepción may have been hesitant to discuss it with José. However, I also noted that *gambiu wida*, as it was explained to Concepción, wasn't a condition that was amenable to any treatments other than those that she was already pursuing for *pisi yawar*. The health-worker at the health post in Chillca had told Concepción that she would simply have to endure *gambiu wida*, and that her symptoms would ease in a few years as she became more accustomed to her "changed life." There was no Quechua word for "menopause," and *gambiu wida* was a direct translation of the Spanish *cambio [de] vida*. It was presented as a distinct life phase, a shift from one part of a woman's life to another: in a pamphlet for Spanish-speaking healthworkers, the Ministerio de Salud translated "menopause" into Quechua in this way: "Juana está con la menopausia / Juanaqa *huk vidawanmi* kashan," literally, Juana is *with another life*.

The notion of menopause as a distinct phase of human life is integral to its biomedical definition as a temporary condition that coincides with the cessation of menstruation and the decline of ovarian function. It is often represented as a period of "degeneration" marked by biological nonreproductivity, and again linked with Western cultural ideas about the blood as the source of vitality (E. Martin 1991, 487). Anthropological research on menopause, however, has destabilized the idea that it represents a universal category of pathological experience, instead revealing its cultural construction (Lock 1995; Lock and Kaufert 2001). Gendered processes of aging are experienced differently throughout the world: as noted in the Japanese condition of *kônenki* (Lock 1995) or the Chinese condition *gengnianqi* (Shea 2020), women's experiences of aging can be long-term, transitional, and social rather than calibrated to a biological event. Symptoms of what we call menopause are heavily inflected by the sensations or experiences that are deemed the most salient, and that correspond to "beliefs about the functioning of the female body and its uses to society" (Lock and Kaufert 2001, 503). In other words, the boundaries of menopause are heavily shaped by cultural expectations of women: particularly women's roles as reproductive mothers, or as caretakers of children, elders, animals, plants, or landscapes.[4]

Concepción didn't consider herself to be entering into another phase of her life, per se, but she did acknowledge that her life was changing. Concepción's understanding of what was happening to her was indeed inextricably embedded within her role as a caretaker of humans and animals, as she noted in her assessment of her decreasing ability to take on practices of care. However, it wasn't so much a decline as it was a fragmentation. A fragmentation of her capacities to feed, be fed, and remain in relation to her animals and landscape. The bodily sensation that Concepción most associated with dying had been that tug, the odd sensation of being pulled backward into unconsciousness just as she was waking. This sensation fit with her general understanding of death as a protracted transition, a notion that is widespread throughout the Andes (Shimada and Fitzsimmons 2015). Beginning months or even years before their death, a person can experience a gradual loss of *animu* (the essence of the living), which slowly dissipates as the person's *alma* (the essence of the dead, often translated as "soul") begins to wander (Ricard Lanata 2007, 88). This dissipation is often palpable: as Catherine Allen suggested, based on ample ethnohistorical evidence of wandering souls in the Andes, "a living person, looking toward death, may recognize signs that his or her soul is wandering" (2015, 312). For Concepción, this was perhaps what she felt in that initial pull as she lay in her bed. And that is what scared her the most, the possibility that this was just the beginning of a longer unraveling. A final fragmentation.

Death and *Drying*

As I came to discover during my time in Chillca, older women talked often of death, and in Concepción's case, this question—what was it, to die?—loomed in her experience of illness. She had, of course, witnessed death in her life. She attributed her waning vision to how much she had cried over the death of her father and her sister, over her own children who had died in infancy. After they had died, she remembers how she had stopped eating and had begun to waste away until she was nursed back to health through her family, her herds, and her coca, which brought back her appetite. And, of course, she had experienced animal death in her life: the young animals that died of starvation or exposure, or were hauled off by a fox or condor, or the old and sick animals that were killed off to make that day's soup. Slaughtering animals was an everyday occurrence. It was often done in a dignified way: the alpacas' eyes were covered with a cloth to decrease their fear, and sometimes coca was placed in their mouth to accompany them on their journey. Death came quickly: the person butchering the alpaca made a swift cut to their abdomen through which they inserted their lower arm and severed the animal's aorta with a thumbnail. Accidental deaths, however, were considered tragic. Earlier in the year, Concepción had lost one of her prized female *suri* alpacas when the animal fell off a steep embankment. She was an older animal, and had reliably given birth to a *cría* almost every other year. Her death was a true tragedy, which Concepción recalled again and again as the animal's head toasted on the stove beside us.

When she articulated her fears around death, it was evident that Concepción was not afraid of pain or suffering, but the rupture of her relationality to her animals, her family, and her community. More than anything, she worried about being forgotten. As I mentioned in chapter 4, forgetting is a social act in the Andes, and upon parting, Andean people often plead the departing person not to forget them (Orlove 2002). In popular love songs, a lover's betrayal is expressed as their having forgotten (*qunqay*) their spurned partner. Older Quechua women like Concepción often articulated their sense of vulnerability in a changing world through the idiom of forgetting. In the songs Concepción sang for Chillca's town anniversary, she expressed her hope that her *waynus* would serve as a memento for her townspeople to remember her by ("may this little *waynu* that I sing be a memento for my town, when I've died, when I've gone"). In one iteration of a song she called "the Bells of Chillca," she rephrased the central theme as a question, asking "when I die, will the bells of Chillca toll for me?" The bells of Chillca were housed in the Catholic church at the town center, which had been in a state of disrepair for years. They were only rung in the event of a wedding or a funeral, but otherwise the structure remained bolted shut. Her question struck

FIGURE 22 A butchered alpaca. Photo by author.

me as a simple, evocative encapsulation of the fears that rooted in her generation, as people moved on and disentangled themselves from the people, animals, and places of Chillca, often departing the localities that used to serve as nexuses of its coherence. She asked the essential question about Chillca's future in a time of change—would the bells toll at all, and would anyone come?

She worried too about her animals—would they, too, be forgotten? Would they begin to forget her? The inability to care for herd animals has been noted elsewhere in the Andes as an constitutive part of a person's death. For example, anthropologist Francisco Pazzarelli wrote that

> with age (or illness), people lose their luck [*swirti*], as if it were fading, and it becomes increasingly difficult for them to take care of (*criar*) animals: the [animals] no longer pay attention and do not want to die in the hands of the elderly . . . Saying that herders cannot control their animals would be another way of saying that they cannot control themselves either. It could be said that, in these moments, the [herding capacities] of people begin

to be erased from this world. The *animu*, then, begins to detach; or, better yet, to *escape*. (2020, 104)

Perhaps we can say the herders' *swirti*, even their *animu*, itself becomes restless.

※

Here I return to my suggestion that a better way to understand Concepción's illness—her life change and her fears of death—is to embed it within the broader processes of restlessness that suffused her community and landscape. If we take health (human, animal, and landscape) as contingent upon practices of keeping beings in relation, the appearance of illness is likewise a signal of broader ecological instability. The shifting quantities of bodily substances like blood, fat, and synovial fluid were both the result *and* the cause of troubled relations between social beings. They signaled the unraveling of collaborative expectations and foretold a continued unraveling unless returned to a state of flow.

It is worth dwelling here in the interstitial spaces between bodies and landscapes where similar processes and distress erupt across socioecological connectivities. In particular, I was struck by the repeated references to a lack of flow, or, indeed, *drying*, as a process linked to that of death and dying. *Pisi yawar*, of course, referenced a lack of blood, as did *gambiu wida*. But even Concepción's assessment of the origin of her illness referenced an improper process of drying, making her more vulnerable to the cold. For José, it was the drying of synovial fluid, of bones and joints. This connection has emerged elsewhere: drawing on the ethnohistorical work of Frank Salomon (1998) and Billie Jean Isbell (1997), Catherine Allen described the widely held understanding in the Andes that the human body moves through stages, from "soft juiciness, to firm adulthood, to dry, seed-like old age, and then death" (2015, 355).

Taken literally, then, the "topographical-hydraulic model of physiology" proposed by Joseph Bastien urges us to consider how the drying of bodies (and their capacity as relational conduits) is emerging within the same historical and material processes of socioecological disruption that are drying the Andean landscape. In Chillca the looming white peak of

Ausangate brought constant reminders of the centrality of glacial water to the well-being of the people, animals, and the landscape. While the southern face of Ausangate still shone bright in 2016, surrounding mountains were starting to lose their ice, causing concern for future water availability. I heard mention of glacial retreat most often in the sectors of Phinaya, Killeta, Antaparara, and Qampa, located at the base of several peaks on which glacial retreat was much more visible. In these sectors, herders tied the darkening of white peaks explicitly to the future loss of lifegiving waters. As an older man in the sector of Antaparara noted, "The wetlands were nicer [in the past]. Now they are drying out." He gestured over to a nearby peak:

> On that white peak over there, the snow is disappearing. [See] how Ausangate is white, right? That's how those mountains used to be. Now they are melting bare, they are turning black . . . The water just isn't like it used to be. Then it will dry out, and there won't be any water [in the future].

Another herder in the sector of Qampa likewise expressed his concern, noting that the water was already diminishing, and it was getting more difficult to gather water for daily household use in the dry season. "When the snow disappears, how are we going to live?" He gestured to the peaks around us: "That part, around there, that was pure white. Those over there were totally white." He turned his attention to a small creek that ran alongside his pastures. "The water was plentiful, now it is little, look. Year after year, I don't know what is going to happen."

The erosion of glacial cover was a grave loss both materially and socially. The centrality of water, and the prevalence of water-related concerns, is evident throughout the high Andes (Brandshaug 2019; Stensrud 2019; Paerregaard 2023). Malene Brandshaug coined the term "aguasociality" to articulate how people in the central Andes are "intimately entangled with the world through water—socially, emotionally, and materially" (2021, 62). The power of water, like blood, resides in its heterogeneity and multiplicity as an "animate substance" that also serves as a "life source [connecting] humans, plants, animals, and spirit" (Stensrud 2016, 86). And when it is threatened, that threat is fractal, extending far into the surrounding community. In a place where the materiality of water and the kinetics of flow are quite literally the conditions of life, water loss is

FIGURE 23 Chillca's glacial waters. Photo by author.

not only personal, emotional, and embodied, but ontological. If water is life, then the consequences of death and drying are the same.

The Bells of Chillca

Concepción did not die that year. In fact, she is very much alive as I write this book. I'd find her, seven years later, still herding her animals in Illachiy—but that is a story for the epilogue. Concepción's mother, Emilia, however, did pass away a few years after I left Chillca in 2016. She was found in the pasture, resting on the bulk of her carrying cloth as if sleeping. Her herd—many of whom were the animals of her daughter, Nikolasa, who had died in the lightning storm—was divided among her children and grandchildren, and the animals continued to reproduce and grow in the pastures of Uqi Kancha.

For now, I want to dwell on the potential to *be well*, or indeed *heal*, in this context. Expanding the "social" to include landscapes in the Andes compels us to consider emergent illnesses and discomforts as inherently linked with climate change in ways that simultaneously impact multiple intersecting bodies. Quechua ontologies of relatedness ground individual bodies within broader collectives that are both social and ecological: an individual body's well-being is dependent upon that broader collective. This inextricability is captured in the concept *allin kawsay* or *sumak kawsay* (translated into Spanish as *buen vivir*) which has recently emerged as a key political ideology and discursive phenomenon across the Andean countries. When encoded in policy, *buen vivir* reinterprets Quechua and Kichwa understandings of socioecological relationality to emphasize ideals of reciprocity, social justice, and sustainability within legal and political spheres (Hidalgo-Capitán and Cubillo-Guevara 2017). Notably, *buen vivir* was drafted into Ecuador's 2008 constitution as a deliberate pivot away from neoliberal, capitalist policies of the previous political administrations toward "a new social pact" (Caria and Domínguez 2016; Radcliffe 2012). There is increasing political recognition that to be well is to be kept in relation to the multitude of human and nonhuman beings with which we sustain our world. Quechua women in Chillca understood this viscerally and experientially, as evidenced by their interpretation of their bodies as deeply entangled within a broader socioecological community, the fragmentation of which had real physical, emotional, and social consequences.

Which returns us again to the potentialities of healing. As disability scholar and activist Sunaura Taylor suggests, recognizing ecologies as injured or disabled can "generate mobilizations that utilize conditions of vulnerability, interdependency, and impairment to build more just worlds" (2024, 24). More just worlds, in which we recognize that human life is not premised upon independence and productivity but inextricably rooted in interdependence and reciprocity. *K'ita*, restlessness—in all its teeming and fragmented agitation—underscores the relations of mutual care, nurturing, and cultivation that hold ecologies together, even in the face of unyielding alterity. The crux is sustaining those nodes of relation, and the practices that hold them in relation.

Concepción herself was incredibly skilled at those practices of relation: mobilizing relations between beings through the therapeutic transference of essences and substances across porous bodies. She did this whenever she brought her animals to the pastures, or fed her family, prepared her *phukuy* each morning, or lovingly administered medicinal therapies—whether burning pumpkin seeds for her sheep, pouring chicha down her alpacas' throats, dripping *ufway suru* in my ears, or placing Tylenol on my pillow. Her children did it too, like when Mario brought irrigation water to Concepción's corral and simultaneously eased his mother's distress. As Elizabeth Cartwright suggested in her work on *susto* and related illnesses in Oaxaca, Mexico, healing often implies not only "curing bodies," but also restoring and sustaining "households, social relationships, and living environments" (Cartwright 2007, 527).

A looming question remains around water, and the future implications of drying bodies and landscapes. In the high Andes, the potentiality of future healing hinges critically on the availability of water, particularly glacial water. Water sovereignty and stewardship will become increasingly critical for glacier-dependent communities. And, as herders live and age in the high Andes, sustaining those socioecological pathways through which vital substances and essences travel—waterways and wetlands, as well as hearths, homes, and broader communities—will be essential for mitigating and alleviating the suffering of both bodies and landscapes. As much as fragmentation continues to pull this landscape and its bodies apart from one another, the flow of water—in all its fluid potentiality as well as its hastening retreat—continuously pulls them back together into collaboration.

When I left her, in August of 2016, Concepción implored me not to forget her and her family. I took this not as a sentimental plea but as a reminder of the "ecology of obligations" (Despret and Meuret 2016) that held me in relation to her, the Rojo family, and the community of Chillca—and also those who hold us all in relation to each other, and to this world more broadly. It was also a reminder to keep people like Concepción and communities like Chillca centered in the broader discussion around potential futures on a shifting planet. In their continued efforts to *puriy*—to endure, and to seek new forms of connection in the face of tension, uncertainty, and fragmentation—herders in Chillca do the arduous and continuous working of striving to be "in good relation" (TallBear 2019), and thereby re-create the conditions of their collective survival in the high Andean grasslands.

CHILLCA CANPANITA (THE BELLS OF CHILLCA)
Kay waynuchallata tukayaramusaq
Kay waynuchallata takiyaramusaq

Wañuqtiy ripuqtiy waqashanankupaq
Llaqtaypi runalla waqayushananpaq

Nuqa ripuqtiyqa
Nuqa wañuqtiyqa
Nuqa ripuqtiyqa
Nuqa wañuqtiyqa
Chillca turrichacha waqayamushanqa
Tukaqqa takiqqa wañukunmi, nispa

Imas kutimuyman
Hayk'as chayamuyman
Imas kutimuyman
Hayk'as chayamuyman
Hallp'aq uhunmanta imas kutimuyman
Hallp'aq chawpinmanta hayk'aq chayamuyman

I'll play this little *waynu*
I'll sing this little *waynu*
To accompany the crying mourners, when I've died, when I've left
To accompany my townspeople as they cry

When I've left
When I've died
When I've left
When I've died
Chillca's tower will be crying out
Saying the musician, the singer has died

How could I come back?
When would I return?
How could I come back?
When would I return?
From the depths of the earth, how could I come back?
From beneath the soil, when would I return?

Epilogue
Returning, 2023

"Huqllatachu kuidashanki?!" the woman called to Concepción as we walked toward the hamlet of Antapata from Chillca. "You're raising another one?!" I knew the woman—her name was Julia, and her husband was a cousin of Concepción's—but she didn't recognize me from her perch above the pasture. Seven years later, my *pullira* and *sumbriru* were replaced by jeans and a baseball cap. I wore glasses now, and my hair was tumbled into a single braid that hid beneath the collar of my jacket. On the cattle truck earlier that day, I'd overheard two women discuss whether I was a man or a woman. "*Warmi*, a woman, I think? Look, her braid is there, hidden."

"Mana, ususichaylla chayamuranlla!" Concepción called back. "No, my little daughter has returned!" A flash of recognition crossed Julia's face as she waved back from the hillside. I had come back for a short visit in May 2023. A lot had changed in seven years: when I left Chillca in 2016, Barack Obama was still president of the United States and Ollanta Humala was the president of Peru. In the seven years since, both countries had undergone a politically tumultuous period. When I arrived in 2023, Peru had just recently descended into a series of protests and violent crackdowns that left forty-nine people dead and unearthed a deep and painful substrate of racism and anti-Indigenous sentiment across the country. The tension continued to linger in the air, as did the uncertainty as to if or when the wounds would be recognized, if ever remedied.

Chillca had managed to weather the COVID-19 pandemic with minimal contagion and mercifully not a single death. We discussed the similarities and differences of our experiences. Mostly, we ruminated on the uncertainty of it all as the pandemic unfolded: not knowing exactly how the virus was transmitted, when it would reach us, and who it might take. Of course, our experiences differed tremendously in terms of our access to health care, social services, and the economic resources necessary to sustain us during the pandemic. Whatever valley of uncertainty I had experienced had been a canyon for people in Chillca: news came in slowly, inconsistently, and full of confusion; the vaccine was late to arrive; and some members of the community felt that they had received minimal support from the regional and national government. The international humanitarian wing of the Seventh-day Adventist Church, the Adventist Development and Relief Agency (ADRA), stepped into the vacuum to provide food assistance and build new houses throughout the Ausangate valley. Most of Chillca's families had moved out of their stone-and-thatch homes into new adobe homes with solar panels, indoor lighting, and passive solar heating. According to most people in Chillca, it was an undeniable improvement, although they felt more ambivalent about the large "ADRA" letters the organization had carved into the hillside above the town.

The biggest change in Chillca, of course, had been the community's decision to divide their lands into individual parcels (*parcelas*) after all. The process began not long after I left, and those whom I talked to described it as a painful period involving roughly twenty-four contentious assemblies over the course of six months. It was decided that every community member who was *empadronado* was entitled to a parcel, and that the households in each sector would decide how to divide their lands equitably. Of course, not everyone agreed that the process unfolded as it should have. Community members who were *empadronado* longer were given larger parcels than those who were more recently incorporated. Several of Chillca's younger residents who hadn't yet gone through *empadronamiento* were left on a waiting list. Some thought that they should have received larger parcels because of their family history in the community. Some received parcels with bountiful wetlands, while others had smaller and drier parcels. Community members yelled, cried, and feuded in the assemblies, but finally they managed to reach an agreement and began running fences along the newly drawn *parcela* borders. "It was shocking," one woman described. "You couldn't walk through the hillsides like before; there were fences everywhere." New roads snaked up the hillsides so that *comuneros* could reach the most remote parcels on motorcycle. The community alpaca herd, the *majada*, was dissolved: each *empadronado* received a couple dozen alpacas, and the rest were sold off to help pay for the construction of the roads and other community projects.

I encountered Antapata as a patchwork. Concepción's parcel included half of the flat pampa of Antapata, and her beloved Illachiy, which I noted with relief. In fact, many people I talked to in the sector of Chillca were satisfied with their parcels. They agreed it was a drastic change in the beginning, but they had become accustomed to herding their animals within their own landholdings. The biggest improvement was the ability to pursue novel forms of *mejoramiento*: of pasture (seeding pastures; removing rocks, prickly plants, and other obstructions; irrigating dry hillsides and expanding the wetlands) and of animals (buying new stud males from Macusani and Puno, the second generation of whose descendants were just being born). Concepción's herd had grown, as had Mario and Maritza's, whose parcel was in the glacial valley surrounding their residence in Uqi Kancha. Those lucky enough to have large and ecologically diverse parcels were able to rotate their herds within their pastures and build additional herding camps and enclosures, and they could do so without coordinating with their neighbors or the broader community. Some community members had multiple landholdings: one which held their pastures and their homes, another their potato farm, and another their reserved enclosure (*tullu kancha*), and they could circulate between the three.

However, from the perspective of the older generation of women herders, the work of herding had become much lonelier. They no longer met spontaneously with other herders in the pasture, stopping to rest, share food, and weave together on the hillsides. There were no more hurried conversations volleyed from across the valley as herders prepared to take their animals out for the day. And they could no longer leave their animals with a neighbor herding in the same valley—the system of *valikamuy* required one herder to leave their parcel for another, which was much more complicated and usually required payment. They didn't overlap with their family members and neighbors in seasonal herding locations where they could share food, care, and labor. And they no longer visited the places they knew so well: Concepción no longer herded in the valleys of Hatun Wayq'u, which now belonged to her neighbor, and she seldom visited Warmi Saya or Palumani up in Uqi Kancha. She wondered if future generations of the Rojo family would know the history, or even just the names, of those places.

If there was anything I learned about being-in-relation during my time in Chillca, it was that living in community is hard. It is constant, tiring, and emotionally fraught work. For all the people who may romanticize the idea of "community," there are many people that would prefer to detach themselves from it. And yet communal management—of resources, knowledge, and care networks—has proven to be a powerful adaptive strategy in the face of many forms of social, ecological, and economic uncertainty. As they navigate a new form of community, the people of Chillca have already begun to forge new practices of collaboration, exchange, and connection in order to circulate resources and knowledge across a fragmented landscape. Instead of coordinating herding migrations, they rent pastures from one another. Community members who are not *empadronado* often leave some of their animals in the larger parcels of their parents. Chillca still had monthly assemblies and periodically held communal work events like the yearly vicuña *chaku* as well as NGO-headed development projects. While *empadronados* no longer paid fees for missing work events, they did still pay fees to the community if their animals repeatedly crossed parcel boundaries. Instead of an irrevocable rupture and fragmentation, I found that new agreements continued to circulate animals, labor, food, and cash, albeit in different ways. Despite some fears, the community of Chillca was still there, still in relation.

※

There is no doubt, however, for both herders and for climate scientists, that people living in the high elevation, glacier-dependent communities of the Andes continue to face a precarious situation. The conditions of that precarity manifest in different ways, depending on the modes of identification and methods of evaluation through which they are made legible. For climate scientists, a clear trajectory of atmospheric temperature increase, glacial retreat, fluctuating precipitation, and shifting ecozones has altered the conditions of life in the Andes, with stark implications for the future. By midcentury, they've estimated, the earth's climate will shift outside the historical range of variability, and the high tropical Andes will be among the first places where the regionalized effects of this epochal shift will become palpably and terrifyingly legible. For herders in Chillca, the conditions of precarity manifest in and through the daily and seasonal spatial practices of animal husbandry and pastoralism, through which they read the traces—the palpable, exposed, and observable *sut'i*—of change. Herders detect trouble in the breakdown of communicative practices between humans, animals, and landscapes. As the rain-fed grasses of the wet season sprout later than usual, the animals become thinner and more agitated. While embarking on their daily herding routes, the animals are increasingly difficult to work with, as predictable forms of cooperative labor break down. Sheep scatter, and alpacas and llamas wander across sectoral boundaries and into reserved pastures, flaunting the established norms of the herders and the regulations of the broader community and leading to human conflict. As drought conditions increase in the southern Peruvian Andes, human-animal communication is a powerful form of knowledge production, and the failure of these interspecies communicative practices indexes the potential for chaotic futures.

In trying to make sense of these changes, I have drawn from the Quechua concept of *k'ita* as a powerful analytic for understanding the world as it is shifting under the conditions of climate change. Restlessness, *k'ita*, neatly articulates the confluence of temporal, spatial, and relational qualities that define precarity in a time of climate change. I draw on an ontological definition of precarity (Han 2018) that emphasizes interdependence as a necessary condition of embodied human life, and I underscore the condition of precarity as a result of the failure of relational networks and the refusal of entities to stay in relation with one another (Butler 2006; 2009). In Southern Quechua ontologies, to be is to be-in-relation: the conditions of precarity emerge in the weakening, severing, or shifting of the significant binds that keep social worlds intact. For Quechua herders, the various components of their world are no longer staying in a recognizable configuration of place and time. Rains no longer arrive at the right time: they fail to quench the grasses at the end of the wet season, and unexpectedly putrefy the potato harvest in the dry season. The sun burns hotter, and the wind blows harder. Animals run off, no longer adhering to the conventional codes of conduct that sustain hierarchical forms of relationality. In detecting these signals of failed relationality in the interactions between humans and animals, herders articulate their own well-being as deeply embedded and emergent within these broader socioecological collectives. Shifts in engagement between humans, animals, and landscapes reveal the rifts in these configurations, and threaten the material and social rupture of livelihoods and communities.

We can see traces of restlessness elsewhere, as phenomena come untethered from their expected and anticipated positions in time and space, and predictable forms of relationality between beings and entities become increasingly elusive. From delayed and absent rains in the Andes, to rapidly melting permafrost and the accelerated collapse of ice shelves in the Arctic, to the shifting migratory patterns and life cycles of some species and the extinction of others. The spatiotemporal shifts of various entities and phenomena mark the global breadth of ruptured relationalities. These shifts put into doubt our ability to make sense of our world, to predict its qualities and respond in turn. And this has implications for how we all will orient ourselves in relational ecologies.

And yet the notion of restlessness leaves the state of things rather open-ended, making room for the endurance of certain ties and the creation of others within historically situated ecologies. It is not quite Donna Haraway's "Chthulucene," for example, an epochal shift through which all beings and entities on the planet become melded into a vast, monstrous compost pile of vibrant "intra-active entities-in-assemblages" (2015, 160; 2016). We can't assume all-encompassing connectivity, nor can we assume complete disconnection: some beings and entities will return from their restless wanderings (the sheep did eventually come home, for example), while other entities will continue to resist their entanglement with others (herders did move to parcelize their lands after all).

I hold us back from apocalyptic notions of Chillca as a community on the verge of collapse, however. Indeed, there has been a widespread assumption—by now heavily critiqued (Bettini 2013; Boas et al. 2019)—

that Indigenous communities throughout the world will face inevitable displacements, relocation, or dissolution as their landscapes bear the brunt of ecological change. This might appear to be the logical end result of *k'ita*, of restlessness—an irrevocable fragmentation that was powerfully punctuated by the barbed wire that marked the enclosure of the commons. However, I want to again emphasize the continued practices of relation that endured through disruption in Chillca. The defeatist inevitability of apocalyptic narratives overlook Indigenous and localized practices—like montane transhumance, seasonal rounds (Whyte, Talley, and Gibson 2019), circular labor mobility (Hirsch 2018; Zickgraf 2022), place-making practices (Farbotko 2022), and "caretaking relations" (Tall-Bear 2019)—that resist the sedentary and fatalistic logics of settler colonialism in many parts of the world (Boas et al. 2022; Hirsch 2023). While projections of climate change often emphasize Indigenous people's vulnerabilities, it is critical to engage with the narratives of hope, persistence, and ingenuity that urge us all to seek out more just, interdependent, and collaborative futures in a restless world.

※

When I stepped out of the car into Chillca's town center in May 2023, Concepción and I embraced for a long time. We were both relieved to find the other person healthy: she looked stronger, I mentioned; I looked fatter, she mentioned. I talked about my children, who were two and four years old by then. She talked about her children: her oldest son, Jorge, had married his long-term partner the previous year, Mario and Maritza had two girls now, and her daughter Vilma had found a kind man in Pitumarca with whom she had a five-year-old daughter. Concepción, as always, was quick to fret: "Here I am, walking around like a corpse," she said, as her children chuckled and shook their heads. When I left, she implored that I come back soon, that I wouldn't let seven years pass like last time. She reassured me, in the Quechua tradition of leave-taking, that she'd be there: "Tupananchiskama," she said. "Until we meet again."

FIGURE 24 Concepción in 2023. Photo by author.

Appendix

Concepción's Waynus

I. Chillca

Chillcapata llaqtayqa	My town Chillca
Ima munayta llanllashan	How lovely it is sprouting
Chillcapata llaqtayqa	My town Chillca
Ima munayta phallchishan	How lovely it is blooming
T'ikachahina llanllashan	Like a little flower
Ima munayta llanllashan	How lovely it is sprouting
T'ikachahina phallchishan	Like a little flower
Ima munayta phallchishan	How lovely it is blooming
Ima munayta llanllashan	How lovely it is sprouting
Chayhinallataq nuqapas	And just like that, I also
T'ikachahina wiñani	Grow like a little flower
Chayhinallataq nuqapas	And just like that, I also
Llaqtay kikichan kashani	I am quite like my town itself
Ima munayta wiñani	How lovely I grow
T'ikachahina wiñani	Like a little flower I grow
Llaqtay kikichan kashani	I am my town itself
T'ikachahina wiñani	I grow like a little flower
T'ikachahina wiñani	I grow like a little flower

Chillca pampata qhawarispa	Gazing upon Chillca pampa
Piru amamá waqankichu	Oh, but don't you cry
Llaqtachallayta rikuruspa	Seeing my town
Piru amamá llakinkichu	Oh, but don't become sad
Chillca pampata qhawariqtiyki	When you gaze upon Chillca pampa
Waqay waqayraq hap'isunki	Crying will overcome you
Llaqtachallayta rikuruqtiyki	Seeing my little town
Sunquchaykiraq nananqa	Your heart will hurt
Waqay waqayraq hap'isunki	Crying will overcome you
Uyachallayta rikuruspa	Upon seeing my face,
Piru amamá waqankichu	Oh, but don't you cry
Karachallayta qhawarispa	Gazing upon my face
Piru amamá llakinkichu	Oh, but don't become sad
Uyachallayta rikuruqtiyki	Gazing upon my face
Sunquchaykiraq nanaqa	Your heart will hurt
Karachallayta qhawariqtiyki	Gazing upon my face
Waqay waqayraq hap'isunki	Crying will overcome you
Sunquchaykiraq nananqa	Your heart will hurt
Ausangati q'uchaman rumichalla chhanqasqay	Having tossed a pebble in Ausangate lake
Ausangati q'uchaman rumichalla wikch'usqay	Having thrown a pebble in Ausangate lake
Maytaq kunankamari kutiramusqan-kich	And (until now) where have you been coming back to?
Maytaq kunankamari vueltaramus-qankichu	And (until now) where have you been returning to?
Kutiramusqankichu	Have you come back?
Chayhinallataq	And like that,
Taytamamay maytaq kutimushanchu	To where are my parents coming back?
Chayhinallataq	Just like that
Mamataytay maytaq wiltamushanchu	To where are my parents returning?
Sapachallay sulachallay	All alone, all on my own
Kay llaqtapi tarikuni	I find myself in this town
Kay llaqtapi rikukuni	I see myself in this town
Kay llaqtapi rikukuni	I see myself in this town

Pipas kashachun	With whomever accompanies me,
Maypis kashachun	And wherever I may be,
Kay waynuypiraq tusuylla tusuyusaq	I will still just dance, dance this *waynu*
Pipas kashachun	With whomever accompanies me,
Maypis kashachun	And wherever I may be,
Kay waynuypiraq takiylla takiyusaq	I will still just sing, sing this *waynu*.

II. Agustu Wayrahina

Yachayurankitaq, sabiyurankitaq
Yachayurankitaq, sabiyurankitaq
Agustu wayrachahina luku kasqaytaqa
Fibriru killachahina waq'a kasqaytaqa

Yachayushaspayki
Sabiyushaspayki
Yachayushaspayki
Sabiyushaspayki
Amacha urpischay waqachiwankimanchu
Amacha sambuschay llakichiwankimanchu

Taytayman mamayman willayapuwanki
Mamayman taytayman willayapuwanki
Warmi wawaykiqa ripushanmi, nispa
Warmi wawaykiqa pasashanmi, nispa

Hinaya ripuchun, nispa niwaqtinqa
Hinaya pasachun, nispa niwaqtinqa
Wichaypas uraypas ripukapunaypaq
Uraypas wichaypas pasakapunaypaq

Rasunta mamay niwaran
Rasunta taytay niwaran
Nuqaña mayta ripuqtiyqa
Maypiraq kallin kallincha
Maypiraq wasin wasincha

Rasunta taytay niwaran
Rasunta mamay niwaran
Nuqaña mana kallaqtiyqa
Maypiraq wasin wasincha
Maypiraq kallin kallincha

You must have known, you may have known
You must have known, you may have known
That I was crazy like the August winds
That I was mad like the month of February

In having known this
In having realized this
In having known this
In having realized this
Don't make me cry, my dove
Don't make me sad, my *sambu*

You'd tell on me to my father and mother,
You'd tell on me to my mother and father,
Saying, "Your daughter is leaving."
Saying, "Your daughter is going away."

Let her go, they'll say about me
Let her go, they'll say about me,
So that I'd go away, ascending and descending
So that I'd leave, descending and ascending

My mother told me the reason
My father told me the reason
Where must I be going
Along which roads
In which neighborhoods

My mother told me the reason
My father told me the reason
Where I mustn't be going

In which neighborhoods
Along which roads

III. Ausangate

Ausangatita qhawarinkichu	Do you gaze upon Ausangate?
Llaqtay lumata qhawarinkichu	Do you gaze upon the hills of my town?
Yanayarintaq yuraqyarintaq	Through black and white
Wayrarimuntaq phuyurimuntaq	Through the winds and clouds
Chayhinallataq nuqapas kani	Just like that, so am I
Así lo mismo nuqapas kani	Just the same, so am I
Ripusaq nini	I'll leave, I say
Pasasaq nini	I'll go, I say
Karu llaqtata ripusaq nini	I'll leave to a faraway town, I say
Ripushaniñan, pasashaniñan	I'm already leaving, I'm already going
Ripushaniñan, pasashaniñan	I'm already leaving, I'm already going
Llaqtamasiypa waqachiwasqan	My fellow townspeople having made me cry
Llaqtamasiypa chiqnikuwasqan	My fellow townspeople having spited me
Ripushaniñan, pasashaniñan	I'm already leaving, I'm already going
Ripushaniñan, pasashaniñan	I'm already leaving, I'm already going
Chillca llaqta dispidikuyki	Chillca town, I say goodbye to you
Chillca llaqta saqirisayki	Chillca town, I will leave you behind
Pitumarka pwintisitucha	Dear Pitumarca bridge
Pitumarka pwintisitucha	Dear Pitumarca bridge
Allillamanta pasarachiway	Let me pass safely
Allillamanta chinparachiway	Let me cross safely
Chinpachapiña willarukusayki	Upon having crossed, I'll tell you
Chinpachapiña willarukusayki	Upon having crossed, I'll tell you
Llaqtamasiypa waqachiwasqanta	Of how my fellow townspeople made me cry
Llaqtamasiypa sufrichiwasqanta	Of how my fellow townspeople made me suffer

Pitumarquiñu sultiritucha	Dear Pitumarca bachelor
Pitumarquiñu sultiritucha	Dear Pitumarca bachelor
Llikllachaytapas hap'ikushaspas	Tugging on my little shawl
Amurchallayta kutichipuway	Return my little affections

Qaparit'i mayutari qhunchuntintachu tumarani	Did I drink from the ice of Qaparit'i river?
Ripuy pasay nishaspapas	So that, while saying "leave, go"
Manalla ripuy atinaypaq	I just couldn't leave
Manalla pasay atinaypaq	I just couldn't go

Qaparit'i unutari laq'intintachu uharani	Did I drink from the spring of Qaparit'i's waters?
Pasay ripuy nishaspapas	So that, while saying "leave, go"
Manalla pasay atinaypaq	I just couldn't go
Manalla ripuy atinaypaq	I just couldn't leave

IV. Ausangatiman Phuyu Tiyayun

Ausangatiman
Phuyu tiyayun qunqaylla
Llaqtay urquta
Phuyu muyumun wayrantin
Chaypa chawpinpi puriyushani nuqaqa
Así es mi vida, así es mi suerte soltero

Haqay chinpa Ausangatiman phuyu tiyayamun
Imaraq viday? Hayk'araq swirtiy?

Haqay urquta
Kuntur muyumun phuyuntin
Llaqtay urquta
Kuntur muyumun wayrantin
Chayllatapis qhawawaqmá chulitu
Chayllatapis qhawawaqmá ingratu

Imallamantaq purishanri, nirani
Hayk'allamantaq hamushanri, nirani
Alpacaytaña mikhuruspa hamusqa
Uwihaytaña mikhuruspa hamusqa

Yanqallanpaqcha ganadira karani
Yanqallanpaqcha alpakira karani
Imanasaqtaq kunanpachari chulitu
Hayk'anasaqtaq kunanpachari ingratu

Imanasaqtaq kunanpachari turachay
Hayk'anasaqtaq kunanpachari ñañachay
Mamataytaycha ripuy, niwanqa turachay
Taytamamaycha pasay, niwanqa ñañachay

On Ausangate
The clouds suddenly settle
My mountain town
Is encircled in clouds and wind
I am walking in the middle of it
That is my life, that is my lonely luck

The clouds settle before me on Ausangate
What of my life? What of my luck?

On yonder mountain
The condor circles in the clouds
Over my mountain town
The condor circles in the wind
Just like that you'd watch me, *cholito*
Just like that you'd watch me, ungrateful one

Where, oh where is he walking, I said
When, oh when is he coming, I said
Only my alpaca, grazing, has come
Only my sheep, grazing, has come

Perhaps in vain I was a herder
Perhaps in vain I was an alpaquera
Whatever will I do now, *cholito*
However will I be now, ungrateful one

Whatever will I do now, brother
However will I be now, sister
Go home to mother and father, my brother will tell me
Get home to mother and father, my sister will tell me

V. Chillca Q'inqu Mayu

Chillca pampaschallay
Q'inqu mayuschallay
Chillca pampaschallay
Q'inqu mayuschallay
Maytataq apanki warmayanallayta
Maytataq apanki warmayanallayta

Uranpas qaqataq
Hawanpas mayutaq
Uranpas qaqataq
Hawanpas mayutaq
Mayninta pasaspan
Yanaywan tupayman
Mayninta pasaspan
Yanaywan tupasaq

Siyilupi quyllurcha
K'anchaykamullaway
Siyilupi ch'askascha
K'anchaykamullaway
Mamataytallayman chayarapunaypaq
Taytamamallayman chayarapunaypaq

Taytayri mamayri
Imanawanqataq
Mamayri taytayri
Hayk'aniwanqataq
Kay runaq llaqtanpin tutayachikuni
Kay runaq llantanpin sapay rikukuni

Suyayki suyayki
Bandurriayta tukaspa
Suyayki suyayki
Wifanuchayta tukaspa
Manaña chayamuqtiyki
Wawqichaykiwan ripuni
Manaña chayamuqtiyki
Runaq llaqtanta ripuni

Manaña chayamuqtiyki
runaq llaqtanta ripuni

My dear pampas of Chillca
My dear Q'inqu river
My dear pampas of Chillca
My dear Q'inqu river
Where are you taking my young beloved?
Where are you taking my young beloved?

Down by the cliffs
Up by the river
Down by the cliffs
Up by the river
Where, wandering
Would I find my beloved?
Where, wandering
Will I find my beloved?

Little Venus in the sky
Shine down on me

Little star in the sky
Shine down on me
So that I can arrive to my mother and father
So that I can arrive to my father and mother

My father and my mother,
What will they do to me?
My mother and father,
What will they do to me?
I spend the night in a stranger's town
I find myself alone in a stranger's town

I wait for you, I wait for you
Playing my bandurria
I wait for you, I wait for you
Playing my *wifanu*
If you don't come
I'll leave with your brother
If you don't come
I'll leave to another town

If you don't come
I'll leave to another town

VI. Bandurriay (My Bandurria)

Bandurriay waqayamuya
Chay kunkaykiwan waqayamuya
Phinaya llaqtaq anivirsariunpaq
Chillca llaqtaq fiyistachallanpaq

Bandurriay waqayamuya
Chay kunkaykiwan waqayamuya
Phinaya llaqtaq anivirsariunpaq
Chillca llaqtaq fiyistachallanpaq

Waqayusqayki tukayusqayki
Waqayusqayki tukayusqayki
Llaqtaypa rikwirduchanpaq
Chhallukuqtiyki ñut'ukuqtiyki
Waqayusqayki tukayusqayki
Waqayusqayki tukayusqayki
Llaqtaypa rikwirduchanpaq
Chhallukuqtiyki ñut'ukuqtiyki

Kay waynuchalla takiyusqaytaq
Kay qinachalla takiyusqaytaq
Llaqtaypa rikwirduchaypaq
Wañuqtiy ripukapuqtiy

Tukayusqayqa takiyusqayqa
Tukayusqayqa takiyusqayqa
Llaqtaypa rikwirduchanpaq
Wañuqtiy ripukapuqtiy

Carrituy suyayullaway
Carrituy suyayullaway
Llaqtayman aparapullaway
Llaqtayman aparapullaway
Carrituy suyayullaway
Carrituy suyayullaway
Llaqtayman aparapullaway
Llaqtayman aparapullaway

My bandurria, cry out to me
With your throat, cry out to me
For Phinaya town's anniversary
For Chillca town's celebration

My bandurria, cry out to me
With your throat, cry out to me
For Phinaya town's anniversary
For Chillca town's celebration

That which you've cried out, that which you've played
That which you've cried out, that which you've played
May it be a little memory for my town
That which you've broken, that which you've crumbled
That which you've cried, that which you've played
That which you've cried, that which you've played
May it be a little memento for my town
That which you've broken, that which you've crumbled

Perhaps this little *waynu* that I've sung
Perhaps this little *qina* that I've sung
Will be my little memento for my town
When I've died, when I've left

That which I've played, that which I've sung
That which I've played, that which I've sung
May it be a memento for my town
When I've died, when I've left

My little car, wait for me
My little car, wait for me
Take me back to my town
Take me back to my town
My little car, wait for me
My little car, wait for me
Take me back to my town
Take me back to my town

VII. Chillca Canpanita

Kay waynuchallata tukayaramusaq
Kay waynuchallata takiyaramusaq
Wañuqtiy ripuqtiy waqashanankupaq
Llaqtaypi runalla waqayushananpaq

Nuqa ripuqtiyqa
Nuqa wañuqtiyqa

Nuqa ripuqtiyqa
Nuqa wañuqtiyqa
Chillca turrichacha waqayamushanqa
Tukaqqa takiqqa wañukunmi, nispa

Nuqa wañuqtiyqa
Nuqa ripuqtiyqa
Nuqa wañuqtiyqa
Nuqa ripuqtiyqa
Chillca canpanita waqayamushanqa
Tukaqqa takiqqa wañukunmi, nispa

Adius niway sanbu
Dispidiway ninru
Adius niway sanbu
Dispidiway ninru
Manañas ichaqa kutimusaqñachu
Manañas ichaqa chayamusaqñachu

Imas kutimuyman
Hayk'as chayamuyman
Imas kutimuyman
Hayk'as chayamuyman
Hallp'aq uhunmanta imas kutimuyman
Hallp'aq chawpinmanta hayk'aq chayamuyman

I'll just play this little *waynu*
I'll just sing this little *waynu*
To accompany the crying mourners, when I've died, when I've left,
To accompany my townspeople as they cry

When I've left
When I've died
When I've left
When I've died
Chillca's tower will be crying out
Saying the musician, the singer has died

When I've died
When I've left
When I've died
When I've left
Chillca's bells will be crying out
Saying the musician, the singer has died

Tell me goodbye, *sambu*
Bid me farewell, *negro*
Tell me goodbye, *sambu*
Bid me farewell, *negro*
I'll never be coming back again
I'll never be returning again

How could I come back?
When would I return?
How could I come back?
When would I return?
From the depths of the earth, how could I come back?
From beneath the soil, when would I return?

VIII. Palumani Urqu (Palumanu Hill)

Palumani urqutaqa	On Palumani mountain
Warmi saya q'asataqa	On Warmi Saya pass
Yana phuyu wasayamun	Dark clouds pass over
Aqarapi chakichayuq	Walking in the frozen dew
Iphu para chakichayuq	Walking in the mist
Chay phuyuq chawpichallanpi	Amid those clouds
Chay rit'iq k'anchallapi	In the brightness of that snow
Maris, maris waqayunay	Why, oh why, must I cry
Waqayuspa puriyunay	Crying, I must go on
Taytamamay uywawasqa	My parents having raised me
Mamataytay uywawasqa	My folks having raised me

Waqaspalla purinaypaq	So that I must go on, crying
Sufrimintu pasanaypaq	So that I must carry on in my suffering
Hinapaqcha swirtiy karan	Like that, just my luck
Aqnapaqcha swirtiy karan	Like that, just my luck
Waqaspalla purinaypaq	So that I must go on, crying
Sufrimintu pasanaypaq	So that I must carry on in my suffering
Sultiruchus kayushayman	Would I be single?
Sapallaychus kayushayman	Would I be alone?
Wichaypas uraycha kanman	Up would be down
Uraypas wichaycha kanman	Down would be up
Mayuq chinpanpi rikushawaspa	Seeing me at the riverbank
Unuq chinpanpi qhawashawaspa	Gazing upon me at the water's edge
Imapaq munayuwaranki	Why did you love me?
Hayk'apaq parlayuwaranki	For what did you talk to me?
Mayuq chinpanpi rikushawaspa	Seeing me at the riverbank
Unuq chinpanpi qhawashawaspa	Gazing upon me at the water's edge
Imapaq munayuwaranki	Why did you love me?
Hayk'apaq parlayuwaranki	For what did you talk to me?
Bandurriaschay nuqa waqachiq	My little bandurria that makes me cry
Charanguituschay nuqa llakichiq	My little *charango* that makes me sad
Pillaraq aparikapunman	Whoever will come to claim it?
Mayllaraq aparikapunman	And where will it be taken?

Notes

Introduction

1. The *Academia Mayor de la Lengua Quechua* (2005) translates *illa* as "a certain slight light that penetrates through a crack or hole into an environment; the penetration of light or clarity in a dark place || [v] to make clear" (69). Other variations include: star (*ch'aska, estrella*) (Herrero S. J. and Sánchez de Lozada 1983, 177); jewel, prize, or amulet (Laime Ajacopa et al. 2007, 32); currency/coin, transparency, or rock that has been struck by lightning (Lira and Mejía Huamán 1984, 89). Catherine Allen translates *illa* as "ray of light" and as a synonym for *inqaychu*, small stone animal amulets endowed with vital force (Allen 2016, 328, 336). For another description of *illa* as amulet, see the work of Jorge Flores Ochoa: "The *illa* are small sculptures that represent alpacas, llamas or sheep. They are made of stone, usually quartzite, basalt, granite or other fine-grained stones. Many are undoubtedly of pre-Columbian origin, of which they are widely known as '*conopa*'" (Flores Ochoa 1974, 249).

2. See, for example, Bebbington and Bury (2009); Boelens (2014); Bury et al. (2013); Buytaert et al. (2017); Carey et al. (2017); Chevallier et al. (2011); Drenkhan et al. (2015); Finer and Jenkins (2012); Pabón-Caicedo et al. (2020).

3. Much like *illachiy*, *sut'i* was a process based on *vision* that could be undertaken by a sighted being—whether human, animal, or landscape being—and required that the phenomena be illuminated, by either a light source or some other means (Orlove 2009, 141).

4. See, for example, Hallowell (1960); Ingold (2000); Kirsch (2006); Nadasdy (2007); Povinelli (2001; 1995); Raffles (2002); Viveiros de Castro (1998); Willerslev (2007); Henare, Holbraad, and Wastell (2006).

5. See, for example, the work of Browman (1974; 1987); Flannery, Marcus, and Reynolds (1989); Flores Ochoa (1968; 1977); Nachtigall (1965); Orlove (1977a); Palacios Ríos (1977); Webster (1973).

6. In his 1968 study of the pastoralists of Paratía, Peru, Flores Ochoa acknowledged that "the care and management of alpacas requires the participation of almost the entire family, men as well as women; from children to adults, all know how to handle the animals" (1968, 114). Steven Webster's suggested that among the Q'ero herders of Peru, however, that "the routine tasks of herd supervision are usually assigned to women or children" (Webster 1973, 119), whereas Bolton et al. acknowledge that "it should be noted that *both* males and females engage in herding, contrary to the general worldwide tendency for herding to be an occupation assigned solely or primarily to men and boys" (Bolton et al. 1976, 467). In *The Articulated Peasant*, Enrique Mayer noted that in the community of Tangor, Peru, in 1969, that "women . . . were responsible for the care of animals . . . Men sometimes tended the animals when the women were too busy, but it was clear that, in doing so, they were essentially performing a woman's task" (2002, 11). However, at the height of the structuralist turn in Andean anthropology, the role of women as herders tended to be underrepresented (Palacios Ríos 1982; Palomino Flores 1984).

7. Pablo Sendón's archival work in the region reveals a long history of occupation by the same families living in Chillca today, evidenced by the appearance of maternal and paternal surnames in census materials from 1883 (eighty-three tax-paying male individuals) to 1888 (eighty-four individuals) (Sendón 2016, 152).

8. Other animals included one to two horses; two herding dogs; often a cat; a handful of guinea pigs; and in rare cases, a couple of chickens.

9. The one annex, Mulluviri, was considered separate from the rest of Chillca in many ways and was not a part of my research.

10. This was similar to a pattern found in many Andean pastoralist communities, where pastures are held communally, with certain usufruct rights allotted to agnatic groupings (Arnold and Yapita 2001; Custred 1977; Flores Ochoa 1968; Palacios Ríos 1977; Postigo, Young, and Crews 2008).

11. In a 2004 study of alpaca and llama diets in Parinacota province of Peru, Giorgio Castellaro and colleagues (2004) determined that the pasturage preferences of both species were dominated by wetland vegetation, with alpacas consuming a much more focused diet of grassy and succulent wetland species.

12. There is the key difference between resting (*samay*) and reserved (*reservado*) pastures: the first is a recognized norm based on the observation of grass conditions, whereas the second is a formalized, regulated use category instituted by a fine.

13. For a detailed description of a year of herding patterns in Chillca, see chap. 5 of Caine 2019.

Chapter 1

1. Verbs in Quechua are typically modified with the infixes *mu-* and *pu-* to indicate directionality. *Mu-* indicates a directional action *toward* the speaker/speech act, or ongoing nondirectional action in a location separate from the speaker/speech act (i.e., *mullumuy*, to round up toward speaker; *michimuy*, to

pasture/herd in a location distant from current speaker/speech act). *Pu-* indicates a directional action *away* from the speaker/speech act (*tirapuy*, to chase away from the speaker/speech act) (Kerke and Muysken 1990).

2. Visual cues like shifts in animal movement likewise communicated vital information back to the herder: a sudden ripple of agitated movement through the herd might let the herder know that the animals had been startled by a predator (or a gust of wind and a flying plastic bag, as was more often the case).

3. The conventionalization of herding whistles is common across herding contexts. In communicative practice between sheep herders and border collies in the United States, for example, there is a consistent correlation between acoustic structures of whistles and desired action: short, rapidly repeated notes with a rising frequency serve as *stimulation* signals, while prolonged, descending single notes are *inhibiting* signals (McConnell and Baylis 1985).

4. Represented in the dictionary of the Academia Mayor de la Lengua Quechua (2005) as "uksi, uksi!—interj. fam. Voz con el que se azuza a los perros a ladrar y envestir [*sic*]," voice with which dogs are incited to bark and pursue. Studies of acoustic signaling in herding contexts often emphasize the mutual training of humans and herding dogs (Despret and Meuret 2016; Queen 2017; Savalois, Lescureux, and Brunois 2013). Dogs are central members of the herd-household and recruited into the work of herding as well as household protection. Beyond *wuqchi*, their commands include *tiray!* (push/propel the herd), and in the event of a predator, *muquramuy* (attack, bite). In the wet season, when condors pose a threat to newly born *uñas*, herders will signal to the dogs the presence of a condor with a low-pitch call *gundur-gundur-gundur*, prompting the dogs to look to the sky, locate the condor, and encircle the herd.

5. I use a pseudonym here due to the tense border relations between Chillca and Pampachiri.

6. See, for example, Academia Mayor de la Lengua Quechua (2005, 90); Cusihuaman (2001, 139); González Holguín (1608, 98); Herrero S. J. and Sánchez de Lozada (1983, 347); Lira and Mejía Huamán (1984).

7. Elsewhere, I've translated this term in Spanish as *desasosiego* or *inquietud* (Caine 2024).

8. Malevolent forces can also *hark'ay*. For example, there is a type of illness caused by malevolent winds that is called *wayra hark'ana*.

9. The alterity of *k'ita* plants is what makes them medicinal, and even domesticated foods retain the healing powers of their *k'ita* ancestors, as Carlos Ríos notes in her research (2015, 396).

Chapter 2

1. In other regions also called *chukcha rutuchikuy* or *chukcha rutuchiy* (Bolin 2006, 50, 167–68; Flores Ochoa 1977, 61). In some regions, it is preceded by a Catholic baptism and the *unuchakuy* baptism, although these were both becoming less common in Chillca by 2015.

2. Women and nonbinary scholars have been particularly attentive to the ways in which Andean women configure and negotiate their identities through labor and affective practices in the household (Bourque and Warren 1981; Deere 1983; Silverblatt 1987) and in agricultural fields and hillsides (Isbell 1985; Maxwell 2011; Paulson 2003) and through routinized performances of socioeconomic exchange in the market (Babb 1998; 2018; Bunster and Young 1988; Seligmann 1989; 1993; 2000; Weismantel 1988; 2001).

3. While wool was the predominant identifying features, other relevant features included species and breed (alpaca: *wakaya*, *suri*; llama: *q'upa*, *q'ara*, *suri*; sheep: *criullu*, *mirinu*), followed by the animal's sex (*china*, female; *machu/ urqu*, male), which was marked by the placement of the ear tassel on the left (male) or right (female) ear, or by leaving longer tufts of fiber (*puchu*) on the chest, sides, or mid-abdomen for female animals, and on the tails or rumps for male animals. The next relevant identifying features was age: *cría* (birth to two years of age); *tuwi* or *tiq'i* (two years and older), or *malta* (female alpaca of a reproductive age). Beyond the key differences in wool texture and length between the *wakaya* and *suri* breeds of alpaca, there were further grades of distinction (*wilma sapa*, *phinu*, *chashka*, etc.). Unlike llama and alpaca, sheep were not usually classified in terms of the texture of their wool. The descriptors *chharqa* (coarse, heavy) and *llamphu* (soft, light) also described fiber texture, but they were only used to describe the wool, not the animal.

4. For further discussion of these classifications in other communities, see Arnold and Yapita 2001 and Palacios Ríos 2000.

5. As Jorge Flores Ochoa noted, these terms of reference were not necessarily hierarchical, but flexible, depending on the precision with which the animal had to be identified from other members of the herd (1968, 146). The most distinguishing feature determined the foremost descriptor: phenotypic variation (i.e., *mut'u*, *q'usi*, *p'arqa*) was noted before coat color (i.e., *yana*, *yuraq makitu*, *muru*) and coat color before age (*tuwi*, *malta*), for example. All those things being the same, the animals would then be distinguished by the quality of their fiber.

6. Anthropologist Olivia Angé also observed that potato farmers in the Cusco region prioritize cultivating happiness, joy, or contentment (*kusisqa*). Like alpacas, potato happiness could be observed in the physical presentation of the plant, especially in the color and shape of the leaves (2021, 21). And, by judging these signs of happiness—the shape, size, and color of the plant—people could predict whether the harvest would be successful (2021, 112). Through planting, cultivating, harvesting, and ritual practices, cultivators accounted for the "emotionality" of potatoes in their pursuit of prosperity, and they did so in a way that invoked surrounding landscape beings, humans, animals, as well as the plants themselves (2021, 108).

7. Bread, rather than being considered a staple, is an especially enticing treat or luxury throughout the Andes: "it is the appropriate gift, the favorite treat" and

as such is "critically important in many social and ceremonial contexts" (Weismantel 1988, 110).

8. Of course, these utterances, while referencing the outward mobility of men, neglect to acknowledge the localized mobility of women herders, who often trekked between six and ten miles following their herds in nearby glacial valleys.

9. The term *valikamuy*, or *valikuy*, was also used in other contexts, such as school cooking responsibilities, animal husbandry tasks (such as shearing, medicating, or castration), and borrowing horses. With agricultural work, *valikuy* referred specifically to requesting help (farm labor) in return for payment (twenty soles/day, at the time). Reciprocal agricultural labor was called *ayni*.

10. Both *ingaray* and *valikuy* are considered forms of *ayni*, unless the labor is exchanged for money or goods, in which case it is no longer *ayni* but *mink'a* (asymmetrical exchange involving payment for a service). The use of llama labor was also *ayni*, although this was organized largely by men. As Mario explained, "With llamas there is always *ayni*. Always. For example, when it's time to transport *guano* [to the potato fields], we will always lend each other llamas. My brother would say to me, 'tomorrow help me transport *guano*,' right? And I must go with my llamas. With my llamas, my ropes, and my sacks. Equally, he must come help me. He must come with his llamas, his ropes, his sacks, to help me."

11. For more on the distinction between formal and informal exchanges and how it maps onto kinship distance in an Andean agricultural community (Tangor, Peru), see the chapter "The Rules of the Game in Andean Reciprocity" in Enrique Mayer's *The Articulated Peasant* (2002). While Mayer writes that "reciprocity among women is a realm onto itself" that he had less access to during his fieldwork, his description of the scale of formality relative to social closeness is similar to what I encountered in Chillca (138n7).

12. Concepción and other women of her generation were often an exception to this rule. Sectoral patrilocality was institutionalized after her husband, Julio, had already moved to Concepción's sector. Given this history, Concepción's oldest son, Jorge, was permitted to move to his wife's sector, Chimpa Chillca, when they married.

13. There appears to have been a general decline in the specificity and range of the lexicon of mixed-coat alpacas, which I noted when comparing wool color terminology in Chillca with that gathered by Jorge Flores Ochoa in Paratía, Peru, in the 1960s (1968, 144). While these differences could also reflect regional variations, it is likely that fewer terms endure given the increasing uniformity of coat patterns.

Chapter 3

1. Penelope Dransart describes a similar ritual practice in which herders in Isluga, Chile, burned flamingo feathers "to discourage their llamas, alpacas and sheep from wandering and to keep them together as a tightly formed herd," much like

a flock of flamingos (2019, 75). In both cases, the desired transformation is mediated through an offering to the surrounding earth beings (*pukara* in Chillca, *uywiri* in Isluga), who will then compel or "inspire" (2019, 89) the animals to change behavior.

2. Feminist scholars working on practices of care likewise emphasize how care is "always shot through with asymmetrical power relations" that organize beings within broader histories of power and privilege (A. Martin, Myers, and Viseu 2015, 627).

3. *Gastillu* was described as a protector, a *pukara* that has a strong affinity for a particular person.

4. See Guillermo Salas's dissertation for more detail on the history of the Maranatha church in the Cusco region (Salas Carreño 2012b, 259).

5. Robert Rhoades, for example, suggested this was the case in Ecuador in the early 2000s when the loss of glacial ice on Mama Cotacachi's led the people of the region to "sense she is dying" and that the region itself is in "social decay" (2008, 48).

6. For similar interpretations, see: Allen (1988); Berg (1989); Boillat and Berkes (2013); Bolin (1999); Cometti (2020); Flores Moreno (2014); Paerregaard (2013); Rivière (2002); Salas Carreño (2012a; 2018); Scoville-Simonds (2018).

7. See also Brugger et al. (2013); Salas Carreño (2021); Jurt et al. (2015); Paerregaard (2013).

8. *P'inqachiy*, while translated here as "to embarrass," relates more broadly to immoral acts or actions out of step with prevailing traditions, customs, or social mores.

9. For similar arguments specifically about the distribution of water in the Peruvian highlands, see Andersen (2018); Brandshaug (2021); Paerregaard (2014); Stensrud (2019).

Chapter 4

1. Single men of a certain age (usually early twenties) who resided in the community were officially considered *empadronados* once they passed through a system of registration that included at least a year of observation and then a community vote. After becoming *empadronados*, they were able to speak and vote in community assemblies and were entitled to a plot of land in the town center. Young women, widows, divorced women, and men who had moved to the community could also become *empadronados* through a community vote.

2. These are approximate years based on self-reporting of the relative ages of Concepción and her siblings during this time. Many of Concepción's paternal cousins still live in Tinki.

3. See, for example, McCay and Acheson (1990); Behnke and Scoones (1993); Berkes et al. (1989); Galvin et al. (2007); Feeny et al. (1990); Ostrom (1999); Trawick (2002); Villarroel et al. (2014).

4.   The evaluation metrics used in livestock competitions are often as follows: fleece fineness (forty possible points), density (ten points), curl and shine (five points), and uniformity (fifteen points); conformation of the head (ten points), height (ten points), wool coverage (five points), and general appearance (five points). The fiber of the *wakaya* breed should be "soft and spongy with waves, and shine when parting the fleece," and can be graded as either high, medium, or low quality by virtue of the diameter of the fiber (less than twenty-two microns; twenty-three to twenty-six microns; or greater than twenty-six microns, respectively). Both *wakaya* and *suri* breeds should have "relatively small triangular-shaped ears, wide nostrils, [a] well-shaped tuft and clean face," which is evaluated as good (*buena*), regular (*regular*), or low (*baja*) quality. Their bodies should demonstrate "proportioned harmony" (*armoniosidad proporcionado*), as evidenced by a "good bodily composure (*aplomos*) denoting the harmonious and slender silhouette of a rectilinear body shape."

5.   As the Marca Perú and Alpaca del Perú brands exemplify, the image of the Indigenous producer is central to Peru's outward image. However, as anthropologist María Elena Garcia argues in her research on the Peruvian gastronomic boom, while these marketing campaigns "seemingly elevate the Indigenous producer and his labor . . . the figure of the producer has been carefully crafted to promote what Anders Burman might call a 'defanged indigeneity'" (García 2021, 99). It is an indigeneity that is deliberately marketable: both in the national labor economy as well as the international wool market. Peruvian developmental efforts contain an implicit contradiction, identified by anthropologist Tania Murray Li as a tension between "the promotion of capitalist processes and concern to improve the condition of the dispossessed" (Li 2007, 31). They "solve" this contradiction by transforming herders into wool producers and leveraging their knowledge as a marketable quality, one that increases the value of the product. People in Chillca were likewise aware of the value of their traditions or *kustunri*, and the power of navigating the market economy as "keepers of tradition."

6.   Early childhood development programs in Chillca often partnered with family planning initiatives that espoused the virtues of having fewer, well-educated children. Although these initiatives were overtly oriented around education, they housed the undeniably painful reverberations and latent logics of past reproductive violence in Peru. In the 1990s Alberto Fujimori's government launched several aggressive family planning initiatives, including the National Program for Reproductive Health and Family Planning (Programa Nacional de Salud Reproductiva y Planificación Familiar), which implemented mass sterilization campaigns aimed at Indigenous, poor, and rural communities. More than two hundred thousand women were forcibly sterilized, often without their knowledge or consent (Ballón Gutiérrez 2014; Defensoría del Pueblo 2002). This state-sponsored violence was enacted in the interest of promoting national

economic development in the wake of widespread neoliberal reform (Boesten 2007; Carranza Ko 2023). Often, at its center, were the images of educated children: the figurations of a prosperous, modernized Peru (Molina Serra 2017; Chaparro-Buitrago and Freeman 2023).

7. Interventions in Chillca contained some familiar linguistic features seen in development initiatives elsewhere, including "workshop talk," which leverages an authoritative register and invokes a mode of participation, and often mirrors "schoolhouse interaction" call-and-response as well as other forms of "public, monologic speech" like community assemblies (Emlen 2020, 150, 190). As Eric Hirsch noted, this sort of linguistic coaching lends itself to the "ethical crafting," that reframes the objective—whether parenting or entrepreneurship—as "not simply an activity but an orientation to the world" (Hirsch 2022, 142). Likewise, childhood development programs were premised upon assumptions of language socialization and personhood, specifically Lockean understandings of rational subject formation that stress the importance of direct, dyadic exchanges between parent and child and discursive bracketing of what one does, thinks, and knows, in order to produce a successful neoliberal subjectivity (Ochs 2018).

Chapter 5

1. Amy Moran-Thomas has made a similar argument regarding diabetes and other metabolic disorders as "para-communicable" with global environmental disruption (Moran-Thomas 2019).

2. Bruce Mannheim provides the example of *runaq allin purinan*, which can be translated as "the well-being of the people" (1998, 269).

3. Pastoralist landscapes (grasslands, shrublands, savannas, tundra, steppe, desert fringes, and alpine areas) have historically been considered "marginal" given the inability of these ecosystems to sustain sedentary agriculture, a livelihood strategy that was privileged by the researchers and policymakers defining the parameters of productivity.

4. Like anemia, menopause is also inextricable from the broader sociopolitical context of Peru, in particular the forced sterilization campaigns of the 1990s (mentioned in notes to chap. 4), in which hundreds of thousands of Indigenous women were forced into menopause. These campaigns mobilized deeply racialized understandings of the female body and its capacities and potentialities, and weaponized these ideas to force the cessation of bodily and social reproduction in Indigenous communities.

Bibliography

Abbink, Jon. 2003. "Love and Death of Cattle: The Paradox in Suri Attitudes toward Livestock." *Ethnos* 68 (3): 341–64.

Abram, David. 1997. *The Spell of the Sensuous: Perception and Language in a More-Than-Human World*. New York: Vintage.

Academia Mayor de la Lengua Quechua. 2005. *Diccionaro Quechua-español-quechua (Qhesqa-español-qheswa: Simi taqe)*. Cusco: Municipalidad del Qosqo, Academia Mayor de la Lengua Quechua (Qhesqa Simi Hamut'ana Kurak Suntur).

Adger, W. Neil. 2000. "Social and Ecological Resilience: Are They Related?" *Progress in Human Geography* 24 (3): 347–64.

Adger, W. Neil. 2006. "Vulnerability." *Global Environmental Change* 16 (3): 268–81.

Adger, W. Neil, Jon Barnett, Katrina Brown, Nadine Marshall, and Karen O'Brien. 2013. "Cultural Dimensions of Climate Change Impacts and Adaptation." *Nature Climate Change* 3 (2): 112–17.

Agrawal, Arun, Maria Carmen Lemos, Ben Orlove, and Jesse Ribot. 2012. "Cool Heads for a Hot World—Social Sciences Under a Changing Sky." *Global Environmental Change* 22 (2): 329–31.

Alaimo, Stacy. 2016. *Exposed: Environmental Politics and Pleasures in Posthuman Times*. Minneapolis: University of Minnesota Press.

Alberti, Giorgio, and Enrique Mayer. 1974. *Reciprocidad e intercambio en los Andes peruanos*. Lima: Instituto de Estudios Peruanos.

Albrecht, Glenn, Gina-Maree Sartore, Linda Connor, Nick Higginbotham, Sonia Freeman, Brian Kelly, Helen Stain, Anne Tonna, and Georgia Pollard. 2007. "Solastalgia: The Distress Caused by Environmental Change." *Australasian Psychiatry* 15 (1_suppl): S95–98.

Allen, Catherine. 1982. "Body and Soul in Quechua Thought." *Journal of Latin American Lore* 8 (2): 179–96.

Allen, Catherine. 1988. *The Hold Life Has: Coca and Cultural Identity in an Andean Community*. Washington, D.C.: Smithsonian Institution Press.

Allen, Catherine. 1997. "When Pebbles Move Mountains: Iconicity and Symbolism in Quechua Ritual." In *Creating Context in Andean Cultures*, edited by Rosaleen Howard-Malverde, 73–84. New York: Oxford University Press.

Allen, Catherine. 1998. "When Utensils Revolt: Mind, Matter, and Modes of Being in the Pre-Columbian Andes." *RES: Anthropology and Aesthetics* 33:18–27.

Allen, Catherine. 2015. "The Sadness of Jars: Separation and Rectification in Andean Understandings of Death." In Shimada and Fitzsimmons, *Living with the Dead in the Andes*, 304–28.

Allen, Catherine. 2016. "Stones Who Love Me." *Archives de Sciences Sociales des Religions* 174 (April): 327–46.

"Alpaca del Perú: Moda y Tradición." n.d. Alpaca del Perú. Accessed March 1, 2023. https://alpacadelperu.com.pe/.

Andersen, Astrid Oberborbeck. 2018. "Purification: Engineering Water and Producing Politics." *Science, Technology, and Human Values* 43 (3): 379–400.

Angé, Olivia. 2021. "Ecological Nostalgias and Interspecies Affect in the Highland Potato Fields of Cuzco (Peru)." In *Ecological Nostalgias: Memory, Affect and Creativity in Times of Ecological Upheavals*, edited by Olivia Angé and David Berliner, 107–25. New York: Berghahn Books.

Arnold, Denise Y. 2022. "Animal Rearing, Hunting, and Sacrifice in the Andes: Rethinking Reciprocal Relations Between Humans and Mountains." In *Cultures in Mountain Areas: Comparative Perspectives*, edited by Tobias Boos and Daniela Salvucci, 57–88. Bolzano, Italy: Bozen-Bolzano University Press.

Arnold, Denise Y., and Juan de Dios Yapita. 2001. *River of Fleece, River of Song: Singing to the Animals, an Andean Poetics of Creation*. Markt Schwaben, Germany: Anton Saurwein.

Arnold, Denise Y., and Juan de Dios Yapita. 2006. *The Metamorphosis of Heads: Textual Struggles, Education, and Land in the Andes*. Pittsburgh: University of Pittsburgh Press.

Babb, Florence E. 1998. *Between Field and Cooking Pot: The Political Economy of Marketwomen in Peru*. Austin: University of Texas Press.

Babb, Florence E. 2018. *Women's Place in the Andes: Engaging Decolonial Feminist Anthropology*. Oakland: University of California Press.

Ballón Gutiérrez, Alejandra. 2014. *Memorias del caso peruano de esterilización forzada*. Lima: Biblioteca Nacional del Perú.

Barnes, Jessica, Michael Dove, Myanna Lahsen, Andrew Mathews, Pamela McElwee, Roderick McIntosh, Frances Moore, Ben Orlove, et al. 2013. "Contribution of Anthropology to the Study of Climate Change." *Nature Climate Change* 3 (6): 541–44.

Barnett, Jon, Petra Tschakert, Lesley Head, and W. Neil Adger. 2016. "A Science of Loss." *Nature Climate Change* 6 (11): 976–78.

Barth, Fredrik. 2002. "An Anthropology of Knowledge." *Current Anthropology* 43 (1): 1–18.

Basso, Keith H. 1996. *Wisdom Sits in Places: Landscape and Language Among the Western Apache.* Albuquerque: University of New Mexico Press.

Bastien, Joseph W. 1978. "Mountain/Body Metaphor in the Andes." *Bulletin de l'Institut Français d'études Andines* 7 (1–2): 103.

Bastien, Joseph W. 1985. "Qollahuaya-Andean Body Concepts: A Topographical-Hydraulic Model of Physiology." *American Anthropologist* 87 (3): 595–611.

Bebbington, Anthony, and Jeffrey T. Bury. 2009. "Institutional Challenges for Mining and Sustainability in Peru." *Proceedings of the National Academy of Sciences* 106 (41): 17296–301.

Behnke, Roy, and Ian Scoones. 1993. "Rethinking Range Ecology Implications for Rangeland Management in Africa." In *Rangeland Ecology at Disequilibrium: New Models of Natural Variability and Pastoral Adaptation in African Savannas,* edited by Royh H. Behnke Jr., Ian Scoones, and Carol Kerven, 1–30. London: Overseas Development Institute, Regent's College.

Berg, Hans van den. 1989. *"La tierra no da así no más": Los ritos agrícolas en la religión de los aymara-cristianos de los Andes.* Amsterdam: Centro de Estudios y Documentación Latinoamericanos.

Berkes, Fikret, David Feeny, Bonnie J. McCay, and James M. Acheson. 1989. "The Benefits of the Commons." *Nature* 340:91–93.

Berkes, Fikret, and Dyanna Jolly. 2002. "Adapting to Climate Change: Social-Ecological Resilience in a Canadian Western Arctic Community." *Conservation Ecology* 5 (2): 18.

Bettini, Giovanni. 2013. "Climate Barbarians at the Gate? A Critique of Apocalyptic Narratives on 'Climate Refugees.'" *Geoforum Risky Natures, Natures of Risk* 45:63–72.

Blanchette, Alex. 2020. *Porkopolis: American Animality, Standardized Life, and the Factory Farm.* Durham: Duke University Press.

Blaser, Mario. 2013. "Ontological Conflicts and the Stories of Peoples in Spite of Europe: Toward a Conversation on Political Ontology." *Current Anthropology* 54 (5): 547–68.

Boas, Ingrid, Carol Farbotko, Helen Adams, Harald Sterly, Simon Bush, Kees van der Geest, Hanne Wiegel, Hasan Ashraf, Andrew Baldwin, et al. 2019. "Climate Migration Myths." *Nature Climate Change* 9 (12): 901–3.

Boas, Ingrid, Hanne Wiegel, Carol Farbotko, Jeroen Warner, and Mimi Sheller. 2022. "Climate Mobilities: Migration, Im/Mobilities and Mobility Regimes in a Changing Climate." *Journal of Ethnic and Migration Studies* 48 (14): 3365–79.

Boelens, Rutgerd. 2014. "Cultural Politics and the Hydrosocial Cycle: Water, Power and Identity in the Andean Highlands." *Geoforum* 57 (November): 234–47.

Boesten, Jelke. 2007. "Free Choice or Poverty Alleviation? Population Politics in Peru Under Alberto Fujimori." *Revista Europea de Estudios Latinoamericanos y del Caribe/European Review of Latin American and Caribbean Studies* 82:3–20.

Boillat, Sébastien, and Fikret Berkes. 2013. "Perception and Interpretation of Climate Change among Quechua Farmers of Bolivia: Indigenous Knowledge as a Resource for Adaptive Capacity." *Ecology and Society* 18 (4): 21.

Bolin, Inge. 1998. *Rituals of Respect: The Secret of Survival in the High Peruvian Andes*. Austin: University of Texas Press.

Bolin, Inge. 1999. "Survival in Marginal Lands: Climate Change in the High Peruvian Andes." *Development and Cooperation* 5:25–26.

Bolin, Inge. 2001. "When Apus Are Losing Their White Ponchos: Environmental Dilemmas and Restoration Efforts in Peru." *Development and Cooperation* 6:25–26.

Bolin, Inge. 2006. *Growing Up in a Culture of Respect: Child Rearing in Highland Peru*. Austin: University of Texas Press.

Bolin, Inge. 2009. "The Glaciers of the Andes Are Melting: Indigenous and Anthropological Knowledge Merge in Restoring Water Resources." In Crate and Nuttal, *Anthropology and Climate Change*, 228–40.

Bolton, Charlene, Ralph Bolton, Lorraine Gross, Amy Koel, Carol Michelson, Robert L. Munroe, and Ruth H. Munroe. 1976. "Pastoralism and Personality." *Ethos* 4 (4): 463–81.

Bolton, Maggie. 2006. "Genetic Defects or Generative Prototypes? Competing Models for Livestock Improvement in Southern Bolivia." *Journal of the Royal Anthropological Institute* 12 (3): 531–49.

Bourdieu, Pierre. 1984. *Distinction: A Social Critique of the Judgement of Taste*. Translated by Richard Nice. Cambridge, MA: Harvard University Press.

Bourque, Susan, and Kay Barbara Warren. 1981. *Women of the Andes: Patriarchy and Social Change in Two Peruvian Towns*. Ann Arbor: University of Michigan Press.

Bradley, Raymond S., Frank T. Keimig, Henry F. Diaz, and Douglas R. Hardy. 2009. "Recent Changes in Freezing Level Heights in the Tropics with Implications for the Deglacierization of High Mountain Regions." *Geophysical Research Letters* 36 (17): L1770.

Brandshaug, Malene K. 2019. "Water as More than Commons or Commodity: Understanding Water Management Practices in Yanque, Peru." *Water Alternatives* 12 (2): 538–53.

Brandshaug, Malene K. 2021. "Water, Life, and Loss: Aguasociality and Environmental Change in the Peruvian Andes." *Kritisk Etnografi—Swedish Journal of Anthropology* 4 (2): 51–66.

Brewer, Jessica D., Maria P. Santos, Karina Román, Amy R. Riley-Powell, Richard A. Oberhelman, and Valerie A. Paz-Soldan. 2020. "Micronutrient Powder Use in Arequipa, Peru: Barriers and Enablers across Multiple Levels." *Maternal and Child Nutrition* 16 (2): e12915.

Brotherston, Gordon. 1989. "Andean Pastoralism and Inca Ideology." In Clutton-Brock, *Walking Larder*, 240–55.

Browman, David. 1974. "Pastoral Nomadism in the Andes." *Current Anthropology* 15 (2): 188–96.

Browman, David. 1983. "Andean Arid Land Pastoralism and Development." *Mountain Research and Development* 3 (3): 241–52.

Browman, David. 1987. *Arid Land Use Strategies and Risk Management in the Andes: A Regional Anthropological Perspective*. Boulder: Westview Press.

Browman, David. 1989. "Origins and Development of Andean Pastoralism: An Overview of the Past 6000 Years." In Clutton-Brock, *Walking Larder*, 256–68. London: Unwin Hyman.

Brugger, Julie, K. W. Dunbar, Christine Jurt, and Ben Orlove. 2013. "Climates of Anxiety: Comparing Experience of Glacier Retreat Across Three Mountain Regions." *Emotion, Space and Society Emotion and Ecology* 6:4–13.

Brush, Stephen B. 1977. *Mountain, Field, and Family: The Economy and Human Ecology of an Andean Valley.* Philadelphia: University of Pennsylvania Press.

Bryant, F. C., and R. D. Farfan. 1984. "Dry Season Forage Selection by Alpaca [Lama Pacos] in Southern Peru." *Journal of Range Management* 37 (4): 330–33.

Bubandt, Nils, and Anna Tsing. 2018. "Feral Dynamics of Post-Industrial Ruin: An Introduction." *Journal of Ethnobiology* 38 (1): 1–7.

Bugallo, Lucila. 2016. "Wak'as en la puna jujeña: Lo fluido y lo fino en el diálogo con pachamama." In *Wak'as, diablos y muertos: Alteridades significantes en el mundo andino,* edited by Lucila Bugallo and Mario Vilca, 111–61. San Salvador de Jujuy, Argentina: Universidad Nacional de Jujuy, IFEA.

Bugallo, Lucila. 2020. "Pachamama y Coquena: Seres poderosos en los Andes del sur." In Muñoz Morán, *Ensayos de etnografía teórica.*

Bugallo, Lucila, and Jorge Tomasi. 2012. "Crianzas mutuas: El trato a los animales desde las concepciones de los pastores puneños (Jujuy, Argentina)." *Revista Española de Antropología Americana* 42 (1): 205–24.

Bugallo, Lucila, and Mario Vilca. 2011. "Cuidando el ánimu: Salud y enfermedad en el mundo andino (puna y quebrada de jujuy, Argentina)." *Nuevo Mundo Mundos Nuevos,* July 13, 2011.

Bullard, Robert D. 2000. *Dumping in Dixie: Race, Class, and Environmental Quality.* 3rd ed. New York: Routledge.

Bunster, Ximena, and Ellan Young. 1988. *Sellers and Servants: Working Women in Lima, Peru.* New York: Praeger.

Burman, Anders. 2017. "The Political Ontology of Climate Change: Moral Meteorology, Climate Justice, and the Coloniality of Reality in the Bolivian Andes." *Journal of Political Ecology* 24 (1): 921–38.

Bury, Jeffrey, Bryan G. Mark, Mark Carey, Kenneth R. Young, Jeffrey M. McKenzie, Michel Baraer, Adam French, and Molly H. Polk. 2013. "New Geographies of Water and Climate Change in Peru: Coupled Natural and Social Transformations in the Santa River Watershed." *Annals of the Association of American Geographers* 103 (2): 363–74.

Butler, Judith. 2006. *Precarious Life: The Powers of Mourning and Violence.* London: Verso.

Butler, Judith. 2009. "Performativity, Precarity and Sexual Politics." *AIBR: Revista de Antropología Iberoamericana* 4 (3): 1–13.

Buytaert, Wouter, Simon Moulds, Luis Acosta, Bert De Bièvre, Carlos Olmos, Marcos Villacis, Carolina Tovar, and Koen M. J. Verbist. 2017. "Glacial Melt Content of Water Use in the Tropical Andes." *Environmental Research Letters* 12 (11): 114014.

Cadena, Marisol de la. 2005. "Are Mestizos Hybrids? The Conceptual Politics of Andean Identities." *Journal of Latin American Studies* 37 (2): 259–84.

Cadena, Marisol de la. 2010. "Indigenous Cosmopolitics in the Andes: Conceptual Reflections Beyond 'Politics.'" *Cultural Anthropology* 25 (2): 334–70.

Cadena, Marisol de la. 2015. *Earth Beings: Ecologies of Practice Across Andean Worlds*. Durham: Duke University Press.

Caine, Allison. 2019. "Restless Ecologies in the Andean Highlands." PhD diss., University of Michigan.

Caine, Allison. 2021. "'Who Would Watch the Animals?': Gendered Knowledge and Expert Performance Among Andean Pastoralists." *Culture, Agriculture, Food and Environment* 43 (1): 4–13.

Caine, Allison. 2024. "El cambio climático y el desasosiego animal en la cordillera de Vilcanota, Perú." *Allpanchis* 51 (93): 343–80.

Callañaupa Alvarez, Nilda, Christine Franquemont, and Joe Coca. 2013. *Faces of Tradition: Weaving Elders of the Andes*. Loveland, Colo.: Thrums Books.

Camino, Lupe. 1992. *Cerros, plantas y lagunas poderosas: La medicina al norte del Perú*. Piura, Perú: CIPCA. http://www.gbv.de/dms/sub-hamburg/043319106.pdf.

Canessa, Andrew. 2000. "Fear and Loathing on the Kharisiri Trail: Alterity and Identity in the Andes." *Journal of the Royal Anthropological Institute* 6 (4): 705–20.

Canessa, Andrew. 2012. *Intimate Indigeneities: Race, Sex, and History in the Small Spaces of Andean Life*. Durham: Duke University Press Books.

Capriles, José M., and Nicholas Tripcevich, eds. 2016. *The Archaeology of Andean Pastoralism*. Albuquerque: University of New Mexico Press.

Carey, Mark, Olivia C. Molden, Mattias Borg Rasmussen, M. Jackson, Anne W. Nolin, and Bryan G. Mark. 2017. "Impacts of Glacier Recession and Declining Meltwater on Mountain Societies." *Annals of the American Association of Geographers* 107 (2): 350–59.

Caria, Sara, and Rafael Domínguez. 2016. "Ecuador's 'Buen Vivir': A New Ideology for Development." *Latin American Perspectives* 43 (1): 18–33.

Carlos Ríos, Eugenia. 2015. "La circulación entre mundos en la tradición oral y ritual y las categorias del pensamiento Quechua en Hanansaya Ccullana Ch'isikata (Cusco, Peru)." PhD diss., Universitat Autònoma de Barcelona.

Carranza Ko, Ñusta. 2023. "Unacknowledged Genocide: Coercive Sterilization of Indigenous Women in Peru." *Violence: An International Journal* 4 (1–2): 11–29.

Carsten, Janet. 2013. "What Kinship Does—and How." *HAU: Journal of Ethnographic Theory* 3 (2): 245–51.

Cartwright, Elizabeth. 2007. "Bodily Remembering: Memory, Place, and Understanding Latino Folk Illnesses Among the Amuzgos Indians of Oaxaca, Mexico." *Culture, Medicine and Psychiatry* 31 (4): 527–45.

Casaverde, J. 1985. "Sistema de propiedad y tenencia de pastos naturales altoandinos." *Allpanchis* 25:271–88.

Castañeda, Claudia. 2002. *Figurations: Child, Bodies, Worlds*. Durham: Duke University Press.

Castellaro, Giorgio, Tamara Ullrich R., Birgit Wackwitz, and Alberto Raggi S. 2004. "Composición botánica de la dieta de alpacas (Lama Pacos L.) y llamas (Lama Glama L.) en dos estaciones del año, en praderas altiplánicas de un sector de la Provincia de Parinacota, Chile." *Agricultura Técnica* 64 (4): 353–63.

Chao, Sophie. 2022. *In the Shadow of the Palms: More-Than-Human Becomings in West Papua.* Durham: Duke University Press.

Chaparro-Buitrago, Julieta, and Cordelia Freeman. 2023. "Reproductive Justice and the Figure of the Child: The Multiple Harms of Forced Sterilization and Abortion in Peru." *Feminist Anthropology* 4 (2): 171–77.

Chevallier, Pierre, Bernard Pouyaud, Wilson Suarez, and Thomas Condom. 2011. "Climate Change Threats to Environment in the Tropical Andes: Glaciers and Water Resources." *Regional Environmental Change* 11 (1): 179–87.

Clement, Floriane, Wendy Harcourt, Deepa Joshi, and Chizu Sato. 2019. "Feminist Political Ecologies of the Commons and Commoning (Editorial to the Special Feature)." *International Journal of the Commons* 13 (1): 1.

Clutton-Brock, Juliet, ed. 1989. *The Walking Larder: Patterns of Domestication, Pastoralism, and Predation.* London: Unwin Hyman.

Cometti, Geremia. 2020. "El Antropoceno puesto a prueba en el campo: Cambio climático y crisis de las relaciones de reciprocidad entre los q'ero de los Andes peruanos." *Antípoda: Revista de Antropología y Arqueología* 38:3–23.

Cookson, Tara Patricia. 2018. *Unjust Conditions: Women's Work and the Hidden Cost of Cash Transfer Programs.* Oakland: University of California Press.

Cooper, David J., Jeremy Sueltenfuss, Eduardo Oyague, Karina Yager, Daniel Slayback, E. Marcelo Cabero Caballero, Jaime Argollo, and Bryan G. Mark. 2019. "Drivers of Peatland Water Table Dynamics in the Central Andes, Bolivia and Peru." *Hydrological Processes* 33 (13): 1913–25.

Crate, Susan. 2011. "Climate and Culture: Anthropology in the Era of Contemporary Climate Change." *Annual Review of Anthropology* 40 (1): 175–94.

Crate, Susan, and Mark Nuttall. 2009. *Anthropology and Climate Change: From Encounters to Actions.* Walnut Creek, Calif.: Left Coast Press.

Cronon, William. 1996. "The Trouble with Wilderness: Or, Getting Back to the Wrong Nature." *Environmental History* 1 (1): 7.

Cruikshank, Julie. 2005. *Do Glaciers Listen? Local Knowledge, Colonial Encounters, and Social Imagination.* Vancouver: University of British Columbia Press.

Cusihuaman, Antonio G. 2001. *Diccionario Quechua: Cuzco-Collao.* Cusco: Centro Bartolomé de las Casas.

Custred, Glynn. 1977. "Las punas de los Andes centrales." In Ochoa, *Pastores de puna,* 55–85. Lima: Instituto de Estudios Peruanos.

Damonte, Gerardo, Manuel Glave, Sandra Rodríguez, and Andrea Ramos. 2016. "The Evolution of Collective Land Tenure Regimes in Pastoralist Societies: Lessons from Andean Countries." Research paper. Lima: Group for the Analysis of Development (GRADE).

Dangles, Olivier, Antoine Rabatel, Martin Kraemer, Gabriel Zeballos, Alvaro Soruco, Dean Jacobsen, and Fabien Anthelme. 2017. "Ecosystem Sentinels for Climate

Change? Evidence of Wetland Cover Changes over the Last 30 Years in the Tropical Andes." *PLOS ONE* 12 (5): e0175814.

Das, Veena. 2013. "Being Together with Animals: Death, Violence and Noncruelty in Hindu Imagination." In *Living Beings: Perspectives on Interspecies Engagements*, edited by Penelope Dransart, 17–31. London: Bloomsbury.

Dave, Naisargi N. 2014. "WITNESS: Humans, Animals, and the Politics of Becoming." *Cultural Anthropology* 29 (3): 433–56.

Deere, Carmen Diana. 1983. "The Allocation of Familial Labor and the Formation of Peasant Household Income in the Peruvian Sierra." In *Women and Poverty in the Third World*, edited by Mayra Buvinic, Margaret A. Lycette, and William Paul McGreevey, 104–29. Baltimore: Johns Hopkins University Press.

Defensoría del Pueblo. 2002. *Informe defensorial no. 69. La aplicación de la anticoncepción quirúrgica y los derechos reproductivos III. Casos investigados por la defensoría del pueblo.* Lima: Defensoría del Pueblo.

deFrance, Susan D. 2016. "Pastoralism Through Time in Southern Peru." In Capriles and Tripcevich, *Archaeology of Andean Pastoralism*, 119–38.

Despret, Vinciane. 2008. "The Becomings of Subjectivity in Animal Worlds." *Subjectivity* 23 (1): 123–39.

Despret, Vinciane, and Michel Meuret. 2016. "Cosmoecological Sheep and the Arts of Living on a Damaged Planet." *Environmental Humanities* 8 (1): 24–36.

Dong, Shikui, Lu Wen, Shiliang Liu, Xiangfeng Zhang, James P. Lassoie, Shaoliang Yi, Xiaoyan Li, Jinpeng Li, and Yuanyuan Li. 2011. "Vulnerability of Worldwide Pastoralism to Global Changes and Interdisciplinary Strategies for Sustainable Pastoralism." *Ecology and Society* 16 (2): 10.

Dransart, Penelope. 2019. "On the Wings of Inspiration: Ritual Efficacy, Dancing Flamingos and Divine Mediation Among Pastoralists and Herd Animals in Isluga, Chile." In Rivera Andía, *Non-Humans in Amerindian South America*, 73–96.

Dransart, Penny. 2003. *Earth, Water, Fleece and Fabric: An Ethnography and Archaeology of Andean Camelid Herding.* London: Routledge.

Drenkhan, Fabian, Mark Carey, Christian Huggel, Jochen Seidel, and María Teresa Oré. 2015. "The Changing Water Cycle: Climatic and Socioeconomic Drivers of Water-Related Changes in the Andes of Peru." *Wiley Interdisciplinary Reviews: Water* 2 (6): 715–33.

Drenkhan, Fabian, Lucía Guardamino, Christian Huggel, and Holger Frey. 2018. "Current and Future Glacier and Lake Assessment in the Deglaciating Vilcanota-Urubamba Basin, Peruvian Andes." *Global and Planetary Change* 169 (October): 105–18.

Drinot, Paulo. 2011. *The Allure of Labor: Workers, Race, and the Making of the Peruvian State.* Durham: Duke University Press.

Dyson-Hudson, Rada, and Neville Dyson-Hudson. 1980. "Nomadic Pastoralism." *Annual Review of Anthropology* 9:15–61.

Eakin, Hallie, and Amy Lynd Luers. 2006. "Assessing the Vulnerability of Social-Environmental Systems." *Annual Review of Environment and Resources* 31 (1): 365–94.

Emlen, Nicholas Q. 2020. *Language, Coffee, and Migration on an Andean-Amazonian Frontier*. Tucson: University of Arizona Press.

Escobar, Arturo. 2011. *Encountering Development: The Making and Unmaking of the Third World*. Princeton: Princeton University Press.

Fabian, Johannes. 2002. *Time and the Other: How Anthropology Makes Its Object*. New York: Columbia University Press.

Farbotko, Carol. 2022. "Anti-Displacement Mobilities and Re-Emplacements: Alternative Climate Mobilities in Funafala." *Journal of Ethnic and Migration Studies* 48 (14): 3380–96.

Farmer, Paul. 1996. "On Suffering and Structural Violence: A View from Below." *Daedalus* 125 (1): 261–83.

Farmer, Paul. 2004. "An Anthropology of Structural Violence." *Current Anthropology* 45 (3): 305–25.

Farmer, Paul. 2009. "On Suffering and Structural Violence: A View from Below." *Race/Ethnicity: Multidisciplinary Global Contexts* 3 (1): 11–28.

Farrell, Ali. 2020. *Pretty Rugged: True Stories from Women of the Sea*. Camden, Maine: Sea Street.

Federici, Silvia. 2018. *Re-Enchanting the World: Feminism and the Politics of the Commons*. Oakland, Calif.: PM Press.

Feeny, David, Fikret Berkes, Bonnie J. McCay, and James M. Acheson. 1990. "The Tragedy of the Commons: Twenty-Two Years Later." *Human Ecology* 18 (1): 1–19.

Ferguson, James. 1994. *The Anti-Politics Machine: Development, Depoliticization, and Bureaucratic Power in Lesotho*. Minneapolis: University of Minnesota Press.

Ferrié, Francis. 2018. "Losing Part of Oneself: Channels of Communication between Humans and Non-Humans." In Rivera Andía, *Non-Humans in Amerindian South America*, 143–63.

Finer, Matt, and Clinton N. Jenkins. 2012. "Proliferation of Hydroelectric Dams in the Andean Amazon and Implications for Andes-Amazon Connectivity." *PLoS ONE* 7 (4): e35126.

Fisher, Chelsea. 2023. *Rooting in a Useless Land: Ancient Farmers, Celebrity Chefs, and Environmental Justice in Yucatan*. Oakland: University of California Press.

Fiske, Shirley J., Susan Crate, Carole L. Crumley, Kathleen A. Galvin, Heather Lazrus, Lisa J. Lucero, Anthony Oliver-Smith, Benjamin S. Orlove, Sarah Strauss, et al. 2014. "Changing the Atmosphere: Anthropology and Climate Change." Final report of the AAA Global Climate Change Task Force. Arlington, Va.: American Anthropological Association.

Flachs, Andrew. 2019. *Cultivating Knowledge: Biotechnology, Sustainability, and the Human Cost of Cotton Capitalism in India*. Tucson: University of Arizona Press.

Flannery, Kent V., Joyce Marcus, and Robert G. Reynolds. 1989. *The Flocks of the Wamani: A Study of Llama Herders on the Punas of Ayacucho, Peru*. Walnut Creek, Calif.: Left Coast Press.

Flores Martínez, Arturo. 2005. *Manual de pastos y forrajes altoandinos*. Lima: Intermediate Technology Development Group (ITDG-Peru), OIKOS.

Flores Moreno, A. 2014. "La reciprocidad puesta a prueba: Hacia una fenomenología social del cambio climático en sociedades pastoriles del sur Andino Peruano." *Estudios de Filosofía* 13:55–82.

Flores Ochoa, Jorge. 1968. *Los pastores de Paratía: Una introducción a su estudio.* Mexico City: Instituto Indigenista Interamericano.

Flores Ochoa, Jorge. 1974. "Enqa, Enqaychu Illa y Khuya Rumi: Aspectos mágico-religiosos entre pastores." *Journal de la Société des Américanistes* 63 (1): 245–62.

Flores Ochoa, Jorge. 1977. *Pastores de puna: Uywamichiq punarunakuna.* Lima: Instituto de Estudios Peruanos.

Flores Ochoa, Jorge. 1986. "The Classification and Naming of South American Camelids." In *Anthropological History of Andean Politics,* edited by John V. Murra, Nathan Wachtel, and Jacques Revel, 137–48. Cambridge, U.K.: Cambridge University Press.

Gade, Daniel W. 2013. "Llamas and Alpacas as 'Sheep' in the Colonial Andes: Zoogeography Meets Eurocentrism." *Journal of Latin American Geography* 12 (2): 221.

Gallopín, Gilberto C. 2006. "Linkages Between Vulnerability, Resilience, and Adaptive Capacity." *Global Environmental Change* 16 (3): 293–303.

Galvin, Kathleen A., Jim Ellis, Roy Behnke, N. Thompson Hobbs, and Robin S. Reid. 2007. *Fragmentation in Semi-Arid and Arid Landscapes: Consequences for Human and Natural Systems.* Dordrecht: Springer.

García, María Elena. 2021. *Gastropolitics and the Specter of Race: Stories of Capital, Culture, and Coloniality in Peru.* Oakland: University of California Press.

Geertz, Clifford. 1983. *Local Knowledge: Further Essays in Interpretive Anthropology.* New York: Basic Books.

Gibson-Graham, J. K. 2006. *A Postcapitalist Politics.* Minneapolis: University of Minnesota Press.

Gil Montero, Raquel. 2009. "Mountain Pastoralism in the Andes During Colonial Times." *Nomadic Peoples* 13 (2): 36–50.

Gilio-Whitaker, Dina. 2019. *As Long as Grass Grows: The Indigenous Fight for Environmental Justice, from Colonization to Standing Rock.* Boston: Beacon Press.

Göbel, Barbara. 2002. "La arquitectura del pastoreo: Uso del espacio y sistema de asentamientos en la puna de Atacama (Susques)." *Estudios Atacameños* 23:53–76.

Göbel, Barbara. 1997. "You Have to Exploit Luck: Pastoral Household Economy and the Cultural Handling of Risk and Uncertainty in the Andean Highlands." *Nomadic Peoples* (New Series, Risk and Uncertainty in Pastoral Societies) 1 (1): 37–53.

Goepfert, Nicolas, and Gabriel Prieto. 2016. "Offering Llamas to the Sea: The Economic and Ideological Importance of Camelids in the Chimu Society, North Coast of Peru." In Capriles and Tripcevich, *Archaeology of Andean Pastoralism,* 197–210.

González Holguín, Diego. 1608. *Vocabulario de la lengua general de todo el Peru llamada lengua qquichua o del Inca.* Lima: Francisco del Canto.

Gose, Peter. 2018. "The Semi-Social Mountain: Metapersonhood and Political Ontology in the Andes." *HAU: Journal of Ethnographic Theory* 8 (3): 488–505.

Govindrajan, Radhika. 2015a. "'The Goat That Died for Family': Animal Sacrifice and Interspecies Kinship in India's Central Himalayas" *American Ethnologist* 42 (3): 504–19.

Govindrajan, Radhika. 2015b. "The Man-Eater Sent by God: Unruly Interspecies Intimacies in India's Central Himalayas." *Unruly Environments (RCC Perspectives)* 3:33–38.

Govindrajan, Radhika. 2018. *Animal Intimacies: Interspecies Relatedness in India's Central Himalayas.* Chicago: University of Chicago Press.

Grasseni, Cristina. 2004. "Skilled Vision. An Apprenticeship in Breeding Aesthetics." *Social Anthropology* 12 (1): 41–55.

Grasseni, Cristina. 2009a. *Developing Skill, Developing Vision: Practices of Locality at the Foot of the Alps.* Oxford: Berghahn Books.

Grasseni, Cristina, ed. 2009b. *Skilled Visions: Between Apprenticeship and Standards.* Oxford: Berghahn Books.

Greenway, Christine. 1998. "Hungry Earth and Vengeful Stars: Soul Loss and Identity in the Peruvian Andes." *Social Science and Medicine* 47 (8): 993–1004.

Gupta, Akhil. 1998. *Postcolonial Developments: Agriculture in the Making of Modern India.* Durham: Duke University Press.

Hallowell, A. Irving. 1960. "Ojibwa Ontology, Behavior, and World View." In *Culture in History: Essays in Honor of Paul Radin,* edited by Stanley Diamond, 19–52. New York: Columbia University Press.

Han, Clara. 2018. "Precarity, Precariousness, and Vulnerability." *Annual Review of Anthropology* 47 (1): 331–43.

Hanshaw, Maiana N., and Bodo Bookhagen. 2013. "Glacial Areas, Lake Areas, and Snow Lines from 1975 to 2012: Status of the Cordillera Vilcanota, Including the Quelccaya Ice Cap, Northern Central Andes, Peru." *Cryosphere Discussions* 7:573–34.

Haraway, Donna. 1988. "Situated Knowledges: The Science Question in Feminism and the Privilege of Partial Perspective." *Feminist Studies* 14 (3): 575–99.

Haraway, Donna. 2008. *When Species Meet.* Minneapolis: University of Minnesota Press.

Haraway, Donna. 2015. "Anthropocene, Capitalocene, Plantationocene, Chthulucene: Making Kin." *Environmental Humanities* 6 (1): 159–65.

Haraway, Donna. 2016. *Staying with the Trouble: Making Kin in the Chthulucene Experimental Futures: Technological Lives, Scientific Arts, Anthropological Voices.* Durham: Duke University Press.

Hardin, Garrett. 1968. "The Tragedy of the Commons." *Science* 162 (3859): 1243–48.

Harris, Olivia. 2000. *To Make the Earth Bear Fruit: Essays on Fertility, Work and Gender in Highland Bolivia.* London: Institute of Latin American Studies.

Harvey, David. 2005. *A Brief History of Neoliberalism.* Oxford: Oxford University Press.

Harvey, Penelope, and Hannah Knox. 2015. *Roads: An Anthropology of Infrastructure and Expertise. Expertise: Cultures and Technologies of Knowledge.* Ithaca, N.Y.: Cornell University Press.

Heath Justice, Daniel. 2018. *Why Indigenous Literatures Matter.* Waterloo, Ontario: Wilfrid Laurier University Press.

Heckman, Andrea M. 2003. *Woven Stories: Andean Textiles and Rituals.* Albuquerque: University of New Mexico Press.

Henare, Amiria, Martin Holbraad, and Sari Wastell, eds. 2006. *Thinking Through Things.* London: Routledge.

Hernandez, Jessica. 2022. *Fresh Banana Leaves: Healing Indigenous Landscapes Through Indigenous Science.* Huichin, unceded Ohlone land, aka Berkeley, Calif.: North Atlantic Books.

Herrero S. J., Joaquín, and Federico Sánchez de Lozada. 1983. *Diccionario Quechua.* Cochabamba, Bolivia: C.E.F.C.O.

Hidalgo-Capitán, Antonio Luis, and Ana Patricia Cubillo-Guevara. 2017. "Deconstrucción y genealogía del 'buen vivir' latinoamericano: El (trino) 'buen vivir' y sus diversos manantiales intelectuales." *International Development Policy / Revue Internationale de Politique de Développement* 9 (October). http://journals.open edition.org/poldev/2517.

Hill, Michael Douglas. 2013. "Growing up Quechua: Ethnic Identity, Narrative, and the Cultural Politics of Childhood Migration in Cusco, Peru." *Childhood* 20 (3): 383–97.

Hirsch, Eric. 2018. "Remapping the Vertical Archipelago: Mobility, Migration, and the Everyday Labor of Andean Development." *Journal of Latin American and Caribbean Anthropology* 23 (1): 189–208.

Hirsch, Eric. 2022. *Acts of Growth: Development and the Politics of Abundance in Peru.* Stanford: Stanford University Press.

Hirsch, Eric. 2023. "Forced Emplacement: Flood Exposure and Contested Confinements, from the Colony to Climate Migration." *Environment and Society* 14 (1): 4–22.

Hodgson, Dorothy L. 2001. *Rethinking Pastoralism in Africa: Gender, Culture, and the Myth of the Patriarchal Pastoralist.* Oxford: James Curry.

Huss, Matthias, Bodo Bookhagen, Christian Huggel, Dean Jacobsen, R. S. Bradley, J. J. Clague, M. Vuille, W. Buytaert, D. R. Cayan, et al. 2017. "Toward Mountains Without Permanent Snow and Ice." *Earth's Future* 5 (5): 418–35.

Ingold, Tim. 2000. *The Perception of the Environment Essays on Livelihood, Dwelling and Skill.* London: Routledge.

Ingold, Tim. 2011. *Being Alive: Essays on Movement, Knowledge and Description.* London: Routledge.

Irvine, Richard D. G., Barbara Bodenhorn, Elsa Lee, and D. Amarbayasgalan. 2019. "Learning to See Climate Change: Children's Perceptions of Environmental Transformation in Mongolia, Mexico, Arctic Alaska, and the United Kingdom." *Current Anthropology* 60 (6): 723–40.

Isbell, Billie Jean. 1985. *To Defend Ourselves: Ecology and Ritual in an Andean Village.* Prospect Heights, Ill.: Waveland Press.

Isbell, Billie Jean. 1997. "De inmaduro a duro: Lo simbolico femenino y los esquemas andinos de genero." In *Más allá del silencio: Las fronteras de género en los Andes,* edited by Denise Y. Arnold, 253–301. La Paz, Bolivia: Biblioteca Andina.

Jomelli, Vincent, Vincent Favier, Antoine Rabatel, Daniel Brunstein, Georg Hoffmann, and Bernard Francou. 2009. "Fluctuations of Glaciers in the Tropical Andes over the Last Millennium and Palaeoclimatic Implications: A Review." *Palaeogeography, Palaeoclimatology, Palaeoecology* 281 (3): 269–82.

Jurt, Christine, Maria Dulce Burga, Luis Vicuña, Christian Huggel, and Ben Orlove. 2015. "Local Perceptions in Climate Change Debates: Insights from Case Studies in the Alps and the Andes." *Climatic Change* 133 (3): 511–23.

Kamp, Ulrich, Karina Yager, Elise Arnett, Krysten Bowen, Kate Truitt, Anton Seimon, Tracie Seimon, and Alvaro Ivanoff. 2021. "Using Repeat Oblique Aerial Photography and Satellite Imagery to Detect Glacial Change in the Cordillera Vilcanota, Peru, Since 1931." EGU General Assembly (online), April 19–30, 2021. https://doi.org/10.5194/egusphere-egu21-139, 2020.

Kerke, Simon van de, and Pieter Muysken. 1990. "Quechua Mu and the Perspective of the Speaker." In *Unity in Diversity: Papers Presented to Simon C. Dik on His 50th Birthday*, edited by Harm Pinkster and Inge Genee, 151–63. Berlin: Walter de Gruyter.

Kimmerer, Robin Wall. 2015. *Braiding Sweetgrass: Indigenous Wisdom, Scientific Knowledge and the Teachings of Plants*. Minneapolis: Milkweed Editions.

Kirksey, S. Eben, and Stefan Helmreich. 2010. "The Emergence of Multispecies Ethnography." *Cultural Anthropology* 25 (4): 545–76.

Kirsch, Stuart. 2001. "Lost Worlds: Environmental Disaster, 'Culture Loss,' and the Law." *Current Anthropology* 42 (2): 167–98.

Kirsch, Stuart. 2004. "Changing Views of Place and Time Along the Ok Tedi." In *Mining and Indigenous Lifeworks in Australia and Papua New Guinea*, edited by Alan Rumsey and James Weiner, 182–207. Oxon: Sean Kingston.

Kirsch, Stuart. 2006. *Reverse Anthropology: Indigenous Analysis of Social and Environmental Relations in New Guinea*. Stanford: Stanford University Press.

Kleinman, Arthur. 1989. *The Illness Narratives: Suffering, Healing, and the Human Condition*. Reprint edition. New York: Basic Books.

Krishnan, Siddhartha, Christopher L. Pastore, and Samuel Temple. 2015. "Unruly Environments." *RCC Perspectives* 3:69–74.

Kronenberg, Marlene, Simone Schauwecker, Christian Huggel, Nadine Salzmann, Fabian Drenkhan, Holger Frey, Claudia Giraáldez, Wolfgang Gurgiser, Georg Kaser, et al. 2016. "The Projected Precipitation Reduction over the Central Andes May Severely Affect Peruvian Glaciers and Hydropower Production." *Energy Procedia* 97:270–77.

La Frenierre, Jeff, and Bryan G. Mark. 2014. "A Review of Methods for Estimating the Contribution of Glacial Meltwater to Total Watershed Discharge." *Progress in Physical Geography* 38 (2): 173–200.

Laime Ajacopa, Teofilo, and Efrain Cazazola, Félix Layme Pairumani, Pedro Plaza Martínez. 2007. *Diccionario bilingüe iskay simipi yuyayk'ancha: Quechua-Castellano, Castellano-Quechua*. 2nd ed. La Paz, Bolivia: AGRUCO-Obras generales.

Latour, Bruno. 1993. *We Have Never Been Modern*. Cambridge, Mass.: Harvard University Press.

Leinaweaver, Jessaca. 2005. "Familiar Ways: Child Circulation in Andean Peru." PhD diss., University of Michigan.

Leinaweaver, Jessaca. 2008. "Improving Oneself: Young People Getting Ahead in the Peruvian Andes." *Latin American Perspectives* 35 (4): 60–78.

Leinaweaver, Jessaca. 2009. "Raising the Roof in the Transnational Andes: Building Houses, Forging Kinship." *Journal of the Royal Anthropological Institute* 15 (4): 777–96.

Lema, Verónica Soledad. 2014. "Hacia una cartografía de la crianza: Domesticidad y domesticación en comunidades andinas." *Espaço Ameríndio* 8 (1): 59.

Lemos, Maria Carmen, Emily Boyd, Emma Tompkins, Henny Osbahr, and Diana Liverman. 2007. "Developing Adaptation and Adapting Development." *Ecology and Society* 12 (2): 26–29.

Leonard, Sonia, Meg Parsons, Knut Olawsky, and Frances Kofod. 2013. "The Role of Culture and Traditional Knowledge in Climate Change Adaptation: Insights from East Kimberley, Australia." *Global Environmental Change* 23 (3): 623–32.

Li, Tania Murray. 2007. *The Will to Improve: Governmentality, Development, and the Practice of Politics.* Durham: Duke University Press.

Linebaugh, Peter. 2008. *The Magna Carta Manifesto: Liberties and Commons for All.* Berkeley: University of California Press.

Lira, Jorge A., and Mario Mejía Huamán. 1984. *Diccionario Quechua-Castellano, Castellano-Quechua.* Lima: Universidad Ricardo Palma.

Lock, Margaret. 1995. *Encounters with Aging: Mythologies of Menopause in Japan and North America.* Berkeley: University of California Press.

Lock, Margaret, and Patricia Kaufert. 2001. "Menopause, Local Biologies, and Cultures of Aging." *American Journal of Human Biology* 13 (4): 494–504.

Loza Herrera, Susi, Rosa Meneses, and Fabien Anthelme. 2015. "Comunidades vegetales de los bofedales de la Cordillera Real (Bolivia) bajo el calentamiento global." *Ecología en Bolivia* 50 (1): 39–56.

Ludovico Bertonio, P. 1612. *Vocabulario de la lengua aymara.* La Paz: Instituto de Lenguas y Literaturas Andinas-Amazónicas.

Maldonado Fonkén, Mónica Sofía. 2014. "An Introduction to the Bofedales of the Peruvian High Andes." *Mires and Peat* 15 (5): 1–13.

Mannheim, Bruce. 1986. "The Language of Reciprocity in Southern Peruvian Quechua." *Anthropological Linguistics* 28 (3): 267–73.

Mannheim, Bruce. 1991. *The Language of the Inka Since the European Invasion.* Austin: University of Texas Press.

Mannheim, Bruce. 1998. "'Time, Not the Syllables, Must Be Counted': Quechua Parallelism, Word Meaning, and Cultural Analysis." *Michigan Discussions in Anthropology* 13 (1): 238–81.

Mark, Bryan G., Geoffrey O. Seltzer, Donald T. Rodbell, and Adam Y. Goodman. 2002. "Rates of Deglaciation During the Last Glaciation and Holocene in the Cordillera Vilcanota-Quelccaya Ice Cap Region, Southeastern Perú." *Quaternary Research* 57 (3): 287–98.

Martin, Aryn, Natasha Myers, and Ana Viseu. 2015. "The Politics of Care in Techno-science." *Social Studies of Science* 45 (5): 625–41.

Martin, Emily. 1991. "The Egg and the Sperm: How Science Has Constructed a Romance Based on Stereotypical Male-Female Roles." *Signs* 16 (3): 485–501.

Martínez-Alier, Joan. 2003. *The Environmentalism of the Poor: A Study of Ecological Conflicts and Valuation.* Cheltenham, U.K.: Edward Elgar.

Mauss, Marcel. 1979. "The Notion of Body Techniques." In *Sociology and Psychology: Essays,* edited by Ben Brewster, 97–123. London: Routledge.

Maxwell, Keely. 2011. "Beyond Verticality: Fuelscape Politics and Practices in the Andes." *Human Ecology* 39 (4): 465–78.

Mayca-Pérez, Julio, Armando Medina-Ibañez, José E. Velásquez-Hurtado, and Luis F. Llanos-Zavalaga. 2017. "Representaciones sociales relacionadas a la anemia en niños menores de tres años en comunidades Awajun y Wampis, Perú." *Revista Peruana de Medicina Experimental y Salud Pública,* September, 414–22.

Mayer, Enrique. 2002. *The Articulated Peasant: Household Economies in the Andes.* Boulder: Westview Press.

McCay, Bonnie J., and James M. Acheson. 1990. *The Question of the Commons: The Culture and Ecology of Communal Resources.* Tucson: University of Arizona Press.

McConnell, Patricia B., and Jeffrey R. Baylis. 1985. "Interspecific Communication in Cooperative Herding: Acoustic and Visual Signals from Human Shepherds and Herding Dogs." *Zeitschrift für Tierpsychologie* 67 (1–4): 302–28.

Mengoni Goñalons, Guillermo Luis. 2008. "Camelids in Ancient Andean Societies: A Review of the Zooarchaeological Evidence." *Quaternary International* 185 (1): 59–68.

Mengoni Goñalons, Guillermo Luis, and Hugo Yacobaccio. 2006. "The Domestication of South American Camelids: A View from the South-Central Andes." In *Documenting Domestication: New Genetic and Archaeological Paradigms,* edited by Melinda A. Zeder, Daniel G. Bradley, Eve Emshwiller, and Bruce D. Smith, 228–44. Berkeley: University of California Press.

Miller, Theresa L. 2019. *Plant Kin: A Multispecies Ethnography in Indigenous Brazil.* Austin: University of Texas Press.

Mol, Annemarie. 2002. *The Body Multiple: Ontology in Medical Practice.* Durham: Duke University Press.

Molina Serra, Ainhoa. 2017. "Esterilizaciones (Forzadas) en Perú: Poder y configuraciones narrativas." *AIBR: Revista de Antropología Iberoamericana* 12 (1): 31–52.

Moore, Katherine M. 2016. "Early Domesticated Camelids in the Andes." In Capriles and Tripcevich, *Archaeology of Andean Pastoralism,* 17–38.

Moran-Thomas, Amy. 2019. *Traveling with Sugar: Chronicles of a Global Epidemic.* Oakland: University of California Press.

Muñoz Morán, Óscar, ed. 2020. *Ensayos de etnografía teórica: Andes.* Madrid: Nola Editores.

Murra, John V. 1972. "El 'control vertical' de un máximo de pisos ecológicos en la economía de las sociedades andina." In *Visita de la provincia de León de Huánuco en 1562*, edited by John V. Murra, 427–76. Huánuco, Peru: Universidad Nacional Hermilio Valdizán.

Mysyk, Avis. 1998. "Susto: An Illness of the Poor." *Dialectical Anthropology* 23 (2): 187–202.

Nachtigall, Horst. 1965. "Beiträge zur Kultur der Indianischen Lamazüchter der Puna de Atacama (Nordwest-Argentinien)." *Zeitschrift für Ethnologie* 2:184–218.

Nadasdy, Paul. 2007. "The Gift in the Animal: The Ontology of Hunting and Human-Animal Sociality." *American Ethnologist* 34 (1): 25–43.

Neukom, Raphael, Mario Rohrer, Pierluigi Calanca, Nadine Salzmann, Christian Huggel, Delia Acuña, Duncan Christie, and Mariano Morales. 2015. "Facing Unprecedented Drying of the Central Andes? Precipitation Variability over the Period AD 1000–2100." *Environmental Research Letters* 10 (8): 084017.

Nielsen, Axel. 2016. "Home-Making among South Andean Pastoralists." In Capriles and Tripcevich, *Archaeology of Andean Pastoralism*, 231–44.

Nightingale, Andrea J. 2019. "Commoning for Inclusion? Commons, Exclusion, Property and Socio-Natural Becomings." *International Journal of the Commons* 13 (1): 16–35.

Nixon, Rob. 2011. *Slow Violence and the Environmentalism of the Poor*. Cambridge, Mass.: Harvard University Press.

Nureña, César R. 2023. "The Kafkaesque Control of Anemia in Peru." *Anthropology News* (blog). November 28, 2023. https://www.anthropology-news.org/articles/the-kafkaesque-control-of-anemia-in-peru/.

Ochs, Elinor. 2018. "The Biopolitics of Baby Talk." Presented at the Michigan Anthropology Colloquia, University of Michigan, October 18, 2018.

Ødegaard, Cecilie Vindal. 2011. "Sources of Danger and Prosperity in the Peruvian Andes: Mobility in a Powerful Landscape." *Journal of the Royal Anthropological Institute* 17 (2): 339–55.

Ødegaard, Cecilie Vindal. 2018. "Prosperity and the Flow of Vital Substances: Relating to Earth Beings in Processes of Mobility in the Southern Peruvian Andes." In Rivera Andía, *Non-Humans in Amerindian South America*, 326–51.

Orlove, Benjamin. 1977a. *Alpacas, Sheep, and Men: The Wool Export Economy and Regional Society of Southern Peru*. New York: Academic Press.

Orlove, Benjamin. 1977b. "Integration Through Production: The Use of Zonation in Espinar1." *American Ethnologist* 4 (1): 84–101.

Orlove, Benjamin. 1982. "Native Andean Pastoralists: Traditional Adaptations and Recent Changes." In *Contemporary Nomadic and Pastoral Peoples: Africa and Latin America.*, edited by Philip Carl Salzman, Studies in Third World Societies no. 17, 95–136. Williamsburg: College of William and Mary.

Orlove, Benjamin. 1985. "The History of the Andes: A Brief Overview." *Mountain Research and Development* 5 (1): 45–60.

Orlove, Benjamin. 2002. *Lines in the Water: Nature and Culture at Lake Titicaca*. Berkeley: University of California Press.

Orlove, Benjamin. 2005. "Human Adaptation to Climate Change: A Review of Three Historical Cases and Some General Perspectives." *Environmental Science & Policy* 8 (6): 589–600.

Orlove, Benjamin. 2009. "The Past, the Present and Some Possible Futures of Adaptation." In *Adapting to Climate Change: Thresholds, Values, Governance*, edited by W. Neil Adger, I. Lorenzoni, and K. O'Brien, 131–63. Cambridge, U.K.: Cambridge University Press.

Orlove, Benjamin, John Chiang, and Mark Cane. 2002. "Ethnoclimatology in the Andes: A Cross-Disciplinary Study Uncovers a Scientific Basis for the Scheme Andean Potato Farmers Traditionally Use to Predict the Coming Rains." *American Scientist* 90 (5): 428–35.

Orr, David M. R. 2013. "'Now He Walks and Walks, as If He Didn't Have a Home Where He Could Eat': Food, Healing, and Hunger in Quechua Narratives of Madness." *Culture, Medicine, and Psychiatry* 37:694–710.

Ostrom, Elinor. 1999. "Revisiting the Commons: Local Lessons, Global Challenges." *Science* 284 (5412): 278–82.

Pabón-Caicedo, José Daniel, Paola A. Arias, Andrea F. Carril, Jhan Carlo Espinoza, Lluís Fita Borrel, Katerina Goubanova, Waldo Lavado-Casimiro, Mariano Masiokas, et al. 2020. "Observed and Projected Hydroclimate Changes in the Andes." *Frontiers in Earth Science* 8 (61): 1–29.

Paerregaard, Karsten. 2012. "Commodifying Intimacy: Women, Work, and Care in Peruvian Migration." *Journal of Latin American and Caribbean Anthropology* 17 (3): 493–511.

Paerregaard, Karsten. 2013. "Bare Rocks and Fallen Angels: Environmental Change, Climate Perceptions and Ritual Practice in the Peruvian Andes." *Religions* 4 (2): 290–305.

Paerregaard, Karsten. 2014. "Broken Cosmologies: Climate, Water and State in the Peruvian Andes." In *Anthropology and Nature*, edited by Kirsten Hastrup, 196–210. London: Routledge.

Paerregaard, Karsten. 2015. *Return to Sender: The Moral Economy of Peru's Migrant Remittances*. Oakland: University of California Press.

Paerregaard, Karsten. 2021. "Lubricating Water Metabolism: How Mountain Offerings Contribute to Water Sustainability in the Peruvian Andes." *Kritisk Etnografi — Swedish Journal of Anthropology* 4 (2): 83–98.

Paerregaard, Karsten. 2023. *Andean Meltdown: A Climate Ethnography of Water, Power, and Culture in Peru*. Oakland: University of California Press.

Palacios Ríos, Félix. 1977. ". . . *Hiwasaha uywa uywataña, uka uywaha hiwasaru uyusitu": Los pastores aymara de Chichillapi*. Lima: Pontificia Universidad Católica del Perú, Programa de Perfeccionamiento en Ciencias Sociales.

Palacios Ríos, Felix. 1982. "El simbolismo aymara de la casa." *Boletín del Instituto de Estudios Aymaras* 2 (12): 37–57.

Palacios Ríos, Félix. 2000. "El simbolismo de las alpacas: Ritual y cosmovisión andina." In *Pastoreo altoandino: Realidad, sacralidad y posibilidades*, edited by Jorge Flores Ochoa and Yoshiki Kobayashi, 190–99. La Paz, Bolivia: Museo Nacional de Etnografía y Folklore.

Palomino Flores, Salvador. 1984. *El sistema de oposiciones en la comunidad de Sarhua*. Lima: Editorial Pueblo Indio.

Parreñas, Juno Salazar. 2018. *Decolonizing Extinction: The Work of Care in Orangutan Rehabilitation.* Durham: Duke University Press.

Paulson, Susan. 2003. "Gendered Practices and Landscapes in the Andes: The Shape of Asymmetrical Exchanges." *Human Organization* 62 (3): 242–54.

Pazzarelli, Francisco. 2020. "Parte-pastor: Notas sobre pastoreo y depredación en los cerros jujeños (Andes meridionales, Argentina)." In Muñoz Morán, *Ensayos de etnografía teórica,* 85–113.

Pazzarelli, Francisco, and Veronica S. Lema. 2024. "La geografía del estómago / el estómago de la geografía: Texturas, cuerpos y ofrendas de arrieros en los Andes argentinos." *Antípoda: Revista de Antropología y Arqueología* 54 (January): 3–25.

Perry, Baker, Anton Seimon, and Ginger Kelly. 2014. "Precipitation Delivery in the Tropical High Andes of Southern Peru: New Findings and Paleoclimatic Implications." *International Journal of Climatology* 34 (1): 197–215.

Picq, Manuela Lavinas. 2018. *Vernacular Sovereignties: Indigenous Women Challenging World Politics.* Tucson: University of Arizona Press.

Polk, Molly H., Kenneth R. Young, Michel Baraer, Bryan G. Mark, Jeffrey M. McKenzie, Jeffrey Bury, and Mark Carey. 2017. "Exploring Hydrologic Connections between Tropical Mountain Wetlands and Glacier Recession in Peru's Cordillera Blanca." *Applied Geography* 78 (January): 94–103.

Postigo, Julio, Kenneth Young, and Kelley Crews. 2008. "Change and Continuity in a Pastoralist Community in the High Peruvian Andes." *Human Ecology* 36 (4): 535–51.

Povinelli, Elizabeth A. 1995. "Do Rocks Listen?" *American Anthropologist* 97 (3): 505–18.

Povinelli, Elizabeth A. 2001. "Radical Worlds: The Anthropology of Incommensurability and Inconceivability." *Annual Review of Anthropology* 30:319–34.

Przytomska-La Civita, Anna. 2020. "La relación de depredación entre humanos y no-humanos en la ontología de los q'ero de la cordillera de Vilcanota, Perú." *Etnografia: Praktyki, Teorie, Doświadczenia* 6 (6): 127–53.

Queen, Robin. 2017. "When a Linguist Talks to a Dog." Presented at the 2017 Linguistic Institute, University of Michigan.

Quijano, Aníbal. 1999. "Colonialidad del Poder, Cultura y Conocimiento en América Latina." *Dispositio/n* 24 (51): 137–48.

Rabatel, Antoine, Bernard Francou, Álvaro Soruco, Joice Gomez, Bolívar Cáceres, Jorge Luis Ceballos, Ruben Basantes, Mathias Vuille, J.-E. Sicart, et al. 2013. "Current State of Glaciers in the Tropical Andes: A Multi-Century Perspective on Glacier Evolution and Climate Change." *Cryosphere* 7 (1): 81–102.

Radcliffe, Sarah A. 2012. "Development for a Postneoliberal Era? Sumak Kawsay, Living Well and the Limits of Decolonisation in Ecuador." *Geoforum* 43 (2): 240–49.

Rado Janzic, Bryan Edmundo. 2011. *Etnobotánica del Distrito de Ocongate—Quispicanchi—Cusco.* Cusco: Universidad Nacional de San Antonio Abad del Cusco.

Raffles, Hugh. 2002. *In Amazonia: A Natural History.* Princeton: Princeton University Press.

Rebhun, L. A. 1994. "Swallowing Frogs: Anger and Illness in Northeast Brazil." *Medical Anthropology Quarterly* 8 (4): 360–82.

Reider, Kelsey. 2018. "Survival at the Summits: Amphibian Responses to Thermal Extremes, Disease, and Rapid Climate Change in the High Tropical Andes." PhD diss., Florida International University.

Rhoades, Robert. 2008. "Disappearance of the Glacier on Mama Cotacachi: Ethnoecological Research and Climate Change in the Ecuadorian Andes." *Pirineos* 163:37–50.

Ricard Lanata, Xavier. 2007. *Ladrones de sombra: El universo religioso de los pastores del Ausangate (Andes surperuanos)*. Lima: Instituto Francés de Estudios Andinos.

Rivera Andía, Juan Javier. 2005. "Killing What You Love: An Andean Cattle Branding Ritual and the Dilemmas of Modernity." *Journal of Anthropological Research* 61 (2): 129–56.

Rivera Andía, Juan Javier. 2018. "Introduction: Towards Engaged Ontographies of Animist Developments in Amerindian South America." In Rivera Andía, *Non-Humans in Amerindian South America*, 1–70.

Rivera Andía, Juan Javier, ed. 2018. *Non-Humans in Amerindian South America: Ethnographies of Indigenous Cosmologies, Rituals and Songs*. Oxford: Berghahn Books.

Rivière, G. 2002. "Temps, pouvoir et société dans les communautés Aymaras de l'altiplano (Bolivie)." In *Entre ciel et terre: Climat et sociétés*, edited by Esther Katz, Annamária Lammel, and Marina Goloubinoff, 357–73. Paris: IRD-IBIS.

Roberts, Elizabeth. 2017. "What Gets Inside: Violent Entanglements and Toxic Boundaries in Mexico City." *Cultural Anthropology* 32 (4): 592–619.

Salas Carreño, Guillermo. 2012a. "Curanderos, peregrinos y turistas: Procesos interculturales en la sociedad cusqueña contemporánea." *Anthropologica* 21 (21): 145–71.

Salas Carreño, Guillermo. 2012b. "Negotiating Evangelicalism and New Age Tourism Through Quechua Ontologies in Cuzco, Peru." PhD diss., University of Michigan.

Salas Carreño, Guillermo. 2016. "Places Are Kin: Food, Cohabitation, and Sociality in the Southern Peruvian Andes." *Anthropological Quarterly* 89 (3): 813–40.

Salas Carreño, Guillermo. 2018. "Evangelicalism in the Rural Andes." In *The Andean World*, edited by Linda J. Seligmann and Kathleen S. Fine-Dare, 280–96. New York: Routledge.

Salas Carreño, Guillermo. 2019. *Lugares parientes: Comida, cohabitación y mundos andinos*. Lima: Pontificia Universidad Católica del Perú.

Salas Carreño, Guillermo. 2021. "Climate Change, Moral Meteorology, and Local Measures at Quyllurit'i, a High Andean Shrine." In *Understanding Climate Change Through Religious Lifeworlds*, edited by David L. Haberman, 44–76. Bloomington: Indiana University Press.

Salomon, Frank. 1998. "How the Huacas Were: The Language of Substance and Transformation in the Huarochiri Quechua Manuscript." *RES: Anthropology and Aesthetics* 33:7–17.

Salzmann, Nadine, Christian Huggel, M. Rohrer, W. Silverio, B. G. Mark, P. Burns, and C. Portocarrero. 2013. "Glacier Changes and Climate Trends Derived from Multiple Sources in the Data Scarce Cordillera Vilcanota Region, Southern Peruvian Andes." *Crysophere* 7 (1): 103–18.

San Martin, F., and F. C. Bryant. 1989. "Nutrition of Domesticated South American Llamas and Alpacas." *Small Ruminant Research* 2 (3): 191–216.

Sato, Chizu, and Jozelin María Soto Alarcón. 2019. "Toward a Postcapitalist Feminist Political Ecology' Approach to the Commons and Commoning." *International Journal of the Commons* 13 (1): 36.

Savalois, Nathalie, Nicolas Lescureux, and Florence Brunois. 2013. "Teaching the Dog and Learning from the Dog: Interactivity in Herding Dog Training and Use." *Anthrozoös* 26 (1): 77–91.

Sax, Marieka. 2015. "On Place, Well-Being, and Illness in the Andes." *INDIANA* 32:47–64.

Schauwecker, Simone, Mario Rohrer, Christian Huggel, Jason Endries, Nilton Montoya, Raphael Neukom, Baker Perry, Nadine Salzmann, Manfred Schwarb, et al. 2017. "The Freezing Level in the Tropical Andes, Peru: An Indicator for Present and Future Glacier Extents." *Journal of Geophysical Research: Atmospheres* 122 (10): 5172–89.

Scheper-Hughes, Nancy. 1993. *Death Without Weeping: The Violence of Everyday Life in Brazil*. Berkeley: University of California Press.

Schlager, Edella, and Elinor Ostrom. 1992. "Property-Rights Regimes and Natural Resources: A Conceptual Analysis." *Land Economics* 68 (3): 249–62.

Schnegg, Michael, Coral Iris O'Brian, and Inga Janina Sievert. 2021. "It's Our Fault: A Global Comparison of Different Ways of Explaining Climate Change." *Human Ecology* 49 (3): 327–39.

Scoville-Simonds, Morgan. 2018. "Climate, the Earth, and God—Entangled Narratives of Cultural and Climatic Change in the Peruvian Andes." *World Development* 110: 345–59.

Seimon, Tracie A., Anton Seimon, Karina Yager, Kelsey Reider, Amanda Delgado, Preston Sowell, Alfredo Tupayachi, Bronwen Konecky, Denise McAloose, et al. 2017. "Long-Term Monitoring of Tropical Alpine Habitat Change, Andean Anurans, and Chytrid Fungus in the Cordillera Vilcanota, Peru: Results from a Decade of Study." *Ecology and Evolution* 7 (5): 1527–40.

Seligmann, Linda J. 1989. "To Be in Between: The Cholas as Market Women." *Comparative Studies in Society and History* 31 (4): 694–721.

Seligmann, Linda J. 1993. "Between Worlds of Exchange: Ethnicity Among Peruvian Market Women." *Cultural Anthropology* 8 (2): 187–213.

Seligmann, Linda J. 2000. "Market Places, Social Spaces in Cuzco, Peru." *Urban Anthropology and Studies of Cultural Systems and World Economic Development* 29 (1): 1–68.

Sendón, Pablo F. 2008. "Organización social de las poblaciones pastoriles de los Andes del sur peruano: Hacia un balance comparativo de un aspecto omitido." In

Perú: El problema agrario en debate—SEPIA XII, edited by Gerardo Damonte, Bernardo Fulcrand, and Rosario Gómez, 327–74. Lima: SEPIA.

Sendón, Pablo F. 2016. *Ayllus del Ausangate: Parentesco y organización social en los Andes del sur peruano*. Lima: Centro de Estudios Regionales Andinos Bartolome de Las Casas.

Shea, Jeanne L. 2020. "Menopause and Midlife Aging in Cross-Cultural Perspective: Findings from Ethnographic Research in China." *Journal of Cross-Cultural Gerontology* 35 (4): 367–88.

Shimada, Izumi, and James L. Fitzsimmons. 2015. *Living with the Dead in the Andes*. Tucson: University of Arizona Press.

Shiva, Vandana. 2005. *Earth Democracy: Justice, Sustainability and Peace*. London: Zed Books.

Silverblatt, Irene. 1987. *Moon, Sun, and Witches: Gender Ideologies and Class in Inca and Colonial Peru*. Princeton: Princeton University Press.

Silverman, Gail P. 2008. *A Woven Book of Knowledge: Textile Iconography of Cuzco, Peru*. Salt Lake City: University of Utah Press.

Smith, Benjamin. 2012. "Language and the Frontiers of the Human: Aymara Animal-Oriented Interjections and the Mediation of Mind." *American Ethnologist* 39 (2): 313–24.

Squeo, Francisco A., Barry G. Warner, Ramón Aravena, and Diana Espinoza. 2006. "Bofedales: High Altitude Peatlands of the Central Andes." *Revista Chilena de Historia Natural* 79 (2): 245–55.

Stensrud, Astrid B. 2016. "Climate Change, Water Practices and Relational Worlds in the Andes." *Ethnos* 81 (1): 75–98.

Stensrud, Astrid B. 2019. "Water as Resource and Being: Water Extractivism and Life Projects in Peru." In *Indigenous Life Projects and Extractivism: Ethnographies from South America*, edited by Cecilie Vindal Ødegaard and Juan Javier Rivera Andía, 143–64. Cham: Springer Nature.

Stepan, Nancy. 1991. *The Hour of Eugenics: Race, Gender, and Nation in Latin America*. Ithaca: Cornell University Press.

Stépanoff, Charles, Charlotte Marchina, Camille Fossier, and Nicolas Bureau. 2017. "Animal Autonomy and Intermittent Coexistences: North Asian Modes of Herding." *Current Anthropology* 58 (1): 57–81.

Stoetzer, Bettina. 2022. *Ruderal City: Ecologies of Migration, Race, and Urban Nature in Berlin*. Durham: Duke University Press.

Strathern, Marilyn. 1992. *Reproducing the Future: Anthropology, Kinship, and the New Reproductive Technologies*. London: Routledge.

TallBear, Kim. 2011. "Why Interspecies Thinking Needs Indigenous Standpoints." *Fieldsights—Theorizing the Contemporary, Cultural Anthropology Online* (blog). April 24, 2011. http://culanth.org/fieldsights/260-why-interspecies-thinking-needs-indigenous-standpoints.

TallBear, Kim. 2019. "Caretaking Relations, Not American Dreaming." *Kalfou* 6 (1): 24–41.

Tapias, Maria. 2006. "Emotions and the Intergenerational Embodiment of Social Suffering in Rural Bolivia." *Medical Anthropology Quarterly* 20 (3): 399–415.

Tapias, Maria. 2015. *Embodied Protests: Emotions and Women's Health in Bolivia.* Urbana: University of Illinois Press.

Taylor, Sunaura. 2024. *Disabled Ecologies: Lessons from a Wounded Desert.* Oakland: University of California Press.

Thompson, Lonnie G., Mary E. Davis, Ellen Mosley-Thompson, E. Beaudon, Stacey E. Porter, S. Kutuzov, P.-N. Lin, V. N. Mikhalenko, and K. R. Mountain. 2017. "Impacts of Recent Warming and the 2015/2016 El Niño on Tropical Peruvian Ice Fields." *Journal of Geophysical Research: Atmospheres* 122 (23): 12688–701.

Thompson, Lonnie G., Mary E. Davis, Ellen Mosley-Thompson, Stacy E. Porter, Gustavo Valdivia Corrales, Christopher A. Shuman, and Compton J. Tucker. 2021. "The Impacts of Warming on Rapidly Retreating High-Altitude, Low-Latitude Glaciers and Ice Core-Derived Climate Records." *Global and Planetary Change* 203:103538.

Thompson, Lonnie G., Ellen Mosley-Thompson, Mary E. Davis, and Henry H. Brecher. 2011. "Tropical Glaciers, Recorders and Indicators of Climate Change, Are Disappearing Globally." *Annals of Glaciology* 52 (59): 23–34.

Thompson, Lonnie G., Ellen Mosley-Thompson, Mary E. Davis, V. S. Zagorodnov, I. M. Howat, V. N. Mikhalenko, and P. N. Lin. 2013. "Annually Resolved Ice Core Records of Tropical Climate Variability over the Past 1800 Years." *Science* 340 (6135): 945–50.

Tichit, Muriel, and Didier Genin. 1997. "Factors Affecting Herd Structure in a Mixed Camelid–Sheep Pastoral System in the Arid Puna of Bolivia." *Journal of Arid Environments* 36 (1): 167–80.

Todd, Zoe. 2016. "An Indigenous Feminist's Take on the Ontological Turn: 'Ontology' Is Just Another Word for Colonialism." *Journal of Historical Sociology* 29 (1): 4–22.

Trawick, Paul. 2002. "Comedy and Tragedy in the Andean Commons." *Journal of Political Ecology* 9 (1): 35–68.

Tripcevich, Nicholas. 2016. "The Ethnoarchaeology of a Cotahuasi Salt Caravan: Exploring Andean Pastoralist Movement." In Capriles and Tripcevich, *Archaeology of Andean Pastoralism*, 211–30.

Tsing, Anna. 2012. "Unruly Edges: Mushrooms as Companion Species." *Environmental Humanities* 1 (1): 141–54.

Tsing, Anna. 2015. *The Mushroom at the End of the World: On the Possibility of Life in Capitalist Ruins.* Princeton: Princeton University Press.

Tsing, Anna. 2018. "The New Wild." *Little Toller Books* (blog), December 6, 2018. https://www.littletoller.co.uk/the-clearing/the-new-wild-by-anna-tsing/.

UNFCCC. 2014. "Peru's Glaciers Shrink 40%." UNFCCC. October 16, 2014. http://newsroom.unfccc.int/action-to-adapt/perus-glaciers-shrink-40-in-40-years/.

Urrutia, Rocío, and Mathias Vuille. 2009. "Climate Change Projections for the Tropical Andes Using a Regional Climate Model: Temperature and Precipitation Simulations for the End of the 21st Century." *Journal of Geophysical Research: Atmospheres* 114:D02108.

Valdivia, Corinne, Jere L. Gilles, and Cecilia Turin. 2013. "Andean Pastoral Women in a Changing World: Opportunities and Challenges." *Rangelands* 35 (6): 75–81.

Valdivia Corrales, Gustavo. 2013. "El neoliberalism y las sociedades pastoriles del sur Andino. Un caso de extrema exclusión y pobreza en los Andes peruanos." In *La construcción social de la pobreza en América Latina y el Caribe: Perspectivas, alternativas y criticas*, 283–316. Buenos Aires: CLACSO.

Van Vleet, Krista. 2008a. "The Intimacies of Power: Rethinking Violence and Affinity in the Bolivian Andes." *American Ethnologist* 29 (3): 567–601.

Van Vleet, Krista. 2008b. *Performing Kinship*. Austin: University of Texas Press.

Veettil, Bijeesh Kozhikkodan, and Sergio Florêncio de Souza. 2017. "Study of 40-Year Glacier Retreat in the Northern Region of the Cordillera Vilcanota, Peru, Using Satellite Images: Preliminary Results." *Remote Sensing Letters* 8 (1): 78–85.

Villarroel, Elena Katia, Paula Lady Pacheco Mollinedo, Alejandra I. Domic, José M. Capriles, and Carlos Espinoza. 2014. "Local Management of Andean Wetlands in Sajama National Park, Bolivia: Persistence of the Collective System in Increasingly Family-Oriented Arrangements." *Mountain Research and Development* 34 (4): 356–68.

Vining, Benjamin. 2016. "Pastoral Intensification, Social Fissioning, and Ties to State Economies at the Formative—Middle Horizon Transition in the Lake Suches Region, Southern Peru." In Capriles and Tripcevich, *Archaeology of Andean Pastoralism*, 87–118.

Viveiros de Castro, Eduardo. 1998. "Cosmological Deixis and Amerindian Perspectivism." *Journal of the Royal Anthropological Institute* 4 (3): 469–88.

Viveiros de Castro, Eduardo. 2004. "Perspectival Anthropology and the Method of Controlled Equivocation." *Tipití: Journal of the Society for the Anthropology of Lowland South America* 2 (1): 1–22.

Viveiros de Castro, Eduardo. 2011. "Zeno and the Art of Anthropology: Of Lies, Beliefs, Paradoxes, and Other Truths." Translated by Antonia Walford. *Common Knowledge* 17 (1): 128–45.

Vuille, Mathias, Raymond S. Bradley, Martin Werner, and Frank Keimig. 2003. "20th Century Climate Change in the Tropical Andes: Observations and Model Results." *Climatic Change* 59 (1): 75–99.

Vuille, Mathias, Mark Carey, Christian Huggel, Wouter Buytaert, Antoine Rabatel, Dean Jacobsen, Alvaro Soruco, Marcos Villacis, Christian Yarleque, et al. 2018. "Rapid Decline of Snow and Ice in the Tropical Andes—Impacts, Uncertainties and Challenges Ahead." *Earth-Science Reviews* 176 (January): 195–213.

Vuille, Mathias, Bernard Francou, Patrick Wagnon, Irmgard Juen, Georg Kaser, Bryan G. Mark, and Raymond S. Bradley. 2008. "Climate Change and Tropical Andean Glaciers: Past, Present and Future." *Earth-Science Reviews* 89 (3–4): 79–96.

Webster, Steven. 1973. "Native Pastoralism in the South Andes." *Ethnology* 12 (2): 115–33.

Weismantel, Mary. 1988. *Food, Gender, and Poverty in the Ecuadorian Andes.* Philadelphia: University of Pennsylvania Press.

Weismantel, Mary. 1995. "Making Kin: Kinship Theory and Zumbagua Adoptions." *American Ethnologist* 22 (4): 685–704.

Weismantel, Mary. 2001. *Cholas and Pishtacos: Stories of Race and Sex in the Andes.* Women in Culture and Society. Chicago: University of Chicago Press.

Weiss, Joseph. 2019. *Shaping the Future on Haida Gwaii: Life Beyond Settler Colonialism.* Vancouver: University of British Columbia Press.

Wheeler, Jane C. 2012. "South American Camelids: Past, Present and Future." *Journal of Camelid Science* 5:1–24.

Wheeler, Jane C., A. J. F. Russel, and Hilary Redden. 1995. "Llamas and Alpacas: Pre-Conquest Breeds and Post-Conquest Hybrids." *Journal of Archaeological Science* 22 (6): 833–40.

White-Nockleby, Caroline, Manuel Prieto, Karina Yager, and Rosa Isela Meneses. 2021. "Understanding Bofedales as Cultural Landscapes in the Central Andes." *Wetlands* 41 (8): 102.

Whitington, Jerome. 2016. "What Does Climate Change Demand of Anthropology?" *PoLAR: Political and Legal Anthropology Review* 39 (1): 7–15.

Whitten, Norman E. 1981. *Cultural Transformations and Ethnicity in Modern Ecuador.* Champaign: University of Illinois Press.

Whyte, Kyle Powys. 2018. "Settler Colonialism, Ecology, and Environmental Injustice." *Environment and Society* 9 (1): 125–44.

Whyte, Kyle Powys. 2024. "Why Does Anything Need to Be Called Wild?" In *The Heart of the Wild,* edited by Ben A. Minteer and Johnathan B. Losos, 71–83. Princeton: Princeton University Press.

Whyte, Kyle Powys, Jared L. Talley, and Julia D. Gibson. 2019. "Indigenous Mobility Traditions, Colonialism, and the Anthropocene." *Mobilities* 14 (3): 319–35.

Wilhoit, Mary Elena. 2017. "'Un Favorzote': Gender and Reciprocity in the Andes: Gender and Reciprocity in the Andes." *Journal of Latin American and Caribbean Anthropology* 22 (1): 438–58.

Willerslev, Rane. 2007. *Soul Hunters: Hunting, Animism, and Personhood among the Siberian Yukaghirs.* Berkeley: University of California Press.

Winchell, Mareike. 2022a. *After Servitude: Elusive Property and the Ethics of Kinship in Bolivia.* Oakland: University of California Press.

Winchell, Mareike. 2022b. "Research Entanglements beyond Predation." *Postmodern Culture* 33 (1).

Winchell, Mareike. 2023. "Critical Ontologies: Rethinking Relations to Other-than-Humans from the Bolivian Andes." *Journal of the Royal Anthropological Institute* 29 (3): 611–30.

Yager, Karina, Manuel Prieto, and Rosa Isela Meneses. 2021. "Reframing Pastoral Practices of Bofedal Management to Increase the Resilience of Andean Water Towers." *Mountain Research and Development* 41 (4): A1–9.

Yarleque, Christian, Mathias Vuille, Douglas R. Hardy, Oliver Elison Timm, Jorge De la Cruz, Hugo Ramos, and Antoine Rabatel. 2018. "Projections of the Future Disappearance of the Quelccaya Ice Cap in the Central Andes." *Scientific Reports* 8 (1): 15564.

Zickgraf, Caroline. 2022. "Relational (Im)Mobilities: A Case Study of Senegalese Coastal Fishing Populations." *Journal of Ethnic and Migration Studies* 48 (14): 3450–67.

Index

About the Author

Allison Caine is an assistant professor of anthropology at the University of Wyoming with an interest in the environment, rural health, and well-being in the Peruvian Andes and the U.S. Mountain West. Her research in Peru takes a multidisciplinary and collaborative approach to understanding contemporary environmental problems in partnership with international and Indigenous citizen scientists. Her ongoing research program aims to understand diverse experiences of health and aging in changing landscapes in Peru and the United States.